TEACHING THE SCREEN

MICHAEL ANDERSON
& MIRANDA JEFFERSON

LONDON AND NEW YORK

Dedicated to all the students and teachers who have taught us so much about film education and especially for the help and support of Robyn Ewing as a mentor and inspirational arts educator over many years

First published 2009 by Allen & Unwin

Published 2020 by Routledge
2 Park Square, Milton Park, Abingdon, Oxon OX14 4RN
605 Third Avenue, New York, NY 10017

Routledge is an imprint of the Taylor & Francis Group, an informa business

© Michael Anderson and Miranda Jefferson 2009

All rights reserved. No part of this book may be reprinted or reproduced or utilised in any form or by any electronic, mechanical, or other means, now known or hereafter invented, including photocopying and recording, or in any information storage or retrieval system, without permission in writing from the publishers.

Notice:
Product or corporate names may be trademarks or registered trademarks, and are used only for identification and explanation without intent to infringe.

National Library of Australia
Cataloguing-in-Publication entry:

Anderson, Michael, 1969-

    Teaching the screen : film education for generation next.

    Includes index.
    Bibliography.

    Cinematography—Study and teaching (Secondary)
    English literature—Film and video adaptations—
    Study and teaching (Secondary).

    Other authors/contributors:
    Jefferson, Miranda.

778.530712

Index by Jo Rudd
Set in 11/14 pt Minion by Post Pre-press Group, Australia

ISBN-13: 9781741757200 (pbk)

Contents

Preface vi
Acknowledgements viii
Introduction ix

1 Teaching, learning and the screen   1
2 Creativity, multiliteracies and screen learning   21
3 Screen theory, practice and learning   36
4 Narrative, genre and film learning   60
5 Scaffolding learning in film aesthetics   77
6 Collaborative learning processes in filmmaking   98
7 Learning from imagining and being in film stories   116
8 Developing a film curriculum   136
9 Assessing the screen   152
10 Researching screen learning in the classroom   167

Appendix: Sample—Scaffolded film learning modules   187
Notes   192
Filmography   195
Bibliography   197
Index   206

Preface

There seems to us to be a mood at the moment for change in education. The emergence of the knowledge economy and the creative industries has created downward pressure on schools to reorient their curriculum to recognise that future economic prosperity may be contingent upon the creation of ideas rather than the manufacturing of things. The children who are currently engaged in schooling are now born into a technology-rich environment. In the midst of this digital revolution, change is a constant and creativity is central to the discussions. One of the gaps that became apparent to us was a place for film, the most pervasive of the arts in many school curricula. We wrote this book to argue that film deserves, and in some ways demands, its own discrete place in the school curriculum. We argue that young people are daily bombarded with filmic images but need quality and systematic teaching in film to make sense of films. As teachers, we know that the only way to improve the quality of teaching is to present an approach to film learning that is clear, authentic, systematic and responds to the realities of schools. We wrote this book in the hope that teachers would be inspired to give film learning a go. While there are undoubted obstacles for some, related to the price and accessibility of the technology, these are diminishing as cameras and screens are integrated and become cheap and ubiquitous consumer items. This book is based on original research carried out by us on film learning in classrooms throughout the world. This research confirms that film learning is popular with young people in schools and given the right approach can be taught very effectively.

We have not written a 'how to' book because there are plenty of excellent resources on filming and editing on the web and in other books. We have instead focused on answering the question 'What does a systematic teaching approach to film look like?' To answer this question, we have drawn from reservoirs of research and practice to examine the forces that have shaped film learning from the past, examined the present practices associated with film learning and imagined what its future might be like. We acknowledge those with whom we have worked as teachers and researchers, our students and colleagues, and we would like to thank them for generously supporting our exploration of film learning and for their influence on us.

Michael Anderson
Miranda Jefferson

Acknowledgements

We would like to acknowledge all the students, teachers and other colleagues who have helped us understand film learning. Special thanks go to the students and staff who worked on the Shostakovich Film Project at Newtown High School of the Performing Arts and Orange High School. For help with this book we would especially like to thank Ula George, James Durran, Kate Early and Isabelle Kim. We would also like to acknowledge Elizabeth Weiss and Angela Handley for their support throughout the project.

'Buffalo Bill 's' is reprinted from *Complete Poems 1904–1962*, by E.E. Cummings, edited by George J. Firmage, by permission of W.W. Norton & Company © 1991 by the Trustees for the E.E. Cummings Trust and George James Firmage.

Introduction

The media often feature discussions about the current generation being out of control and disengaged. Of course, this is a media cliché that has been around since at least the 1960s and probably longer. The media mythology usually suggests that today's youth are disengaged and disinterested in the world. We have between us been involved in teaching for over 40 years. Young people were engaged and excited in learning then and they are now. What has changed is technology in all aspects of our society. In our time, we have seen incredible changes in the technology that young people use. If we had suggested even five years ago that it was possible to shoot and edit films on a mobile phone, most people would have thought we were delusional.

When we began teaching, we found ourselves among engaged, inspired and creative young people and we still do today; what has changed is the *opportunity* they have to create, thanks to the huge advances in creative technologies. The means of creative production affords new capabilities to all of us. The once unattainable or awkward, like film production, can now be a classroom reality. Technology is only one of the challenges. Controlling the technology is a problem, but more problematic is understanding, controlling and being creative with the art form of film. For this to be possible, learning and teaching must catch up with technology and recognise the need for a systematic approach to teaching film.

We use the term 'film' as a way of differentiating ourselves from the way moving image is taught in other fields. Film is the generic term for narrative in film, film as an art form and the word we use for the language of film. While not denigrating in any way the influence of media studies or English, or any other curriculum area, we use the term 'film' to mean a narrative-based form of drama made for the screen, whether that screen be in a cinema, on a television, or part of a phone or computer. The story being told is the most important feature of film learning, and the location and nature of the screen or the capture and recording device (film stock, video, digital) are largely irrelevant to us.

This book emerged from a desire to develop a discussion on teaching film beyond the 'how to' approach. We wanted to develop a holistic understanding of how theories of film and theories of learning could be integrated to create a comprehensive and clear understanding of film learning. We approach film learning not from a media studies background, nor an English teaching background (although both of us have taught these areas at one time or another), but rather from an arts education background.

The primary objective of this book is to investigate the pedagogy of film in the classroom. As you will see, we have drawn on our own research and the research evidence of others in the field so that other investigators in the field may build and extend on our work, use our research and explore other research questions. Our hope is that this book will contribute to a community of practice of researchers, teachers and students that supports the sustainable growth of film learning.

As we began to teach film, it became starkly apparent that this area of education did not fit neatly within other subjects. It demanded its own space for students to engage with the distinctive challenges of the art form. What was required then, and is required now, is an integrated way to teach film that does not bifurcate filmmaking and film appreciation and analysis. It conceptualises filmmaking and film appreciation and analysis as two parts of the one process of film learning. This book is an attempt to situate film learning squarely within the best democratic traditions of arts education, where students analyse what they are watching critically and are given the tools of creation to make their own voices heard through filmed narrative in this pervasive medium.

Young people are, of course, right now all over the world attempting to make film by pointing a camera and shooting and then transferring the product on to YouTube. To us, this is not really filmmaking. It is the digital equivalent of doodling with pen and paper. There is often no understanding of the aesthetics of film or of how to use those aesthetics to communicate effectively. *Teaching the Screen* is an attempt to use what has been learnt through this familiarity with film technologies as a starting point and enrich it by bringing to it aesthetic control.

In Chapter 1, 'Teaching, Learning and the Screen', we propose an outline of our approach to film learning with a focus on the creation of narrative through appreciating the aesthetics of film and gaining control over those aesthetics. Chapter 2, 'Creativity, Multiliteracies and Screen Learning', discusses how screen learning is a creative practice that depends on a critical and engaged understanding of a range of literacies. Chapter 3, 'Screen Theory, Practice and Learning', examines the tenets of screen theory and explores how these concepts can lay the foundations of film learning in the classroom. In Chapter 4, 'Narrative, Genre and Film Learning', we examine the structure of narrative and storytelling, and discuss how understanding narrative supports development of learning and teaching about the screen. Chapter 5, 'Scaffolding Learning in Film Aesthetics', begins the discussion about how deep learning is possible through an engagement in making and appreciating film. The development and discussion of film learning is extended in Chapter 6, 'Collaborative Learning Processes in Film Making', where we argue that film learning is a socially mediated collaborative practice. Chapter 7, 'Learning from Imagining and Being in Film Stories', discusses the centrality of imagination and acting in film learning. In Chapter 8, 'Developing a Film Curriculum', we discuss the structure of a continuum of film learning from early childhood to post-compulsory schooling and examine two case studies of how film learning works in practice. In Chapter 9, 'Assessing the Screen', we discuss how teachers might construct an authentic and engaging approach to assessment that recognises the interdependence of making and appreciating processes in film learning. Finally, in Chapter 10, 'Researching Screen Learning in the Classroom', we invite further discussion through an introduction to teacher research for film in the classroom.

In a sense, *Teaching the Screen* is a melding of research practice and learning theory as a way of inviting everyone involved in education to engage seriously with screen learning. It is our fervent hope that it will spark debate, interest and engagement in film, which promises to be the most pervasive art form of the twenty-first century.

1
Teaching, learning and the screen

> You cannot endow even the best machine with initiative;
> the jolliest steamroller will not plant flowers.
> —*Walter Lippmann*

At the beginning of a book that deals with machines and education, it may serve us to remember the place of the machine—in this case, the digital video camera—in the human endeavour. All a machine will do is reflect the creativity and the initiative with which we fuel it; to expect more is unrealistic. In our case, film technology is neither good nor bad, aesthetically appealing nor disgusting. What matters is the way we use it—or, in relation to this book, the way it is taught and learnt. The melding of teacher skills and intuition with student imagination and creativity is a powerful and grossly under-utilised resource in modern secondary schooling. It is our intention to redress this deficit by providing a series of rationales and approaches for teaching screen narratives in the classroom.

Why teach the screen?

The long answer to this will hopefully unfold for you over the course of this book, but there are two short answers. We teach film because, like the other arts, it is an intrinsically important part of our understanding of ourselves and of human experience. Elliot Eisner (2004) argues that the arts affect consciousness in a number of ways:

> They refine our senses so that our ability to experience the world is made more complex and subtle; they promote the use of our imaginative capacities

so that we can envision what we cannot actually see, taste, touch, hear, and smell; they provide models through which we can experience the world in new ways and they provide the materials and occasions to grapple with problems that depend on arts-related forms of thinking (2004, p. 19).

Learning about and learning to make film is important because it raises our consciousness and awareness of life. The power of the lens is its ability to communicate detail, to convey the subtlety of nuances such as the power and meaning of a look. While all of these qualities have important ramifications for learning across the curriculum, we should not necessarily rely on pragmatic arguments. While we would argue that film can and does teach many things that are useful outside film learning itself (literacy, social skills, and so on), that should not be the sole reason for teaching the screen. Film should be taught because it is intrinsically worthwhile as an area of schooling, and ultimately a way for us to understand others, our world and ourselves. The second 'short answer' is that we increasingly have no choice. Students are now born into a media-rich world where most of the time they are being recorded and often they are recording. Marc Prensky (2001) calls these students digital natives because they have not had to struggle like their digital immigrant elders to get used to the technology that is swirling around them.

Access to the camera and the moving image is not a recent phenomenon, but the 'massification' and consequent democratisation of the form certainly are. Students in Western economies have access to inexpensive cameras, phones and film editing programs that means they can produce, shoot and edit their stories without buying professional or specialised equipment. In a recent study (Carroll, Anderson and Cameron, 2006), first-year education and media students at two universities were surveyed about their use of technology. The survey sampled 210 first-year communication students and 280 education students (pre-service teachers) in 2005. The study found that not only did students use technology constantly, but many of them own digital devices. Not surprisingly, mobile telephones have achieved almost complete penetration.

Mobile phones (more often than not equipped with video cameras) are a key device in the lives of students, for whom interactive technologies are entertainment, identity maintenance and communication devices—all at the same time. With the integration of filming capacities on almost all mobile phones, almost everyone has the capacity to shoot film of some quality. Of course, the quality is often the issue.

The place of film learning in the curriculum

You might be forgiven for thinking that, with the overwhelming penetration of these kinds of technologies, there would be a headlong rush by educators to engage with film learning, and schooling systems would be supporting the development of curriculum in the area. Sadly, there is little evidence of this. Rather, its place in the curriculum is patchy and support for teachers interested in developing the teaching of film in their classrooms is patchy as well.

Film learning has suffered from its relatively late development (in the late nineteenth century) as a discrete art form and consequently a discrete curriculum area. While arts curriculum has suffered from marginalisation (O'Toole, 1998; Anderson, 2004), the study of film narrative is often so marginal it does not appear in the curriculum in several schooling systems. In *A Guide to Teaching Practice* (Cohen and Manion, 2004), self-described as 'the major standard text for teachers on initial teacher training in the UK', there is no mention of film learning in any context. In a chapter on information and communication technology, the only passing comment relevant to film argues that 'multimedia' can 'overemphasise image over content, presentation over substance and entertainment over learning' (2004, p. 64). While this might be true of the worst kind of learning in multimedia or indeed film, it overlooks the possibility that film could indeed both engage and teach. The writers of *A Guide to Teaching Practice* are not alone. There has been an over-emphasis on the tools related to traditional learning and teaching, such as spreadsheets, word processors and the like, that has under-estimated the capacity of other technologies related to creative pedagogies (the camera and editing technologies). Perhaps the relative inaccessibility of the technologies of filmmaking until recent times has also provided obstacles and discouraged teachers and schooling systems from teaching film. Whatever the case, we have now entered an era with exciting possibilities for film. Our students are aware of the technology, and the technology is both affordable and accessible. What is required now is a methodical and clear approach to teaching this art form.

Why teach digital narratives?

Teaching the Screen is focused on the development of film narratives. We are not suggesting here that other forms of screen expression are less valid, but there are many resources that focus on what is referred to as 'media' in many schooling systems. This is an important connected area, and much of our discussion here is possible because of the work that has been done in theory and research in that area. We are focusing on narrative because we believe the development of stories is vital to the way our community passes on what it knows and allows us to communicate with each other. It is crucial that young people have the control of a form of communication so they can enter into dialogue in their communities. Narratives are the way we construct meaning about our world and how we as individuals and communities communicate and construct our own identities. Polkinghorne (1988) argues that narrative is 'the primary form by which human experience is made meaningful' (1988, p. 1). He further argues that narrative organises human experience into temporally meaningful experiences. Film's capacity to organise, rearrange and manipulate time makes it an ideal form for the communication of human experience. The film *Babel* (2006) is a strong example of how narrative can be organised to create dramatic meaning for the audience. *Babel* tells four stories that, when intertwined, reveal the profound inequities between 'haves' and 'have nots'. The power of this film and many others to manipulate time and space makes it one of the most powerful narrative forms. Allowing young people, who are already 'connected up' to the technology, to access film narratives is an important responsibility for educators and schooling systems.

For the individual, narrative has the power to build empathy and a deep understanding of the 'other'. The world of film and cinema has afforded its audience priceless access to such diverse experiences. Through films such as *The Queen* (2006), we saw into the imagined world of the British Royal family around the death of Diana, through *American Beauty* (1999) the world gazed into the lives of Middle America and in *Rabbit-Proof Fence* (2002) audiences gained an understanding of the plight of the Stolen Generation of Indigenous Australians.

While this could be dismissed as mere entertainment, Roslyn Arnold (2005) argues that these narratives, wherever they are found, have an important role in the development of empathic intelligence:

> Through the stories of real and imagined life we become aware of ourselves as feeling and thinking beings who belong in a world potentially richer than, or very different from, our own everyday existence. The culture of narratives experienced through reading, viewing and even participating in dramas can forever stimulate our minds and hearts (2005, p. 72).

Teaching, learning and the screen   5

Figure 1.1 This image from *Babel* occurs at a moment where the other narrative threads are being interlaced with this narrative.

Figure 1.2 *Rabbit-Proof Fence* is an example of a film world that is often imagined by the audience, but rarely experienced.

Fundamentally, an understanding of narrative and the way it is communicated is essential to the development of young people's control over their stories. This book attempts to engage with intuitive understandings already present, and seeks to shape that understanding into a more aesthetically rigorous understanding of film. This in turn will help young people to control and create with film.

Teaching versus learning the screen: A useless dichotomy

As you will have noticed, we are placing an emphasis on teaching in our discussions. We believe that a properly resourced expert teacher makes all the difference in student learning. The research evidence has confirmed this conviction. A study that reviewed 500 000 studies on teacher effectiveness demonstrated the centrality of expert teachers in learning: 'Students who are taught by expert teachers exhibit an understanding of the concepts targeted in instruction that is more integrated, more coherent, and at a higher level of abstraction than the understanding achieved by other students (Hattie, 2003, p. 15).

We are not discounting the importance of the learner—the student—in this relationship; quite the contrary. The discussion you will find here acknowledges that teachers are crucial in the learning of their students. As Ramsden (2003, p. 6) argues: 'The aim of teaching is simple: it is to make student learning possible.' We start from the premise that teaching involves a range of approaches that will sometimes include direct instruction, sometimes facilitation and sometimes informal group collaboration, to name just a few. Skilled teachers understand that learning is not made possible with just one approach. Teaching film will make diverse demands on teachers to vary their approaches. In the space of one lesson, the teacher could be asking analytical questions, providing instruction on the use of an editing program, discussing the aesthetic elements of a mid-shot and so on. Each one of these learning objectives demands a different approach, and an effective teacher of film will use a variety of approaches. The student's familiarity with technology and their own cultural background is central to the learning and teaching; however, without the guidance, provocation and engagement of the teacher, the learner's background knowledge remains just that. Students do have a wealth of implicit knowledge about film that has been absorbed from popular culture. They know about film in the same way that young children know about language: they have been immersed in it and so learn from that immersion. As young children need support and scaffolding to develop language skills, so too do students learning film. Through film learning, their inherent understanding of film grows into aesthetic control and understanding.

Film learning as a sociocultural approach

Sociocultural theories such as that of influential Russian education theorist Lev Vygotsky suggest knowledge is 'constructed by individuals interacting with tools, language and groups in their cultural context'. A further feature of this approach is that Vygotsky argues that learning differs depending on the curriculum context, so learning in geography differs from learning in film. A sociocultural approach argues that learning occurs within specific social and cultural contexts, and cannot be removed from these contexts. It rejects the idea that learning is an individual, solitary endeavour.

Film learning is an example of a sociocultural approach to learning because learning in this area relies heavily on the collaboration of learners who bring their own unique knowledge and backgrounds to the creative learning process. Film is a collaborative art form. Even the auteur relies on others to act and design the films they make. Jerome Bruner (1996) explains that learning in the arts is being able to use the 'cultural toolkit' (1996, p. 4) of the specific learning area skilfully. Film is a collaborative, interactive pedagogy that values and communicates the cultural context. It demands teams of actors, designers, technicians, and so on to contribute to the learning at hand in a specific cultural location.

Our approach to film learning is predicated on the sociocultural approach to learning, where what students learn is heavily dependent on their knowledge of their own context. So for film learning a student's understanding of the aesthetics of film is sometimes discovered almost unconsciously by being an audience member of a constant stream of film and television. This is crucial to their ongoing understanding, analysis and creation of film. Arising from the sociocultural approach is an understanding of screen learning as a 'mediated community of practice' (Carroll, Anderson and Cameron, 2006).

Film learning as a form of experiential learning

We believe film learning is a form of experiential learning. As students experience film through the processes of appreciating and making film, they are using all of their intellectual and physical resources to learn about film and to learn how to make film. The model presented in this book imagines students engaging in their own work and learning through that experience. A central and unequivocal part of that learning is the teacher who acts as guide, support and at times provocateur, leading the student to deeper levels of engagement with the art form.

Kolb (1984) argues that experiential learning is 'the process whereby knowledge is created through the transformation of experience. Knowledge results from the combination of grasping and transforming experience' (1984, p. 41).

A central feature of Kolb's definition is the rigour implicit in 'grasping and transforming experience'. In this view, experience is not sufficient on its own. Experience must be grappled with and changed to make it meaningful for the learner. In the context of film, it is not sufficient just to imitate or derivatively reproduce the work of 'great filmmakers'; it is the recognition and integration of this great work into the student's own aesthetically controlled understanding and practice of film that counts. This kind of experience-based learning is perhaps one of the most difficult areas with which to engage in the curriculum. As leading nineteenth- and twentieth-century educationalist John Dewey (1939) said: 'There is no discipline in the world so severe as the discipline of experience subjected to the tests of intelligent development and direction' (1939, p. 681).

Film learning applies Dewey's rigorous maxim well. The discipline of filmmaking engages students in a collaborative endeavour of their imagination, creativity and knowledge that is undertaken kinaesthetically. They must also interpret their understanding of a dynamic aesthetic and control a diverse range of human and technological resources. Above all, they must interpret their past experience of film appreciation and practice, and apply it to their current and situated experience of filmmaking. Young people in film learning must deal with the challenges of adapting their skills to a dynamic learning situation. For instance, if they are going to shoot a film and their project is interrupted by weather, misfortune or other factors, they must improvise a response using creative group problem-solving. These are the very skills demanded for living as an active and productive world citizen in the twenty-first century.

Film learning: One of *the* productive pedagogies

Film learning is ideally placed to fit within the 'productive pedagogies', 'new basics' or 'quality teaching' movement. Emerging from American research into 'authentic pedagogies' (Newmann and Associates, 1996) was the Queensland School Reform Longitudinal Survey (Hayes et al., 2006), which provided the most recent impetus for this approach. This research argued for four dimensions of classroom practice that particularly supported learning of students who had been marginalised by traditional schooling (Hayes et. al., 2006, p. 8). The dimensions they uncovered were:

- intellectual quality
- connectedness
- a supportive classroom environment, and
- working with and valuing difference (Hayes et. al, 2006, pp. 22–3).

There are strong claims that drama is an excellent fit with the productive pedagogies model (O'Toole, 2002; Martello, 2002). John O'Toole recognised what many drama teachers already implicitly understand, that 'drama in schools can amply fulfil all twenty requirements of the Productive Pedagogies, as a Productive Pedagogy singular. Could drama be the new basic? Based on children's play, it is certainly the oldest of Old Basics' (2002, p. 52). In many of the same and some different ways film is a productive pedagogy as well. Table 1.1 outlines how film learning fulfils the elements of productive pedagogies.

Table 1.1 How film learning fulfils the elements of productive pedagogies

New basic/ productive pedagogy	Dimensions of productive pedagogy	Film
Intellectual quality	<ul><li>Higher-order thinking</li><li>Deep knowledge</li><li>Deep understanding</li><li>Substantive conversation</li><li>Knowledge as problematic</li><li>Meta-language</li></ul>	<ul><li>Understanding the relationship of film form and function, and filmic codes and conventions as social, cultural constructs</li><li>Creating film by constructing and deconstructing cinema aesthetics for narrative meaning</li><li>Problem-solving through the augmenting and dialectical process of creativity in the filmmaking process</li><li>Communicating using meta-language to create film media and critically appreciate them, orally and in writing</li></ul>
Connectedness	<ul><li>Knowledge integration</li><li>Background knowledge</li><li>Connectedness to the world</li></ul>	<ul><li>Integrating knowledge of filmic form in a world of pervasive mediated reality</li><li>Understanding their world through creativity of self-expression in filmic form</li></ul>

Table 1.1 How film learning fulfils the elements of productive pedagogies
continued

		• Problem-based curriculum	• Interacting with 'real-world' phenomena and concerns through the experience of filmmaking • Collaborative processes of film involving communication, negotiation and problem-solving • Processing the reception of spectators' perceptions of screened film works
Supportive classroom environment		• Student direction • Social support • Academic engagement • Explicit quality performance criteria • Self-regulation	• Group practice of collaboration with peers in filmmaking • Undertaking and recognising the symbiotic roles involved in filmmaking, and recognising their contribution to the process and its outcome • Engaging theoretical understanding of cinema aesthetics and film form and function, orally and in writing through the practical process of filmmaking • Recognising how form and function criteria can structure and measure outcomes in process learning and screened outcomes
Recognition of difference		• Cultural knowledges • Inclusivity • Narrative • Group identity • Active citizenship	• Understanding film's function as a social, cultural and artistic form and a construct that recognises difference, change, attitudes and values • Self-expression through the creativity of filmmaking in narrative form and understanding of how the expression of their own stories can explain, examine and explore their world

			<ul><li>Collegiality and cooperation in the collaborative process of film creation</li><li>Processing how the spectator's reception actively engages them in 'real world' concerns</li></ul>

Source: QSRLS (2001).

There is now an inevitable and inexorable pressure on schools to be more effective with the way they use appropriate technologies and intergrate them into the curriculum. As demonstrated above, when taught effectively, film learning offers a productive pedagogy that integrates technology appropriately rather than its being added on in an ad hoc fashion to a learning area.

Screen learning as a flow experience

Flow theory argues that for students to be engaged, the learning activity must feature concentration, interest and enjoyment. Mihaly Csikszentmihalyi's theory (Shernoff et al., 2003) argues that flow is a deep absorption (concentration) where students are motivated to learn a topic for its own sake (interest). They may also find the intellectually demanding activity pleasurable and engaging. These tasks might also include significant creativity and curiosity that 'builds a bridge' to more complex learning (Shernoff et al., 2003). Screen learning conforms to the features of flow theory in the following ways:

- *Concentration.* For any film learning to be effective, students are required to remain focused on the demands of the project and to have shared ownership of the project. Irrespective of the phase of the project—pre-production, production or post-production—there is an intensity of concentration that occurs frequently in arts education. The concentration required for filming a scene often sees participants 'lose track of time' as their energies are focused on the task. Csikszentmihalyi (Shernoff et al., 2003) nominates this quality as evidence that a flow experience is occurring.
- *Interest.* The strong numbers of students interested and maintaining interest in film is witnessed by teachers offering this option. In the New South Wales secondary curriculum, film is offered as a minor elective of a predominantly live theatre course. The numbers of students taking the video drama (film) option have risen dramatically, making it the fastest growing

area in that syllabus (Carroll, Anderson and Cameron, 2006). One student, 'Lloyd', explains the interest young people have in film:

> When film came up as one of the electives it was a really popular subject because technology is becoming such an important factor in our society. It's really prevalent (Early, 2006).

- *Enjoyment.* As Douglas Rushkoff (2005, p. 106) argues, 'the driving force of our new renaissance society is play'. Film learning at its best should be enjoyable, with a sense of play. While film learning is by its nature highly structured, that does not deny the possibility that it can be intrinsically enjoyable. The enjoyment in film learning often stems from the creativity and collaboration inherent in film learning processes. We have included in Table 1.2 an outline of the features that Csikszentmihalyi nominates as integral to flow (1990) and how they might be experienced in effective film learning. As Csikszentmihalyi says, not all of these factors are occurring all of the time in a flow experience.

Table 1.2 Film learning as a flow experience

Feature of flow experience	Examples of flow features in film learning
Clear goals	The development of the film is the clear overall goal but the progressions within the overall project must also be clear, for example, developing a script and storyboard, refining a script, developing a shooting plan, editing for pace and rhythm.
Concentration	In the editing process, students are required to technically and aesthetically manage a complex and consuming task.
A loss of the feeling of self-consciousness	While this is difficult in any area of arts education, authentic acting for camera demands that students resolve and challenge their natural feelings of self-consciousness. This is also required in effective direction and camera operation.

Distorted sense of time	Students in the filming and editing process often lose track of time.
Direct and immediate feedback	Film allows students to see their work at all stages of the process. After filming, they see the rushes and the editing process shows the progress of their storytelling.
Balance between ability level and challenge	Film requires students to engage rigorously with the aesthetics, processes and technology of film. Skilled film educators arrange this alignment as they meet each new set of students.
A sense of personal control over the situation or activity	While in collaborative work this can sometimes be difficult, personal creative control is present in the editing, directing and writing processes.
The activity is intrinsically rewarding	There is often intrinsic reward in the process of making film. The thrill of capturing a meaningful moment on film during the process and the screening of the completed work for an audience response can be intrinsically rewarding parts of the process.

Flow can be experienced in the film classroom. The features elaborated in this table are present in film learning where the teaching is organised and effective. This book is devoted to supporting teachers in achieving effectiveness in their own classrooms.

Teaching film

One of the essential steps on the journey toward a cohesive pedagogy is to articulate what a screen learning framework could be. In the remainder of this chapter, we outline a framework to support those interested in teaching film narrative in the classroom. This framework, shown in Figure 1.3, is not immutable, but it does provide a starting point for those attempting to conceptualise their pedagogy in this area. In the remainder of this chapter, and in the rest of this book, we will develop and extend the concepts in this framework.

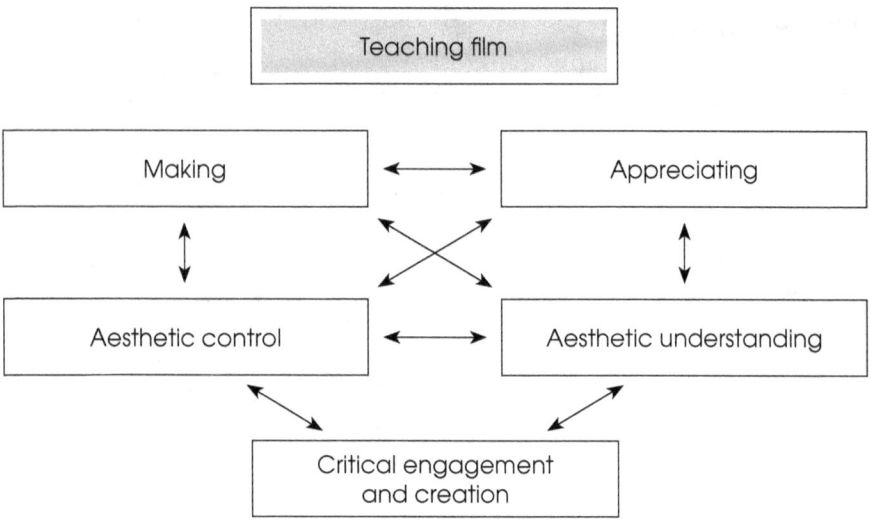

Figure 1.3 Teaching film.

The two pillars of this model consist of terms that are familiar to arts educators: making and appreciating. They are intricately and irrevocably linked concepts. We believe that teaching filmmaking substantially contributes to appreciating, and vice versa. When students develop in this way, they become critically engaged with film aesthetic as makers and appreciators of the art form. We believe that when students have had the opportunity to make film, they can then appreciate film. These pillars are also codependent. In our experience, it is next to useless to expose students to the techniques of a great director and then expect them to reproduce the techniques. Not only does this have the potential to lead to uninspiring derivative work, it assumes that seeing a film will allow the audience to innately understand the techniques and approaches used. In the same way, allowing students to 'run riot' with a camera without being exposed to any filmmaking will see them reproducing what they know, which often results in second-rate parodies of soap operas and reality television. We are not claiming that this is a new approach in arts education. Drama education especially has understood the importance of making and appreciating for decades (Anderson, 2004). In media education, David Buckingham has been calling for a similar engagement between making and appreciating film (Buckingham, 2003). Our framework recognises the antecedents of this approach and proposes elaborations to it that we hope will help practice in this area to evolve further.

Making

We start with making because it is the central and perhaps the most important part of this model. For us, it is central to most of what happens in education. In the development of film narrative, an intimate understanding of the processes involved provides the best preparation for an understanding of how narrative makes the journey from the imagination to the screen. Prioritising making is also a political stance. Making releases the control of the process from the teacher's hands and places it into the hands of the students. By giving students the tools of creation and guiding them in the development of their own work, they come to understand the aesthetic of film by being active participants within it. As Dorothy Heathcote argues (in Carroll, Anderson and Cameron, 2006), schooling and society generally do not value this shift of status:

> The big shift is to move from holding the information and doling it out like charity, to creating the circumstances where it is imperative to inquire, search out and interrogate the information we locate. At present it isn't possible to merge the work of adults and students because we don't value the contribution young children can bring to cultural development of the world's good … (Carroll, Anderson and Cameron, 2006, p. xiii).

David Buckingham (2003) suggests there is a tradition of withholding status and attacking student making that cites the low quality of the productions. Perhaps this is the point. When students attempt to understand narrative and storytelling, their initial attempts will be clichéd, banal, ham-fisted and excruciating to watch at times. This ensues when students are not supported in the development of aesthetic control and understanding. The gap between student attempts and professional quality film can be a harsh disincentive for students to persist with film.

At times, students' first attempts in film are made worse because of the saturation in popular culture of professionally made film that acts as a brutal comparison to students' first, stumbling attempts. English teachers would not consider ignoring writing because the first poetry that students produce is almost unreadable. Beyond the classroom, there are surely several writers, directors, designers and actors who pray that their first efforts may never see the light of day. Ultimately, student development in film should be guided by learning that supports greater control and understanding.

What is required in these cases is not an abandonment of student making but a redoubling of our efforts as teachers to develop our students' aesthetic control. Aesthetic control can only be understood as students actually inhabit the processes of film production. This takes time, and in other areas of the arts—such as music—many schooling systems begin the learning process in preschool and make learning available right up to matriculation level. This learning continuum is predisposed to creating deeper aesthetic control and understanding. The advent of affordable and simplified technologies has allowed students and teachers better access to these processes, and will allow teachers to bring making to the centre of their learning and teaching activities.

Aesthetic control

The main feature of the making process is aesthetic control. This is the extent to which the student can control and manipulate the technical and aesthetic elements of film. These elements include, but are not restricted to, the following:[1]

Pre-production
- Development of a directorial vision that will engage an audience.
- Development of a compelling narrative using dramatic elements such as tension, and expectation.
- Use of film language and film grammar to convey the narrative.

Production
- Skilful direction of the film.
- Skill in framing the action. This will usually employ:
  - camera angles
  - focus
  - shot length
  - shot size
  - movement
  - light, perspective, and/or
  - special effects.
- Skilful direction using production elements that may include:
  - acting
  - location
  - lighting
  - sound capture

- costume, and
- casting.

Post-production

- Editing to convey the dramatic meaning of the film that uses:
  - tension
  - pace
  - mood.
- The employment of sound and music to convey the dramatic meaning of the film.

While these aspects have been listed in an atomised fashion here, aesthetic control also needs to be present in the filmic 'organism' itself. The whole film is often far more than the sum of the elements described here, but if it is to be aesthetically proficient in all of these elements, it must be controlled and understood.

Aesthetic control is more than technical skill. Student access and use of computer-based editing resources are now reasonably commonplace. The inclusion of free editing packages in computers and phones with filming and editing features has seen an explosion in the access the community has to editing. There has, however, been no commensurate rise in the skills young people are demonstrating in the classroom when it comes to editing. Access is not the same as control. The role of the teacher of film is to provide learning that moves young people beyond the technical skills of editing and on to the aesthetic control required to make a successful film. Many young people can now 'drag and drop' clips together, but that is not editing. It is merely a cut and paste exercise. The aesthetic control emerges when young people can use tension, pace and focus to tell a story. These are skills that are rarely learnt in isolation.

Appreciating

The kind of appreciation we envisage in this model is not an antiquated and distant survey of dead white filmmakers. Appreciation for us is an active interaction with the art form that is linked vitally to the production process. As the model suggests, production informs appreciation and appreciation informs production. In practice, this means that teachers can use film (often sparingly and in parts) to assist students' understanding of a technical or aesthetic aspect of filmmaking. What it does not mean is long and unstructured hours sitting in front of 'a classic' in the vain hope that students will somehow osmotically absorb the greatness of the film. An active appreciation involves students watching, actively responding and then experimenting with their appreciation in the making of their own work.

Aesthetic understanding

Aesthetic understanding, like aesthetic control, is focused on students' ability to appreciate effective films and to apply the elements of those films to their own work. The immediate concern here is that often students do not have the resources—financial or otherwise—to apply the principles they have learnt through their appreciation. While this is true when it comes to production values, there are elements of all filmmaking that are essential for students making their own work to understand. The uses of sound, images and editing in filmmaking constitute essential understandings. While the production values of *The Untouchables* (1987) are unsustainable for students, an appreciation of the editing and storytelling involved is an invaluable support for their making processes.

Critically appreciating film

Postmodernism has challenged the high art/low art divide and made it possible for us to recognise aesthetic achievement in many cultural spheres. While postmodernism has opened up analysis of many types of artistic movements and approaches, it has also sought to question judgements about what constitutes excellence. This has acted as a dead hand at times on the teaching of film (and the arts generally), where teachers have felt disinclined to make judgements about filmmaking by their students and others. When teachers are approaching film, they should model a critical and informed appreciation that is not afraid of making and defending aesthetic judgements about film. A robust critical environment in the film classroom (or any classroom, for that matter) ensures that students strive for aesthetic achievement.

David Buckingham (2003) recalls the clamour in media education scholarship in the 1980s to deride student work and earnestly warn teachers against students gaining access to the means of production. While this seems odd three decades later, it does perhaps highlight a problem with the way media and film were taught in an age where technology was not so readily accessible. Technology has made the making process relative to a decade ago a much more feasible classroom activity.

While there is no doubt that there is integrity in young people's work that must be nurtured and appreciated, it must also be supported by promoting depth of understanding of the film aesthetic. Peter Slade's (1954) *Child Drama* is emblematic of a progressivism that sought to leave the work of children untouched. His approach to drama education as outlined in *Child Drama* sat well within the progressivism of the day. *Child Drama*, as a book and as a theory, valued the child's drama as an art in itself that needed to be lovingly nurtured. Slade also stressed that the child's work should not be judged by adult standards. One of the main critiques of this approach comes from David Hornbrook (1989), who writes: 'If the teacher's relationship with *Child Drama* was vitally non-critical then how was it possible to know what educational aims were being realised?' (1989, p. 10).

An important part of Slade's contribution was to acknowledge and prioritise the artistic ability of young children. The enduring critique of this approach, however, is that it is not at its core educative. The process of education and aesthetic education in particular is to develop making and appreciating skills to the point where students are accomplished and confident enough to develop their own artistic practice. This empowerment occurs when they are informed by an appreciation of the art form within which they are working.

Critical engagement

The ultimate aim of this model of film learning is that students will become critically engaged with film and visual culture. You will notice that we have not suggested that all students should become filmmakers any more than any history teacher would suggest that all of her students become historians or archaeologists. While the film industry may be an option for some of our students, the development of an understanding of this ever-present art form is far more important. The pervasiveness of film and visual culture more generally makes a more critically engaged and literate population crucial. What this model adds to the engagement is an active understanding of the processes that make film work, rather than a passive armchair response. Film curriculum developed and offered in this way has the potential to create a greater depth of understanding of this art form.

We have endeavoured in this opening chapter to locate film learning within some of the dominant debates and discourses in education. This chapter is a rationale and an explanation of where film fits in the curriculum and why film learning matters to our society. We believe that we ignore film in the curriculum at our peril. As young people engage with this art form in ever increasing numbers, schools and systems that ignore film learning run the risk of becoming irrelevant to the young people they serve. Now is the time to act and provide a more prominent place for this exciting area of learning.

In the chapters that follow, we will explore some of these issues in more depth, and provide detailed guidance on the implementation of effective film learning in the classroom. Chapter 2 examines how film learning informs and is informed by creativity and literacy.

2
Creativity, multiliteracies and screen learning

>   Buffalo Bill 's
>   defunct
>   who used to
>   ride a watersmooth-silver
>   stallion
>   and break onetwothreefourfive pigeonsjustlikethat
>   Jesus
>   he was a handsome man
>   and what i want to know is
>   how do you like your blueeyed boy
>   Mister Death
>   —E.E. Cummings

'Buffalo Bill 's' (1994) is one of E.E. Cummings's best-known poems, and demonstrates succinctly how literacy and creativity are interdependent. In 'Buffalo Bill 's', Cummings's audacious (for the time) and creative poetic expression is only possible with a masterful understanding of literacy. As a poet, he knew the rules well enough to break them creatively. He is all at once creative, literate, imaginative and in control of the language as he fondly remembers Buffalo Bill and shakes his metaphoric fist at 'Mister Death'.

We begin this chapter with a poem because it quickly and efficiently makes the point that when we work in the arts, literacy and creativity are inseparable. If we were to show you a filmic example, we might choose *Mad Max* (1979), *Three Colours Blue* (1993), *Battleship Potemkin* (1925), *Citizen Kane* (1941), *The Godfather* (1972), *The Third Man* (1949) or *Babel* (2006). In this chapter, we argue that for students to learn about narratives on screen, they need to be literate in narrative forms of all kinds, but especially film, and they need to be able to use that literacy to create their own work. For instance, when discussing the best way to teach literacy no one seriously suggests that conventional literacy consists just of appreciating or interpreting language (listening and reading). Any conventional teaching of literacy also includes the creation of language through speaking and writing. In film learning, we are arguing that the same relationship exists. In the New London Group's (NLG) (1996) introduction of multiliteracy theory, they make the crucial and under-recognised link between creativity and literacy. The NLG argues that people design meaning through a process that recognises 'available designs' and creates new ones:

> In an economy of productive diversity, in civic spaces that value pluralism, and in the flourishing of interrelated, multilayered, complementary yet increasingly divergent lifeworlds, workers, citizens, and community members are ideally creative and responsible makers of meaning. We are, indeed, designers of our social futures (NLG, 1996, p. 88).

Linking creativity and literacy allows young people to design their own future and engage with issues that relate to their worlds. It recognises that they have a responsibility to interpret current social construction but also to create the new worlds that they and their descendants will inhabit. We are already seeing strong evidence of this in film. Young people are combining linguistic conventions with new ideas, just like E.E. Cummings did. They are designing the future of communication by engaging with emergent technology to create new communication. The machinima movement is a recent example of how young people are using established forms—in this case, video games—to create innovative narratives. A typical machinima production sees young artists using gameplay animation to create stories that are posted online, seen and critiqued by their audiences. Like E.E. Cummings, machinima artists are engaging with literacy as they creatively test the boundaries of language and art to create new forms of communication. They can only do this if schools recognise that literacy, screen literacy and creativity are critical and connected features of learning.

Creativity

Creativity is one of those words that suggests loose, abstract individualism, and as such the term is rarely employed (although much talked of) in the service of schooling. Politicians and policy-makers extol the virtues of creativity, presumably because they now see it as a driver of economic activity through the processes of innovation and entrepreneurship. Although discussion about creativity has been more vociferous lately, there is still a significant gap in the research evidence that might tell us what it is and how it can be taught (Kaufman and Sternberg, 2006).

There are many reasons why creativity has trouble finding traction in schools and universities. Perhaps the suspicion of creativity has emerged from the vagueness of the concept for most people. It is vague because it is 'large, unwieldy and hard to grasp' (Kaufman and Sternberg, 2006, p. 3). What we have in mind is something far more tangible and teachable than the vagueness that the term 'creativity' sometimes evokes. A useful definition comes from a report on creative education from the United Kingdom. The authors of this report argue that creativity is 'imaginative activity fashioned so as to produce outcomes that are both original and of value' (Robinson, 1999, p. 30). The same report also identifies three features of creativity: using imagination; pursuing purposes; and being original.

Creativity and schooling

The debate over creativity within schooling generates quite a lot of heat but very little light. There are frequent (often well-meaning) inclusions of the term 'creativity' within syllabus and policy documents, but there is little in the way of real curriculum time devoted to serious engagement with creativity. If creativity is engaged, it is often through the arts and then not always in a rational and systematic way. As Ken Robinson (2001) argues, schools often extol the virtues of creativity but are organised against any possibility of it actually emerging: 'if the government were to design an education system to inhibit creativity, it could hardly do better ... Governments throughout the world emphasise the importance of creativity, but often what they do in education suppresses it' (2001, p. 41).

The difficulty for institutions when it comes to developing creative thinking is that creative thinking often challenges the status quo. The role of the arts, and in particular drama and film, is to question creatively our community's 'taken for granted' assumptions about the world. Schooling systems also rely heavily on order and, as those working first hand with creativity and students know, censorship and restriction are never far away. We would now like to identify some features of screen learning that situate the pedagogy as a potent creative process. These features are elements of creativity that are not always uncontroversial but are identified in the research literature and relate directly to screen learning. They are designed to refute some of the rather romantic notions of creativity. David Buckingham (2003) argues that these attitudes to creativity make it unattainable except for the few:

> creativity is seen in individualistic terms, as the emanation of some kind of 'personal vision'—a matter of an authentic 'self' finding its 'expression'. From this perspective creativity is an essentially unmediated process, a spontaneous outpouring of feeling which is not subject to established conventions and structures. And creative products are seen as somehow self-sufficient: they 'speak for themselves', and hence any kind of analysis will only reduce or destroy them (2003, pp. 127–8).

This attitude makes creativity unattainable, unteachable and individualistic—remote from the everyday student in the everyday classroom. These views, which have been widespread, seriously corrode teaching in film and all of the arts. If creativity cannot be analysed, learnt or taught, it remains the hobby of those who have mystically attained it and worthless to the rest of us. We believe that creativity should be central to all schooling, and that it is a fundamental feature of film learning. Here, we articulate what we consider to be the principles and features of teaching creatively in film learning.

Everyone can be creative

One of the dominant mythologies that surrounds creativity is that it is only available to the elite genius few. The term 'creatives' is often bandied about in industries such as film and advertising. This nomenclature is designed to delineate the 'creatives' from the 'non-creatives'—or the more widely used euphemism, the 'technicians'. This dichotomy entrenches the old idea that some are born to creativity and some are born to technicality, as if these two cannot interact. Of course the technicians often practise a great deal of creativity. In the making of film, if those who are called 'creatives' have no understanding of the technical aspects of their work, their creativity is likely to founder. Aesthetic control and understanding are always predicated on a sound base of technical understanding.

Creativity is part of our daily lives and is exercised by us all. Craft (2002) calls this 'lifewide creativity' because it is manifested throughout our daily lives and seen not just in education. This is the starting point of film learning. Film creativity, as we have argued, is an educative process that begins with the students' immersion in screen culture and then seeks to build aesthetic understanding and aesthetic control. For instance, when students first begin to understand and use the camera deliberately, they have begun to engage in a creative process. While this may be seen by some as elementary in the development of students' understanding of film form and techniques, it is original for the individual student. Robinson (1999) nominates originality as a feature of creativity. Crucially, this report defines originality as original for the individual involved in the activity. This is a fundamentally democratic approach to creativity that frees educators to focus their pedagogy on all students rather than just those that might one day have the potential genius required for a more restricted definition of creativity. This approach does not deny that there are different qualities of creativity; it simply argues that all students provided with the necessary resources can be creative.

Creativity is collaborative

In some places, creativity has been depicted as an individual's struggle for greatness devoid of any real support—the artist alone and starving in a garret, writing the next great novel, play or film. This is perhaps the most debilitating and anti-intuitive myth that relates to creativity for film educators—that it is an individualistic cognitive skill that has no relationship to others. As Fischer et al. (2005) argue: 'Much human creativity arises from activities that take place in a social context in which interactions with other people and the artefacts that embody group knowledge are important contributors to the process. Creativity does not happen inside a person's head, but in the interaction between a person's thoughts and a socio-cultural context' (2005, p. 485). This complex interplay is difficult to measure with tests, but it is a truism of creativity in film learning that it is not an isolated cognitive skill, but rather a complex interaction of the individual learner, their learning context, their fellow learners and film technology.

A cursory understanding of the collaborative processes involved in drama, music and film argues against this stereotype of isolated creativity. In the case of film, it is very much the exception that the individual is capable of creating a film. Creativity in this area routinely relies on the interplay of several creative approaches at once for anything to actually be created. While research has focused more heavily on the sources of individual and personal creativity

(Jeffrey and Craft, 2001), there is evidence that creativity can be and is achieved in group contexts. Holbrook Mahn and Vera John-Steiner (2002) argue that in collaboration participants create mutual zones of proximal development for each other where their intellect and emotions are brought together in a unified whole. They explain how collaborative creativity actually works in the process of filmmaking:

> In producing texts partners share each other's early drafts; they strive to give shape to their communicative intent by combining precision—or word meaning—with the fluidity of the sense of the words. They live, temporarily, in each other's heads. They also draw on their mutuality as well as their differences in knowledge, working styles and temperament (2002, p. 51).

The same processes are taking place in film learning. Students discuss the development of a shooting script, provide different perspectives over the development of images and dialogue on a storyboard, direct acting for the camera, discuss the placement of characters within a shot, and examine how the rhythms of the piece can be manipulated through the editing process. The learning taking place here relies on the student working with the group in cooperation with the aesthetic demands of the form.

As teachers who have worked in the arts well know, the products of these collaborations are not always creative. They are often banal and plodding; however, the potential for creativity is enhanced when the teacher is able to develop a learning environment that makes aesthetic control and aesthetic understanding prominent. Learning to be creative is an evolutionary growth that begins with students making original discoveries (for themselves) and then building on those discoveries in a broader social context.

Teaching for creativity

One of the persistent myths about creativity and learning is that it cannot be taught or fitted within a system of any sort. This view suggests that creativity is inborn and cannot be taught, enhanced and developed in any way. The research evidence suggests that creativity can be developed, taught and supported in schools and other places (Kaufman and Sternberg, 2006). We argue that effective teaching and creative teaching are actually one and the same thing. If you are to teach your students creativity in the context of film learning, you must approach your own pedagogy with a creative orientation. Teaching in this way will see the teacher work flexibly, drawing on all their pedagogical skills. As the influential British report on creativity *All Our Futures* (NACCE, 1999) suggests, there is 'a balance in all good teaching between formal instruction of content and of skills, and giving young people the freedom to inquire, question, experiment and to express their own thoughts and ideas' (1999, p. 105). If the teacher is able to teach creatively, then the preconditions are emerging to teach creativity. Teaching creativity is an awkward idea because the pedagogy demands flexibility and innovation that are in direct conflict with the prescription and testing-based curriculum that is so prevalent in many Western nations (Abbs, 2003, p. 1). Effective teaching for creativity will model creativity and provide learning experiences that support its growth in students:

> There is an obvious sense in which children cannot be 'taught' creativity in the way that they can be taught the times tables. Creative processes do draw from knowledge and practical skills. It is also the case that there are various techniques to facilitate creative thinking (NACCE, 1999, p. 103).

The development of creativity in film sees the melding of aesthetic control and aesthetic understanding. In this process, there will be times when students are left to experiment and other times when they are directly taught the principles of the art form. The modelling of creative approaches has the potential to deliver rich learning experiences that foster innovation and creativity rather than teach students to produce banality and derivative art works.

Creativity in film learning cannot take place without skills in the creation of film. The rest of this chapter discusses the changing nature of literacy in the classroom, and discusses how teachers might support students in developing screen literacy. We argue that literacy and creativity are interdependent in film learning, and that the skills in this area must be developed sequentially. We begin by discussing the importance of literacy, multiliteracy and screen literacy.

Literacy, multiliteracy or cineliteracy?

In any discussion of literacy, there are terms that have the potential to be confusing. Here, when we refer to 'literacy' we are discussing the traditional forms of literacy. The *Oxford English Dictionary* (2006) defines this as: 'The quality or state of being literate; knowledge of letters; condition in respect to education, esp. ability to read and write.' When we discuss multiliteracies, we are referring to a broader definition of literacy that embraces digital and other texts. When we refer to screen literacy or cineliteracies, we are referring directly to literacies that relate to appreciating and making film. Let's begin with a discussion of the place of literacy in today's classrooms.

Literacy

The narrow-minded political posturing that sometimes passes for debate in this area often reduces the debate about literacy to a cliché. This is irritating and a cause for concern because there are significant issues of social justice and access to cultural capital that tend to be overshadowed by narrow political positions. As bell hooks argues:

> When teachers support democratic education we automatically support widespread literacy ... Everyone that knows how to read and write has the tools to enter higher learning even if that learning can not and does not take place in a university setting (hooks, 2003, p. 43).

Literacy has a vital role to play in providing all students with the opportunity to democratically engage with their community. Critical literacy has a strong role to play here as well. The critical literacies approach commits this kind of aspiration to action. This approach is heavily influenced by the work of Paulo Freire (1972) who stressed the importance of active learning rather than traditional direct instructional models of filling 'empty vessels'. Luke and Freebody (1997) argue that those practising critical literacies are 'a coalition of educational interests committed to engaging with the possibilities that technologies of writing and other modes of inscription offer for social change, cultural diversity, economic equity and political enfranchisement' (1997, p. 1). This social change potentially comes about when citizens focus on and question the context and the motivation of the messages with which they are bombarded.

While critical literacy may seem like the very basis of education for many educators, it has garnered significant criticism from traditionalists. Kenneth Wiltshire (2006) wrote:

> By its own admission it [critical literacy] is about things such as revealing the purpose and motives of the composers of texts and their lack of neutrality, the way alternative views are silenced, the power of language, providing students

with opportunities to clarify their own attitudes and values, take a stance on issues and take social action ... This sort of thinking is a recipe for laziness, indifference and unwillingness to identify standards and common values. It inevitably leads to dumbing down of the curriculum and therefore the students ... Should *The Diary of Anne Frank* be replaced with *The Emails of Tom Cruise* or *The Text Messages of Shane Warne*?

This critique of critical literacy uncovers two issues. The first is whether messages should be analysed with reference to their context, and the second is that any form of communication that is electronically mediated is less valid than the written word. The effect of this criticism is that it diminishes the importance of understanding multiple messages and their sources. Its denigration of emerging literacies resorts to the lowest common denominator of celebrity trivia. While this has been a popular stalking horse of political conservatives, there is little evidence that any education system has seriously resorted to the excesses shown here. To suggest that teachers would seriously consider teaching trivia rather than literature under-estimates the professionalism of teachers generally.

Teachers of film will need to defend critical literacy as a valid, and indeed prominent, way of examining their media. As Buckingham (2003) argues: 'media literacy is a form of critical literacy. It involves analysis, evaluation and critical reflection. It entails the acquisition of a metalanguage that is a means of describing the forms and functions of different modes of communication, and it involves broader understanding of the social, economic and institutional contexts of communication' (2003, p. 38). The ability to analyse and then respond to film—be it *Macbeth* (1971) or *Star Wars* (1977)—is central to the practice of making and appreciating classical and more contemporary works. Arguments that focus on whether young people should examine *Pride and Prejudice* (1995) or *Raiders of the Lost Ark* (1981) are distractions at best. As teachers of the screen, we must draw from the best of all traditions to support the learning of our students, and ignore the trivial and aesthetically bankrupt.

Unfortunately, the political posturing that sometimes surrounds the debates about literacy has the potential to pigeonhole this area of learning and restrict students' access to literacy learning that is relevant and relates directly to the world they inhabit. As the New London Group (NLG) argues:

> Literacy pedagogy has traditionally meant teaching and learning to read and write in page-bound, official, standard forms of the national language.

> Literacy pedagogy, in other words, has been a carefully restricted project—restricted to formalised, monolingual, monocultural and rule governed forms of language (NLG, 1996, p. 61).

Multiliteracy theory argues that it is no longer sufficient to pretend that the printed word is the dominant medium. They argue that, in modern societies, diversity and the prevalence of digital technologies require a literacy that will support readings and creation in multiple forms of literacy. The implication for developing critical, active and democratic citizens within our schools is that they will need to interpret and create messages beyond the written word. If they are to do this effectively, schooling must engage with literacy forms beyond the printed page. While this theory has come to currency lately, multiliteracy as a social practice has been around since perhaps before the written word. Elizabeth Daley (2003) argues that multiliteracy was the first literacy:

> The concept of a language composed of elements other than word and text is neither fundamentally new or particularly revolutionary. Rather, this concept is an evolutionary development of the ideas and practices that have been with us since people first struggled to leave records and tell stories. Technology is simply enabling these alternative ways of communicating to penetrate our lives more directly and in more powerful ways (2003, p. 187).

Multiliteracy as a social practice

The social nature of learning in film is inescapable. When it comes to screen literacy, student learning is also socially mediated and situated. We understand screen literacy as learning that is socially constructed, mediated and regulated, not as an individual psychological intelligence. This flies in the face of those who would argue for literacy as a narrow skills-focused form of cognition. In the US context, Cherland and Harper (2007, p. 154) decry this narrow understanding of literacy. They argue that 'the United States Department of Education supported by the American president continues to support laws and policies that assume literacy to be a purely psychological skill, or set of skills, the same for every individual of every race, gender, ethnicity, and class'. By contrast, teachers who understand literacy as a social practice recognise the backgrounds of students and create classrooms where that understanding informs and energises literacy learning.

The understanding of literacy as a social practice has two strong implications for film learning. First, literacy—and film literacy in particular—is inherently social in nature (Buckingham, 2003, p. 38). Anyone who has taught film knows that it is almost impossible to develop an effective filmed narrative without using a social setting to create the learning. The process of storyboard development provides a good example of screen literacy as a social practice. As students develop an understanding of film literacy, you often see them huddled over a storyboard discussing dialogue, the angles of the shot, how the scene will cut up, and so on. While this may seem like an informal process, these students are actively and energetically involved in the process of applying themselves to screen literacy. The visual nature of film learning repositions students. Instead of being sole authors, they are co-writers and collaborators as they work together to exercise aesthetic control of film. This is screen literacy in action, and it is achieved and understood as a process of negotiation, discussion and trial and error.

The second implication is that literacy (for our purposes, screen literacy) can only be understood in the context of the social milieu of the learners. At its core, multiliteracy values a diversity of voices in a community of practice. The New London Group (1996) argues: 'When learners juxtapose different languages, discourses, styles, and approaches, they gain substantively in meta-cognitive and meta-linguistic abilities and in their ability to reflect critically on complex systems and their interactions' (1996, p. 7). The strength of a social approach to literacies is in the diversity of learners applying themselves to the learning.

Children and multiliteracy

Children come to formal schooling more prepared for understanding literacy related to the screen than any other form of literacy. According to an American study undertaken in 2006, about two-thirds (66 per cent) of children aged six months to six years watch television *every* day for an average of one and a quarter hours a day. The study found that the average time children spend reading or being read to was 40 minutes (Kaiser Family Foundation, 2006, p. 7).

There are some valid concerns about this rate of screen media consumption, including potential lessening of physical activity and exposure to inappropriate content. There is an opportunity here to use all this media exposure (which is not the same as aesthetic understanding or aesthetic control) to develop critical readings of the eight and a half hours of media messages they receive on a weekly basis (Kaiser Family Foundation, 2005, p. 57). This ultimately helps them make their own decisions about the media they watch and the media that they produce.

In practice, this area of literacy is largely ignored by schooling systems, or teaching is provided in a piecemeal and patchy fashion. The massive experience that students have in reading screen images lies mostly untapped. Perhaps more than ever, schooling is losing connection with young people as they consume media that schools mostly ignore. Ken Robinson's (2001) argument that schooling is based on hopelessly outmoded practices is evidenced by the way screen learning is currently overlooked in learning. As he (2001, p. 41) argues: 'The system [of education] we have now evolved from a political need to face the challenges and consequences of the industrial revolution.' We are now in the midst of a digital revolution—our schooling systems are still coping with the last revolution. What is required now is a reform of schooling—a reform that recognises the lived realities of young people living with a digital revolution and counts their exposure to media as an asset.

This exposure is an extensive and deep reservoir of film experience, but not necessarily of understanding and control. The challenge for schools and schooling is to construct a screen literacy that supports the development of critical and creative young people who not only read film critically but also create their own work. The answer lies in developing a framework for screen literacy that does not displace other literacies, but rather recognises and supports the need to understand multiple literacies or multiliteracies (Cope and Kalantzis, 2000). The theory of multiliteracies argues that, rather than reading and writing with text, students should develop through education an ability to read and create in multiple media. These readings should not be siloed, but interact and support each other. In the classroom, film is perhaps the most accessible and most easily managed of multimodal texts. When students make and watch film, they are examining image composition, sound, setting, point of view, design elements, and so on, and looking at how these are composed to create meaning. For young people who now require a multimodal understanding of the world, film provides a stronger starting point than traditional printed forms of language.

Film literacy

'Literacy' is a term that, with the advent of the multiliteracies approach and the prevalence of screen-based messages, can no longer be confined to print-based work. There is, however, a need to provide a foundation for the particular kinds of literacy learning that are going on in film learning. This is not to uncouple film literacy from other types of literacy, but rather to see film literacy in the context of a complex and convergent conceptualisation of media. As Sue Brindley (2005) argues: 'Literacy needs to be conceptualised within a broader social order … this new communication order takes account of the literacy practices associated with screen-based technologies. It recognises that reading and writing practices, conceived traditionally as print-based and logo-centric, are only part of what people have to learn to be literate' (2005, p. 39).

There have been some valuable recent contributions to the discussion of film literacy. The British Film Institute's Film Education Working Group's (FEWG 1999) 'cineliteracies' provides a structure for teachers to work towards where there is an absence of coherent policy support for screen literacies. The strength of these structures is that they begin to define the ground that cinema literacy might inhabit. As Buckingham (2003) points out, this is not the first attempt at categorisation of screen literacies (2003, pp. 40–1), but it does constitute an important marker in the journey toward a coherent discussion of screen literacies. The Film Education Working Group (1999) Stage 5 outcomes appear in Table 2.1 as a point of comparison with the development of film literacies in other contexts.

Table 2.1 The Film Education Working Group Cineliteracies for Stage 5

Language	• Explain how FVT (Film as Visual Text) styles and narrative forms can relate to authors, production context, social and cultural context • Use film language to construct moving image narratives • Identify and describe the contributions of different skills in an FVT text
Producers and audiences	• Describe and explain how authors, genres and stars are meaning-bearing systems and how they can be used to market FVT • Identify and describe some of the ways in which FVT institutions relate to social, cultural and political contexts • Describe the economic organisation of FVT institutions and the relationship between producers, distributors, exhibitors and audiences

Messages and values	• Use key words to discuss and evaluate ideological messages in mainstream FVT texts • Describe and account for different levels of realism in FVT texts • Explain relationships between aesthetic style and social/political meaning
In addition they should be able to	• Assemble research findings into clear argument or exposition • Create moving image texts for specific audiences and purposes in specific styles and genres • Develop independent judgements about the value and relevance of critical theories

The focus of the cineliteracies here is on the appreciating of film as visual text and not on the development of literacies through engagement with the form. Perhaps the rapid evolution of screen technology in the years since this framework was developed has seen a change in emphasis, as production becomes a far more feasible classroom activity. New conceptions of screen literacy should recognise the centrality of making in the process of becoming literate in the art form.

Concluding reflections: The link between creativity and literacy

Very young children have an inbuilt, innate capacity for creativity that they exhibit in their play. As they grow older, the education system tends to discourage playfulness, experimentation and creativity in favour of 'learning'. The creative environments of the primary years give way to often-sterile classrooms that discourage collaboration and encourage competition (Arnold, 2005, p. 69). Putting arts at the centre of schooling could change that orientation. As Elliot Eisner (2004) argues, 'shifting the paradigm of education reform and teaching from one modelled after the clocklike character of the assembly line into one that is closer to the studio or innovative science laboratory might provide us with a vision that better suits the capacities and the futures of the students we teach'.

Our outmoded schooling environment is nurtured by the testing regimes that have proscribed school curriculum and organisation at the expense of creativity and discovery. We have often heard teachers say: 'I have no time for making film—I need to get the kids ready for their literacy test.' We are not arguing here that measurement is unimportant. In a balanced curriculum, it is vital. Nor are we arguing that we should drop literacy from classrooms. On the contrary, we are arguing for classrooms—and indeed schooling—that recognise the interdependence of creativity and literacy to engage students. They are interdependent in pedagogy because literacy is one of the bases of creativity. Without a fluency in the language and features of a particular aesthetic, there is little chance that creativity can be a consistent feature of teaching. Research evidence suggests that when creativity and literacy are developed sequentially in the classroom, students achieve strong outcomes in both creativity and literacy:

> Both literacy and the creative arts are about communication and expression. In effective projects, teachers and arts partners created contexts for learning within which language and literacy developed and flourished, always alongside other forms of symbolizing (CLPE, 2005, p. 41).

Effective and engaging film learning will take place when teachers embrace multiliteracies and creativity as interlinked concepts for students of all ages. This relationship forms an essential basis for creating a classroom where aesthetic engagement and production are not only possible, but are an expectation of students and teachers alike. In the next chapter, we consider how screen theory and practice can be used for student learning.

3
Screen theory, practice and learning

> The better one reads an image, the more one understands it, the more power one has over it.
>
> —James Monaco

The film semiotician Christian Metz (1974) famously said: 'A film is difficult to explain because it is easy to understand.' This is the dilemma teachers and students encounter when they analyse film in the classroom. Everyone watches and comprehends moving pictures in cinemas, on television, and on computers and phones, but can they really explain them? Is there a language we can learn to explain moving pictures and understand how they work? Monaco (2000) argues that if audiences understand more how films work, 'the better the balance between observer and creator in the process' and 'the more vital and resonant the work of art' (2000, p. 159). These ideas have ramifications for student learning. As students make films, they must understand how to read images so they have the power to work vitally with the art form, and in doing so become more discriminating consumers of the medium:

> In quantitative terms, the more people who are exposed to a work of art, the more potential effect it has. In qualitative terms, the observer/consumer does have it within their power to increase the sum value of the work by becoming a more sophisticated, creative, or sensitive participant in the process (Monaco, 2000, p. 36).

To read the images of film effectively, we believe it is necessary to learn and control the aesthetic of film. In this chapter, we examine how screen theory and practice provide a key to understanding the film aesthetic and also provide structures for a pedagogy in film learning.

Where do we begin?

Recently we came upon a primary school DVD promising parents 'see your children as you've never seen them before on the big screen!' We anticipated seeing the beginning of classroom innovation in technology and creative arts learning, with primary children knowing how to use film to tell their stories. Viewing the primary DVD, however, took us back in time rather than into the possibilities of the future. It was a flashback to 1902 and the George Méliès film, *A Voyage to the Moon*.

Figure 3.1 Theatrical film stills from George Méliès's film, *A Voyage to the Moon* (1902).

As a stage magician and early filmmaker, Méliès drew on the conventions of theatrical staging to tell his fictional stories in moving pictures. The camera frame was like theatre's proscenium arch, and outside the frame were the wings for the actors to enter and exit. The ornate and fantastical sets filled the frame, within which actors wildly gesticulated actions and reactions. The story was propelled forward by changes of scenes that began and ended with a fade to black, like the dropping of the curtain to conceal a set change. The delight and magic in Méliès's films was his use of celluloid and the cinematograph to tell stories of the imagination capturing three-dimensional events in a two-dimensional projection, existing forever on celluloid for future generations to enjoy. In the development of film, Méliès is also recognised for his abilities to manipulate the technology of early film and create special effects in stop action (people appearing to disappear) and double exposure (the moon appears with a human face). However, his films still appear as theatrical tableaux because the camera has one fixed perspective of the action; it is the view of the best seat in a theatrical auditorium. The capacity to manipulate the viewer's perspective by changing the camera's distance, shot size and angle, and filming with a camera in motion, had not been utilised in either Méliès's film or the primary school flick. We begin with the notion of changing visual perspective as the engine of film's power as an art form—but how do we explain its effect?

Identification and the 'psychic strength of the lens'

The psychological effect of the camera's ability to be mobile is viewed by film theorist Béla Balázs (1970; first published 1952) as 'identification':

> In the cinema the camera carries the spectator into the film picture itself. We are seeing everything from the inside as it were and are surrounded by the characters of the film. They need not tell us what they feel, for we see what they see and see it as they see it. Although we sit in our seats for which we have paid, we do not see Romeo and Juliet from there. We look up to Juliet's balcony with Romeo's eyes and look down on Romeo with Juliet's. Our eye and with it our consciousness is identified with the characters in the film, we look at the world out of their eyes and have no angle of vision of our own (1970, p. 48).

The spectator in film inhabits the characters' world because the camera takes us there. The identification or relationship between the spectator and the characters, actions and landscapes in the film is dependent on how the camera captures the world of the film. The camera choices affecting the audience's identification are based on a highly complex system of communication and aesthetic. In *A Personal Journey with Martin Scorsese Through American Movies* (1995), Scorsese discusses how the early film pioneers explored a new 'poetic' language based on images rather than words, and understood the power of the 'psychic strength of the lens' to create and heighten the illusion of reality and identification, where 'one close-up was worth a thousand words'. Realising the full potential of the camera's psychic capability for identification is what filmmakers have been discovering and developing since the Lumière brothers first screened their 50-second films in 1895.

What is screen learning?

Like Méliès, the primary school flick uses technology to capture and edit its dramatised narratives, but ultimately they are filmed tableaux of theatrical-like performances. They do not fully engage the spectator in a cinematic sense. By not exploring 'the psychic strength of the lens', the primary school DVD merely becomes a two-dimensional recording of a three-dimensional theatrical event, and loses the power of a theatrical experience based on 'liveness' and three dimensions. Such narratives cannot 'live' through the screen without a fundamental metamorphosis into something new.

That metamorphosis is the concern of screen learning. Since its beginnings, film has taken elements from drama and theatre, the visual arts, novels and music. In many ways, learning about film is characterised by understanding and using the elements of these art forms as they come together to create the hybrid of film. Film also has essential elements intrinsic to its own form that must be recognised to fully appreciate the art form. Screen learning recognises film as developing its own aesthetic principles informed by film practice and screen theory.

The productive pedagogy research in *Teachers and Schooling Making a Difference* (Hayes et al., 2006) found that deep knowledge and deep understanding of an operational field contributed to student learning of a higher intellectual quality:

> *Deep knowledge* concerned the central ideas and concepts of a topic or discipline, and such knowledge was judged to be crucial to a topic or discipline. Knowledge was deep when relatively complex relations were established to central concepts ... For students, knowledge was deep when they developed relatively complex understandings of these central concepts (2006, p. 43).

In teaching filmmaking and appreciation, screen theory helps to unlock the essential and fundamental concepts of the learning area. To use an automotive metaphor, to make a car we have to understand what a car's function is and how it works. Knowing how to drive a car is not enough, although driving does contribute to and support our understanding of how to make it. To be able to make a film, we have to know what film's function is and how it works. Screen theory and practice take us deep into the engine of film, and guide us to set up frameworks for sequential and effective learning in filmmaking and appreciation. These structures are expanded upon later in the book; the focus of this chapter is to illustrate how screen theory helps to create a pedagogical vocabulary of film and a pedagogical framework. At the very base of this framework, we begin by addressing what film essentially is because it illuminates more understandings, not only about how film works, but also about how to *make* film work.

How does film work?

In 1915, Vachel Lindsay in *The Art of the Moving Picture* advocated that the new phenomenon of film should be recognised as an art form with its own genius of expression. Lindsay said presciently: 'The invention of the photoplay is as great a step as was the beginning of picture-writing in the stone age.' These words have deep resonances for us today:

> It is obvious that cinematic and electronic technologies of representation have had enormous impact upon our means of signification during the past century ... whether or not we go to the movies, watch television or music videos, own a video tape recorder/player, allow our children to play video and computer games ... we are all part of a moving-image culture and we live cinematic and electronic lives (Sobchack 2000, p. 67).

Certainly moving pictures are ubiquitous in our world of mass communication, and although the technical hardware of celluloid and splicing can now be done by digital tape and computer editing software, the genesis of moving pictures in the late nineteenth century and its development in the twentieth century have shaped what is essentially a 'filmic aesthetic' as a communication sensibility.

The filmic aesthetic, or 'language of film', has developed and continues to develop because of the collusion between filmmakers and the audience to

Figure 3.2 Cross-cutting images from D.W. Griffith's *Death's Marathon* (1913).

make meaning from the way moving pictures are used. When D.W. Griffith first used rapid cross-cutting between three scenes in *Death's Marathon* (1913), the distributors were concerned the audience would be confused by such an innovative technique.

The phone call between the father and his child held in his wife's arms is intercut with the police in a car on their way to capture him. The tension is heightened as the film cross-cuts between the police getting closer and the heartbreaking conversation between the father and his family. Suspense is added for the audience since they can see that the father has a gun. The father is on the phone, the baby listens to daddy, the police arrive, the father raises the gun, over the phone the wife hears the gunshot, the father slumps to the table: he has committed suicide. Three scenes and actions happening at once can feature in the structure of a novel but here film represents it through rapid visual imagery. The audience not only understands how three interrupted and intercut scenes tell one story, but the rhythm and fragmentation of the cross-cutting enhances the tension and quickens the heartbeat of the audience. The audience has conspired with the filmmaker to make meaning of cross-cutting and establish a convention in the aesthetic of filmmaking. Film theorist Christian Metz (1974) says: 'It is not because the cinema is language that it can tell such fine stories, but rather it has become language because it has told such fine stories' (1974, p. 47).

For school students to tell their own stories, they have to control the conventions and aesthetic of filmic language to communicate in the film form, particularly by understanding the fundamental role of movement.

The importance of movement in visual imagery

Herbert Read's simple definition in *Towards a Film Aesthetic* (1932, pp. 7–10) provides the basis for screen learning:

> Film is the art of space–time: it is a space–time continuum. There are at least three directions (or dimensions) in which movement may take place:
> 1. Movement of the camera
> 2. Movement of light
> 3. Movement of the object photographed
>
> Combinations of such movements produce almost endless possibilities of plastic form.

Movement is requisite not only to the aesthetic of a film's form but also to the *construction* of its form. Two-dimensional motion is an illusion of perception for the spectator. The Victorian children's toy, the zoetrope, illustrates this. The zoetrope has still images of a juggler's arms and the trajectory of a juggled ball depicted on the inside of a cylindrical drum. When the drum is spun, the ball appears to be thrown and to move through the air. In 1877, Eadweard Muybridge's photographed stills of a horse galloping were animated by the zoetrope. The possibility of creating the illusion of movement through the use of moving pictures emerged. Muybridge's photographs not only demonstrated the impression of motion, but his moving photographic images of real objects appeared to represent the 'reality' of the world even more than still photography.

Semiotician Roland Barthes describes the observer's engagement with the 'realness' of a still photograph as 'has been there'. Instead, Christian Metz (1974) argues that the film spectator is absorbed by a sense of 'there it is'. This impression of a 'there it is' reality is created by the illusion of movement giving objects in the two-dimensional frame the appearance of volume. The spectator also believes it to be alive because it moves. The difference between still photography and moving pictures is illuminating for students learning the aesthetics integral to film. Although design elements of the two-dimensional visual arts (compositional elements such as balance, proportion and perspective) inform the aesthetics of framing in film, cinematic images involve the animation of 'moving' two-dimensional visual design components. So the arms and ball of the juggler in the zoetrope contribute to the aesthetic of composition in the changing spatial coordinates occurring in the moving frames.

Movement in film creates the impression of 'realness' or 'aliveness', even in an impressionistic or expressionistic sense. When a non-realistic filmic style is used to create an atmosphere or emotional state, movement still gives it life. The

Figure 3.3 The zoetrope, a Victorian children's toy that when spun creates the illusion of movement.

plastic bag caught by the wind in *American Beauty* (1999) appears to dance, and its movement is an expression of great abstract beauty. In the openings of *Witness* (1985) and *Gladiator* (2000), the close-up shots of wheat in a field are 'alive' and 'dynamic' because the wheat moves in the breeze. A shimmering heat haze moves the atmosphere in the most desolate and still desert landscapes of *Lawrence of Arabia* (1962). When the landscape doesn't move, the camera will. For instance, in *Rear Window* (1954), after the spectator reads the high temperature on the thermometer in a static shot, the camera moves to peer out the window. Significantly, movement in the frame or by the frame creates the illusion of 'aliveness' in film. However, movement is also important in other ways.

In film, as in theatre, movement is a dynamic element used to control the spectator's focus on action within the frame, and in this way movement can pull focus in an intended or unintended way. The speeding car far off in the background of a long shot can take the spectator's eye away for a split second from the dramatic focus in the foreground, interfering with the audience's complete engagement. When we watch a film, the design or arrangement of the characters, set, objects, light and landscape within the frame controls our reading of the image. Orson Welles eloquently demonstrated the use of these arrangements throughout *Citizen Kane* (1941)—for example, in the blackmail

Figure 3.4 A still from Orson Welles's *Citizen Kane* (1941) demonstrates how the manipulation of *mise en scène* elements such as lighting, character placement and movement affect dramatic meaning.

scene between Kane, Gettys, Emily and Susan where the proximity of the characters to each other and to the camera, and the dramatic use of light and shadow, illustrate the shifting power relationships between them.

The design of the image and the movement within the frame are part of the aesthetic of film's *mise en scène*. *Mise en scène* describes the manipulation and articulation of space in cinematic imagery, and it affects the information digested by the spectator as they engage with and make meaning of the film. Students need to control images and movement to communicate clearly and expressively in film.

Motion is also the metaphorical glue of the editing process. The editing or montage of shots being brought together means they are connected by illusions of movement, rather like the sleight of hand of a stage illusionist. In montage, this is a way to change the camera's perspective in a scene and change from one scene to the next. The juxtaposition of images in montage distorts real space and time, but movement helps to create an illusionary connection between space and time, and hence a 'there it is' reality. Therefore, a lack of movement in the frame or by the camera can—intentionally or unintentionally—interrupt the fluidity of shot montage and the engagement and meaning that it generates. For example, François Truffaut interrupts the flow of montage at the end of his film *400 Blows* (1959) by freezing the frame on the

Figure 3.5 The frozen frame at the end of François Truffaut's *400 Blows* (1959) disrupts the flow of montage and movement and creates a dramatic effect.

young Antoine, bringing the film to an abrupt end and creating an arresting and ambiguous closure for the audience.

Motion helps to explain what film is, and in creating and controlling moving visual imagery we recognise a vital element in the aesthetic of film; however, moving visual imagery is not the only element—others are sound, speech, music and graphics.

Sound

Herbert Read claimed in 1932: 'It is difficult to see any art-form evolving out of the talkie … The talk interrupts the continuity of the movement, or at least delays it … This does not imply that the talkie has no future. But its laws will not be the laws of the pure film, and the sooner it works out its own salvation, the better' (1932, pp. 7–10). The talkies' redemption is that they have contributed significantly to the aesthetic of 'pure film'. However, Read's analysis does illuminate how the silence of early film contributed to the development of a visual language in the aesthetic that he calls 'pure film', and it draws attention to how images, movement and sound must have a symbiotic aesthetic to work together effectively. It also highlights the primacy of image over sound, where the spectator engages with or believes what they see before what they hear. The revelation of the talkies was the potency of sound and speech to further enhance the sense of 'realness' or 'aliveness' that moving pictures created. When we hear an ambient sound of the environment we are watching, it unconsciously intensifies our belief and engagement in the 'there it is' reality of the film world.

Speech

Dialogue adds another layer of communication and sense of 'realness' to the cinematic experience, but it is a contrived dialogue to further the artistic and dramatic intent of the film's objectives. Just as film's imagery draws from and metamorphosises the aesthetic of design in the visual arts, film does the same with the functioning of dialogue from the dramatic arts. Elements contributing to the dialogue of theatre are similar to those of film, but they are also different. This is because of dialogue's subservience to the power of visual language and how it accommodates the predominance of changing imagery and perspective in film. This, and the effect of juxtaposing images in editing, changes the role, rhythms and meanings of dialogue in film to something different from that of the stage play.

Music

In conjunction with moving pictures, the abstraction of music has augmented an expressionistic and impressionistic texture to the film aesthetic. Nineteenth-century melodrama in theatres and the early silent films were often accompanied by live music to punctuate and heighten emotions and moods in the dramas being enacted. Film uses the components that make music an expressive art form for its own purposes. The principles of music composition underlie the making of music for film, but once again film transforms music as an element because it is not alone: it is combined with images, actions, dialogue, sound and montage to serve the dramatic and artistic purpose of the film. For example, the lush, whimsical John Williams score for the film *Harry Potter and the Philosopher's Stone* (2001) may heighten a student's film about life at school to an emotionally melodramatic and epic level that is inappropriate for the student's work—unless, perhaps, it is used ironically.

Whether music appears as part of the action in the scene (synchronous) or as an unseen accompaniment to the drama (non-synchronous), an aesthetic and meaning are created both when it is there and when it is not. This emphasis on meaning and affect being created with or without music is important in teaching the screen because it demonstrates and focuses the role and power of each element in the aesthetic and the need to control it to serve the filmic intent. A reliance on music alone to tell the drama limits students' capacities and possibilities when it comes to telling their stories cogently and potently.

Graphics

Graphics are word and sign images, and are usually titles and credits in films. They are a visual aesthetic that needs to be manipulated to serve the film's meaning and engagement with the audience. With graphics, the audience reads the semiotics of font, size and design and associates meanings drawn from them. Graphics in titles and credits are part of the visual and dramatic stylistic unity of the whole film and affect audience expectations. Pedro Almodovar's bright and colourful patterns in his title credits for *Volver* (2006) are part of his design palate that takes the audience into the flamboyant, camp aesthetic of his filmic world of melodrama and passion.

How do visual images, sound, speech, music and graphics play a role in the pedagogy?

Communication in film is transmitted through the visual image, sound, speech, music and graphics. The visual image and sound are nearly always present in the aesthetic, but speech, music and graphics are not a given; they are choices made according to the artistic expression and intent of the filmmaker. For students learning about film, it is important to compartmentalise film into these five parts, clearly crystallising the function and effect of the aesthetics' components. Combining all these elements at the beginning of learning can muddy students' understanding when it comes to discerning the components' significance and expressive function. Recognising the parts helps students control each of them as expressive tools. This approach informs the structuring of gradual skill and knowledge acquisition, and enables achievable outcomes, which are based in part on recognising the components discussed: visual image, graphics, sound, music, speech and their combinations. The pedagogical model we have developed is a framework of scaffolded, short filming exercises which focus the learning on parts of the aesthetic and elements within them. The exercises become more complicated and sophisticated as skills are acquired. We have determined the parts that contribute to the whole film form, but we haven't defined what conditions define film as film.

A definition of film that provides parameters to the learning area

A definition of film not only provides underlying principles and guides the framework of screen pedagogy; it also allows for the possibility of film's stylistic development in the future. We have used Noel Carroll's (1996) five necessary conditions to define moving pictures to provide parameters for screen learning (see Table 3.1).

This definition first releases film from the strictures of medium-essentialism—that is, it is not defined by any specific medium or material or technology, such as a projector or film stock. It allows for the stylistic diversity and technological transformations already evident in film's evolution. For example, the technical and artistic developments we have witnessed from celluloid to digital adhere to the five defining conditions. The definition of a screen, the impression of movement, a template artwork as a fixed token

Table 3.1 The application of Carroll's five necessary conditions to define what the motion picture or film is

The screen	The moving image is presented as a detached display where the audience is alienated or disembodied in spatial terms from the cinematic images; instead, in the theatre, the audience is oriented in real space with the performers.
Movement	The imagery belongs to the class of things where the impression of movement is technically possible, so it is not a painting or slide show.
A template	The 'performance' of the motion picture is generated from a template which cannot change (a token), unlike the play performance which is interpretative (a type). The template can be a film print, a DVD, a tape, etc., and exists in one definitive version, so there can only be one 'performance' of Fellini's film *La Dolce Vita*, but in a theatrical performance there is a new interpretation of Shakespeare's *Much Ado About Nothing* every time it is done.
A token, not a type	The performance of showing the moving picture (the token) is not an art work in its own right, whereas the performing of a play or playing music is. A successful projection of a film does not warrant aesthetic appreciation; the projectionist does not interpret the film in an artistic sense like a conductor and orchestra does with music. The film's screening is a technical task, not an aesthetic accomplishment.
Two-dimensionality	The moving images are two-dimensional, so for example the wind-up music box ballerina that fulfils the other four conditioning factors is not two-dimensional and therefore not a moving picture. Balinese shadow puppets are two-dimensional but they are a type, whereas film is generated by templates that are tokens in themselves.

and two-dimensionality create the given conditions of what we call 'film', and provide parameters for the art form and the learning in the area. From this, an aesthetic is developed based on the components of film—the visual image, sound, music, speech and graphics. How the aesthetic is formed is dependent on its function to create meaning. To consider how meaning is created in film helps us to discern and establish how the aesthetic actually works.

How is meaning created in film?

Meaning in film is made through the collusion of filmmaker and audience. The film form functions as a communication device between the two, and from that communion a film language has developed. James Monaco (2000) discusses how Sergei Eisenstein, the Russian filmmaker and theorist, reasoned that the system of film was not based on the relationship between the artist and their raw materials, but on the filmmaker's relationship with the audience. The interdependence of film's form and its function for an audience is a concept which helps to explain how meaning in film is created at many levels. The levels or contexts from which form and function can be examined in film are neatly described by Eisenstein with his filmic metaphor in *A Close-Up View* (1945). He uses the 'long-shot' to characterise film analysis that is concerned with the big picture of the social cultural context and the political and economic ideology. The 'medium-shot' represents the focus on the human scale of film criticism which is the domain of the film reviewer, 'where the spectator is, before all else, in the grip of the story, the event and the circumstances', and the 'close-up' analysis breaks film down into its parts and 'resolves film into its elements' (Eisenstein, 1945, pp. 151–2). Each level or viewpoint of film analysis is interrelated and shapes the others, and by breaking down the parts their connections are demonstrated.

Eisenstein's breakdown helps to illustrate how we can create a structure to learn the making and appreciation of film and the creation of meaning. As with scaffolding the learning of the components of film (visual image, sound, speech, graphics and music), the elements that make meaning in film can be learnt incrementally. The relationship between the form (film) and its function (communicating to an audience) can be structured by microscoping down to its elements (the 'close-up' view of semiotics) and telescoping out to the artwork as a whole (the 'mid-shot' view of the narrative), to the social and political context (the 'long-shot' view) (see Figure 3.6).

The close-up view of semiotics

Film semiotics is in the realm of 'close-up' theory, and it is this microscopic approach that lays the basis for learning the syntax of film's aesthetic. It is the ability to control the codes of communication in film language that enables students to create and express themselves in the film form. To control the

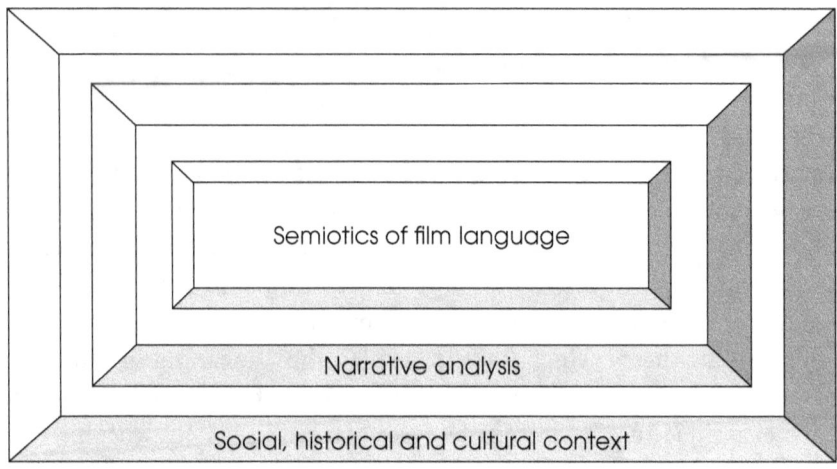

Figure 3.6 Eisenstein's viewpoints of film analysis helps to scaffold learning.

reins, Monaco (2000) says filmmakers must ask themselves three fundamental questions:

1. What do I shoot?
2. How do I shoot it?
3. How do I present it?

The process of creating a film is shaped by the choices made in answering these questions, and the choices are informed by an understanding of the form's function, which is to perceive the effect it will have on an audience. Understanding the connection between form and function is central to how the communication of film language's semiotics works. This begins with understanding the function of *mise en scène.*

Meaning and *mise en scène*

What to shoot is part of the visual aesthetic of *mise en scène*, the manipulation of the image or space within the frame. The frame is a rich palette and the audience can read meaning from everything in the space of the frame. The choice of characters and their placement, costume, movement, landscape, objects, set, décor, light and how they are arranged assists the control of the degree of artifice, focus, space and composition in the frame and creates meaning for the spectator. Space in the frame that is not effectively controlled to make meaning is a dead space or distracting space. Dead space and irrelevant imagery can confuse meaning for the audience, and lose the tension and dynamic of the audience's engagement. The meaning made from *what to shoot* is described as 'denotative', which refers to what is physically in the frame and read by the spectator.

How to shoot it involves the choices of the camera's perspective, which is determined by frame size (long-shot, mid-shot, close-up) and angle (high or low), whether the camera is in motion (panning, tracking, dollying, craning, handheld), how the lens is focused and from what perspective the audience is seeing or identifying. The form of the shot's framing is part of conceiving the *mise en scène*, and it signifies meaning to the audience. In this case, the meaning is 'paradigmatic' and 'connotative' because the spectator reads and understands the semiotic of the visual image because of an association they make between what is in the frame and how it is being shot. For example, an object filmed as a high-angle shot diminishes the power of the object, and so weakened power is a connotation made with the object. If the viewer tracks with a fast-moving object, they identify with it and its sense of speed. A pan identifies for the spectator a sense of discovering and unveiling the world they gradually see more of.

Figure 3.7 An example of a high-angle shot from Sergei Eisenstein's *Battleship Potemkin* (1925) illustrates how the framing diminishes the power of the character.

What to shoot and *how to shoot it* work together to create the *mise en scène*. By recognising the elements of *mise en scène*, students begin to control part of the aesthetic of film's form and its function to communicate meaningfully to an audience. It is also important to realise the power of association to create meaning in film. Meanings by association can be used metonymically through a detail or notion to convey a larger idea, or synecdochically where a part indicates a whole. Metonymy is a cinematic shorthand, so for instance when Hitchcock wants to evoke the abstract quality of heat in *Rear Window* (1954) he focuses on beads of sweat on L.B. Jefferies' face, shows a couple waking from sleeping outside on the cool of the balcony and reveals the high reading on the thermometer. A cinematic synecdoche shows a part, such as marching feet to represent the whole of an army, or spurs to signify the whole cowboy, or a shot through the cowboy's legs to signify a shootout. Describing and clarifying how meaning is made through visual association in film helps to fuel students' awareness and control of expression in filmmaking.

Meaning and montage

The other significant partner to *mise en scène* in the film equation of creating meaning is montage. This is *how to present it*, and it is the placing of shots together to make meaning. Montage (putting together) or editing (cutting) creates a syntagmatic connotation because meaning is made through the association shots make with each other, such as the cross-cutting in the silent film *Death's Marathon* (1913), where the audience sees the father on the phone, and the child and mother on the phone. The audience determines that they must be talking to each other. The juxtaposition of shots forms the complex system and aesthetic of montage that is the element most specific to the art form of film. Choosing the sequence of images following one another structures and communicates meaning for the audience within a scene and between scenes. The type of shots and the timing of the sequencing also create rhythm and pace that affect atmosphere, mood and style, the perception of time and the desired engagement with the spectator. Eisenstein's epic scene of the Odessa Steps massacre in *The Battleship Potemkin* (1925) is seminal in illustrating the power of montage to manipulate time, space and rhythm, and to affect the audience with violent juxtaposed images as well as intellectual dialectics.

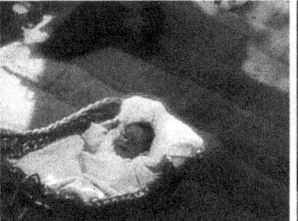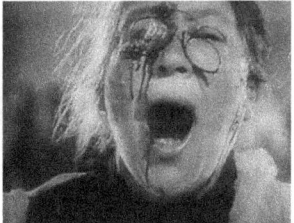

Figure 3.8 This montage from the Odessa Steps scene in Sergei Eisenstein's *Battleship Potemkin* (1925) demonstrates how space, time, rhythm and juxtaposition are manipulated for dramatic effect.

Controlling *mise en scène* and montage for meaning

Jean-Luc Godard (1972) compared *mise en scène* and montage to the inextricable link that exists between melody and rhythm, for 'what one seeks to foresee in space, the other seeks in time' (1972, p. 39). In other words, what happens in the 'space' of *mise en scène* determines the 'time' montage occurs. *Mise en scène* and montage, in their symbiotic relationship, work together to create the language of film and make meaning for an audience. For instance, consider the form and function of a pan shot from one cowboy to another in a Western shootout. Is the audience interested or does it need to be engaged with the space between the two characters and the time the pan takes to travel between them? Does the long pan shot and whatever is in the space between them capture the metaphorical distance of understanding between the two, or does a juxtaposition of two opposing mid-shots of the cowboys create greater tension and a more human level of engagement with the characters? Both space and time are being manipulated, and the choice depends on how the filmmaker wants to tell the story and what they want the spectators to be engaged with. The choices involve the marrying of form—which is the shots and editing—to their dramatic function and the desired effect on the audience.

Techniques of *mise en scène* and montage

Mise en scène and montage are the basis of film language and the organising principles of their aesthetic are called codes or techniques. Some of the codes are already established in the aesthetic of other art forms, such as the elements of two-dimensional design in the visual arts, the expressive tools of music, the narrative construction of the novel and the dramatic elements of the theatre. The codes of these art forms are utilised by film but undergo a metamorphosis when they are combined with each other in film, and must serve the filmic forms of *mise en scène* and montage, constructing codes distinctive and indigenous to film.

For example, the actor's gesture and proximity to objects and people in the *mise en scène* illustrates a code or sign we read as an audience in a theatre performance as well as in film—although the way the code precisely manifests itself is changed to create meaning in the differing art forms. Gesture and proxemics are read differently in the three dimensions of theatre to the two dimensions of film because perspective is manipulated in the two dimensions of film to give the effect or illusion of three dimensions. Often what appears close in proximity in the reality of three dimensions looks far apart through the two-dimensional frame of a shot. The multi-directional and telescopic perspective of the camera in film impacts on the way gesture is communicated. In the theatre, the actor's gesture must be telegraphed to all the members of the audience, and the size, direction and energy of the gesture is determined by the extent of the auditorium. In film, shot size affects and varies the size of the actors' performance and there is an intimacy and subtlety offered by the mid-shot and close-up that significantly reduces the size and energy of an actor's performance. The difference between acting for film and acting for theatre illustrates how the same code is manipulated in different ways in the two art forms.

Film techniques as conventions

The codes or techniques that have been developed by filmmaking over time are cultural constructs, just as with other art forms like music, theatre and painting. The ubiquitous Hollywood film sometimes prevents students from realising that film aesthetics are based on conventions shaped by cultural and economic considerations. For example, the politics and economics of post-war Europe and America shaped not only the content of the style we call film noir but also the aesthetic of its film language—for example, the way it uses black and white, voiceover and flashback. Film noir reflects a bleak, disillusioned world, but it also generated a style that grew from necessity, the constraints of a low budget. Eisenstein's dialectical ideas about intellectual montage and using symbolic shots to interrupt the flow of narrative were formulated with Marxist principles in mind, with the slaughtered cow in *Strike* (1924), for example, representing the treatment of the striking workers. Certainly this form of montage provides a different function and aesthetic of film language rarely embraced by Hollywood filmmakers. Exposing students to films outside the mainstream

Hollywood approach allows them to recognise the concept of non-absolutes in the construction of codes and conventions, and gives them an insight into what Eisenstein (1945) termed 'long-shot' social analysis of film and its impact on 'close-up' semiotic theory. It is apparent that technology continues to affect the aesthetic, but so do ideology, economics and culture.

Film techniques as innovations

Monaco (2000) describes a 'trope' as a technique used in an unusual way to create new meanings. Alfred Hitchcock's montage of 50 fragmented shots from numerous varying angles in *Psycho*'s (1960) famous two-minute shower scene is an example of his cinematic genius to create a trope.

Figure 3.9 Alfred Hitchcock's montage in the shower scene from *Psycho* (1960) illustrates how filmic codes can be used in innovative and unusual ways for dramatic effect.

The rhythms of the cross-cutting, and unusual choices of perspective and images, create a sense of frenzy and a feeling of tension and unease in the spectator. The film form of montage has been manipulated in a new way to engender meaning. It can be the originality of the filmmaker that instigates a trope, but sometimes it is the development of technological innovation that allows the filmmaker to be state of the art. In *Citizen Kane* (1941), Orson Welles and cinematographer Gregg Toland worked with lenses and lighting to generate deep focus that allowed the background and foreground to be in sharp relief and so conceived a new way to manipulate and read the *mise en scène*.

Figure 3.10 The technical innovation of deep focus developed by Orson Welles and Gregg Toland in *Citizen Kane* (1941) allowed the *mise en scène* to be read in a new way.

Filmic codes and learning

Recognising techniques as codes and tropes in film language provides organisational principles for learning. For example, in terms of the image aesthetic, codes of two-dimensional design are expressed through arranging elements of composition (horizontals, verticals and diagonals), balance, space, light and colour to create and focus the meaning in the frame. These elements also compose proximity and perspective in the shot, and the illusion of three dimensions. The framing of the image is made by the choice and dynamic of the camera shot, such as the emotional intimacy of the close-up or the comfortable, conversational distance of the mid-shot or the character contextualised by a landscape in a long-shot, and affects how the drama is being signified to the spectator. All the arrangements in the frame are crucial to how the images are read, and with that are layered the textures of the filmic codes and tropes of sound, music, speech and graphics in the film aesthetic. All these elements synergise to create the cinematic forms of *mise en scène* and montage, which have their own codes and tropes as well. Film at the semiotic 'close-up' level allows us to understand and control the micro-dynamics of film language that then creates meaning at the narrative 'mid-shot' level.

'Mid-shot' theory and the creation of narrative

Eisenstein's 'mid-shot' metaphor explains the layer of the audience level of understanding in film where the mechanics of narrative come into focus. At this level, film reviewers analyse a film with regard to its story, ideas and characters, acting, style and genre, and how these ingredients engage with the audience as an experience. Narrative in film has used elements of storytelling from literature but has developed narrative techniques specific to the cinematic form and evolved codes specific to styles and genre of film. We explore screen theory of narrative and genre and its relationship to learning and pedagogy in Chapter 4. Film at the narrative level of analysis is contextualised by society at large, and shapes the kind of stories that are told.

'Long-shot' analysis and the social context

The 'long-shot' picture of screen theory illustrates the social and political function of film, and it is important to recognise since it provides the prime justification for teaching and learning filmmaking and appreciation with students. Walter Benjamin (1935) argued that once the arts became mechanically reproduced, they no longer depended on a community's ritual for their existence and authenticity, but were based on the practice of mass dissemination and politics. As a reproduced art form, the audience does not mutually authenticate film. Screen theorist, Béla Balázs wrote in 1949:

> we all know and admit that film art has a greater influence on the minds of the general public than any other art ... And unless we study its laws and possibilities very carefully, we shall not be able to control and direct this potentially greatest instrument of mass influence ever devised in the whole course of human history (Balázs, 1970, p. 17).

Cinema in the twentieth century has now splintered into the digital media communications of television, computers and games, and Balázs' impassioned plea for film education rings even louder today. Young people need to be given the tools to deconstruct and engage more actively and assertively with film because of its omnipotent social role.

Balázs (1970) describes film as a product of a large-scale industry, functioning in an economic as well as cultural sphere of influence. Film as an art form, as Siegfried Kracauer says in *Theory of Film: The redemption of physical reality*

(1960), has the power to reflect, confront and manipulate images of the social world. A student who is literate and creative with film is better equipped to realise the potential of film's capacity to influence as a pervasive and persuasive social medium of communication. To return to Monaco's (2000) sentiments at the beginning of the chapter, a film-literate audience can affect the process of consumption and creation of the art form, better authenticating it and having power over it.

What can we learn from screen theory and practice?

In an educational setting, screen theory is the lens that breaks film down into its components, atomises a working pedagogical vocabulary and provides a framework for a pedagogy that leads to effective learning, enabling students to understand and control the film aesthetic.

The framework is built on the foundation of a definition of film that has five conditioning factors (screen, movement, template, token and two-dimensionality). As an art form, its essence is its capacity to capture movement; that is integral to how it works (perception of movement) and its aesthetic (it appears real because it moves). The unique attribute of the camera to change the identification of the spectator affects the relationship between the audience and the world of the film. The primacy of the moving visual image and the role of the components—sound, speech, music and graphics—contribute further to that identification and meaning for the audience. Telescoping from the close-up view of semiotics to the mid-shot view of narrative to the long-shot view of social context provides viewing platforms of the structures of filmmaking, not just analysis. What is apparent and essential in understanding all the components and elements central to film is that its forms of *mise en scène* and montage, and all the techniques or codes associated with them, must have a dramatic or filmic function. Without functioning as meaning for an audience, filmic form is ineffective as an expressive and engaging means of communication, being instead a mere recorder of events.

Screen theory and practice help to focus on the central ideas of the learning area, and provide a foundation on which to build a pedagogical framework and pedagogical vocabulary for teaching students filmmaking and appreciation. Teaching the screen is about giving students the means to use film as an effective tool of expression with purpose. It is about how students can understand and explain moving pictures so they tell their own stories and understand other stories in film with greater skill and potency. The next chapter examines the potential of screen learning to communicate through narrative and genre.

4
Narrative, genre and film learning

> Stories are impossible, but it's impossible to live without them.
> —Wim Wenders

Our focus is on students engaging with the stories and story-making of narrative film. The paradox of storytelling is that stories make our complex and chaotic lives structured and comprehensible. Film director Wim Wenders (1991) (*Wings of Desire*, 1982; *Paris, Texas*, 1984; *Buena Vista Social Club*, 1999) refers to stories as the 'biggest lie' for 'they show coherence where there is none' (1991, p. 59). But he says stories are necessary, powerful and profound as they 'give people the feeling that there is meaning' (1991, p. 54). We need stories to make sense of the world. They appear to make a confused world into understood phenomena through the contrivance of a beginning, an end and connections in between. The narrative form structures and creates the meaning of life as it unfolds in its telling. The majority of films made for and seen by a mass audience have been narrative films.

This chapter explores how the screen theory and practice of narrative, genre and the auteur inform film learning for students. Understanding the mechanics of narrative and genre provides students with the tools for making film stories. Narrative and genre are integral to the expectations and experience of the audience's engagement with film. Storytelling is about making coherence of the world for the audience, but it also creates meaning of the world for our young filmmakers making the films. The 'lie' of stories demonstrates the very process of storytelling structuring a coherent meaning of life and the world around us.

The subservience of the image to tell the story is integral for students' understanding of how to control the meaning of narrative film. Wenders (2002) fears that many young filmmakers living in the audiovisual culture of music videos and commercials work with images without understanding their function in telling a story. A director's duty in narrative film, he says, 'is to have something to say: he or she needs to tell a story' (2002, p. 73). Jean-Luc Godard (2002) (*Breathless*, 1960; *Alphaville*, 1965; *Two or Three Things I Know About Her*, 1967) says a lot of gratuitous camera effects remind him of 'certain operas, where most of the effects are there not to help the story but to offer a distraction because the story is boring' (2002, p. 213). It can be argued that film may be drawing on new styles and forms from other media forms as an adjunct to the narrative experience. However, whether this is true or not, students need to learn how to tell stories in film, and to do that they need to know what narrative film is and what it is not.

What is not a narrative film?

The screen theory of film language discussed in Chapter 3 can apply to all forms of film. The use of film language is dictated by its function to make meaning for any film form, whether there is a story or not. Table 4.1 categorises the nature of film forms according to the definitions put forward by Bordwell and Thompson (2004).

Meaning in categorical, rhetorical, abstract and associational films is not created through the structure of narrative form; however, as Thomas Leitch points out in *What Stories Are* (1986), there are films that are a hybrid of narrative and other film forms. Non-narrative elements can operate in the narrative form to add another dimension in meaning. Leitch uses Marv Newland's cartoon *Bambi Meets Godzilla* (1969) as an example: Bambi peacefully browses in the grass as the credits roll—'Directed by Marv Newland ... Screenplay by Marv Newland ... Bambi's wardrobe by Marv Newland', etc. After the credits finish, Godzilla's foot comes down from the top of the screen and crushes Bambi, and then Godzilla's toes curl. Leitch explains that Newland's film uses the categorical form of film credits as a set-up for the film's joke, and also abstraction because the audience is noticing the material qualities of film's medium by juxtaposing categorical with narrative form. The expectation of an extended narrative is thwarted, but the pattern of narrative causality is there ever so briefly, layered with meaning from the categorical and abstraction film forms. In school curricula, students may be exploring any of these film forms (narrative, categorical, rhetorical, abstract and associational) but they need to understand how the forms work to create meaning so they can express and communicate in those forms. Our focus is students knowing how to tell stories through the narrative form.

Table 4.1 An explanation and example of different film forms based on Bordwell and Thompson's definitions (2004)

Film form	Definition	Example
Narrative	Narrative films tell a story structured by a chain of events in cause–effect relationship occurring in time and space.	The film classic *Citizen Kane* (1941) by Orson Welles, although unusual in terms of style, utilises principles of narrative.
Categorical	'Categorical' describes documentary films that use groupings to organise information and a view of the world.	Leni Riefenstahl's *Olympia* (1936), as a record of the Berlin Olympics, is a classic example of the categorical form.
Rhetorical	The goal of a rhetorical film is to persuade the audience of a certain point of view.	Guggenheim's film about climate change, *An Inconvenient Truth* (2006), presented by Al Gore, is rhetorical.
Abstract	Abstract films use the material qualities of film's form as a medium for expression. This is done though the shaping and patterning of visual aesthetics of colour, shape, size and movement and the aural aesthetics of sound.	Fernand Leger and Dudley Murphy's influential *Ballet Mécanique* (1924) is one of the earliest examples of abstract films.
Associational	Associational form is like poetry of imagery with metaphorical connections and, unlike abstract film, interpretations from the juxtaposed images can be made in associational film.	The images in *Baraka* (1992) by Fricke and Magidson depict the beauty and destruction of nature and humans without a narrative.

What is a narrative film?

Storytelling has made its way from oral traditions to epic poetry, to plays, to novels and into films. In each art form, the style of storytelling changes, but common to them all is an organisation and construction of meaning. Edward

Branigan in *Narrative Comprehension and Film* (1992) argues that narrative is more than a text type; it is 'a perceptual activity that organises data into a special pattern which represents and explains experience'. The spectator perceives narrative because of an arrangement of 'spatial and temporal data into a cause–effect chain of events with a beginning, middle, and end' (1992, p. 3). Narrative arrangements come in many shapes and sizes, but fundamental to its creation is the causal relationships amongst events and how they connect and thrust the story forward, and the audience with it. From this pattern of cause and effect come consequences. More simply, this can be expressed as the idea that for every action there is a reaction which then triggers off further actions and reactions.

Causality or a perceived causality, and a resultant tension, are the essence of narrative. Cause and effect creates a change, or transformation and tension, in the situation or the character or object in the film. Branigan demonstrates causality with examples from E.M. Forster and Gerald Prince (1992, p. 11):

These do not qualify as narratives:
(1a) The king died and then the queen died [chronology].
(2a) Mary ate an apple.

These are narratives:
(1b) The king died, and then the queen died of grief [causality].
(2b) Shirley was good then she drifted into a life of crime.

Causality for (1b) is apparent, but in (2b) Shirley didn't drift into crime because she was good. However, there is an inference that something caused Shirley's change in circumstances, and certainly the fact that she was good sets up a tension in the journey of her changing situation. Examples like this are a way for students to access and grapple with the organisational mechanics of storytelling at a simple but sophisticated level. Students often mistake events, situations, actions, ideas, characters, special effects, music, images and editing for the framework used to construct a narrative. Instead it is the structures and patterns of cause-and-effect relationships that reveal and unravel a story and determine the events, situations, actions, characters, and so on. Narrative theory helps to guide students' literacy and creativity in narrative construction, and the control and appreciation of a story's engagement with an audience. In particular, two aspects of storytelling from the Russian formalists, the 'fabula' and 'syuzhet', help to explain film narrative construction.

The fabula and syuzhet

The fabula describes the story of a film as a succession of events in chronological order, and a film summary in a magazine can describe a film's story in such a way. However, this story is not the experience of what is seen watching the film. How the audience witnesses the story unfolding is called the syuzhet or plot, and it is this narrative construction that provides the causal links in the cause–effect chain of events of the film narrative. Let's use a limerick as an example:

> A jolly young fellow from Yuma
> Told an elephant joke to a puma;
> Now his skeleton lies
> Beneath hot western skies—
> The puma had no sense of huma.
>
> —Ogden Nash

The fabula is that our fellow told a joke to a puma which didn't tickle the puma's fancy so the puma ate the fellow. The syuzhet is that the fellow tells a joke to a puma then the fellow is no more than a skeleton in the desert because the puma had no sense of humour. Both are versions of the same story, but the cause-and-effect relationship is manipulated in the limerick version so we understand the precise cause of the fellow's demise at the end, which provides the element of surprise and humour to the limerick. It doesn't actually say the puma ate the fellow, but perceptually the reader makes that 'internal' story meaning from the 'external' plot.

The syuzhet elucidates how there is logic to the causality of events that is externally understood and explicitly read by the audience as events occur in the plot. At the same time, there is an internal logic that operates in the telling of the story, and this impacts on screen writing and acting in the story. In the original *Star Wars* trilogy (1977–1983), for example, those in the audience who saw the last film in the series—*Return of the Jedi* (1983)—before the prequel trilogy (1999–2005) was made, discovered Darth Vader was Luke's father when Luke found out. For the audience, this is the external perception of the story through the plot, but in hindsight the internal logic of events also makes sense of the fact that Darth Vader was Luke's father all along although the audience didn't realise until it was revealed. The internal logic was there in the screenplay for the actor playing Darth Vader, but hidden from the audience.

The syuzhet and fabula are two significant concepts in viewing a film, because the syuzhet gives the events logical and causal links from which the spectator formulates a fabula and understands the story. A film audience absorbs and organises on-screen events by piecing together the motivations and causality of all the action and events, and combines the threads of the syuzhet to make a meaningful fabula or story from the experience. At the same time, the manipulation of the telling of the story through the syuzhet affects the audience's reception and engagement with the story. What the story is (the fabula) and how it will be received, perceived and understood by the audience (the syuzhet) are important for any filmmaker. This affects every choice by filmmakers, from what the spectator sees in a film (how is the story told) to how the spectator sees it (the *mise en scène* and montage).

The fabula and syuzhet also provide an insight into why the arrangement of 'spatial and temporal data' (Branigan, 1992) is included in a definition of narrative's cause and effect. Space and time are integral to the filmic elements of *mise en scène* and montage, and are also inherent in the creation of narrative form. Time and space should be imagined as elastic elements that serve the cause and effect of events in a film's narrative.

In *Rear Window* (1954), the spectator never sees space beyond Jeffrey's apartment and his view from his rear window. An establishment shot of the Manhattan skyline would be irrelevant spatial data in the film's narrative and meaning. There are spatial and auditory cues in the *mise en scène* that place the apartment setting in a metropolis so the context is there without being shown. Similar manipulations occur with temporal data. Real time can be suggested by the fabula (story), but in syuzhet (plot) terms, time can be manipulated to affect the audience's perceived experience. Citizen Kane's life can be reduced into the length of a feature film. The audience experience of the Odessa Steps massacre in *The Battleship Potemkin* (1925) is longer than the time of the actual massacre itself. *Russian Ark*'s (2002) one take of 90 minutes in real time captures changes in space and historical time through control of the longest running *mise en scène*. *Babel*'s (2006) three plots are told individually in temporal order but are intentionally asynchronous in their time relationships to each other, and *Memento* (2000) reverses the temporal order. All these examples illustrate how time and space are elastic in operating to serve the narrative structure of the syuzhet (plot), but create a coherent fabula (story). Student awareness of controlling time and space demonstrates an understanding of narrative construction and how to create meaning through the manipulation of space and time. To engage an audience with the world of

Figure 4.1 The image of the apartment building and auditory cues in Alfred Hitchcock's *Rear Window* (1954) are all that is required to establish the metropolis setting of the story.

a narrative film requires the establishing and building of a tension of expectation in the audience.

The creation of tension and expectation

All aspects of film images are read by the audience for meaning, and although not everything is equally important, every element in the frame contributes to the film's narrative meaning. To engage the spectator in making that meaning, the narrative must generate intrigue in resolving the questions 'What is going to happen next?' and 'When and how will it end?' This is the 'big picture' or overall cause and effect of the whole film narrative. Branigan (1992, p. 14) uses the following schema to explain the narrative pattern for an entire film. His schema illustrates how an audience's comprehension and expectation are shaped by this organisation of a chain of events:

1. introduction of setting and characters;
2. explanation of a state of affairs;
3. initiating event;
4. emotional response or statement of a goal by the protagonist;
5. complicating actions;

6. outcome;
7. reactions to the outcome.

It is the expectation that narrative will follow this pattern, and in so doing set up a sense of curiosity, suspense or surprise in the audience as to how the issues resulting from the established narrative pattern will be resolved. Audiences know the narrative pattern because stories are everywhere—'narrative is international, transhistorical, transcultural: it is simply there, like life itself' (Barthes, 1977, p. 79). Audiences may know the pattern unconsciously, but filmmakers have to work with the narrative structure consciously to make it work effectively. How, then, do filmmakers use the predicable narrative pattern to create a tension of engagement with the audience?

To care about what happens next, Bordwell and Thompson (2004) argue that the audience has to have invested some emotion in the situation, and this may occur if the audience has identified with the characters. For example, in Peter Jackson's *Lord of the Rings* trilogy (2001–03) the audience ultimately wants the protagonists Frodo and Sam to get home safely from their adventures because the audience, through identification, know that Frodo and Sam love The Shire and want to return there. Once there is identification and investment, the audiences' expectations can be manipulated by the narrative pattern. Bordwell and Thompson (2004, p. 54) describe the manipulation of audience expectation in three ways:

- delayed fulfilment
- gratified expectations, and
- cheated expectations.

The audience's wish fulfilment that Frodo and Sam get home causes anxiety or sympathy, and once they are home the viewers' expectations are gratified, producing relief and satisfaction. When it is realised that Frodo cannot stay home, sympathy and pathos come into play because fulfilment is delayed. When expectations are cheated, the audience experiences puzzlement and a keener interest in what may happen, and this element is used in the narrative treatment of films:

- *In the Mood for Love* (2000)—Is there a love affair?
- *Hidden* (2005)—Who is involved in the surveillance?
- *Babel* (2006)—How are the stories connected?

Narrative pattern can be likened once again to a limerick, especially one by Ogden Nash, because there is the expectation something dreadful and humorous will be revealed at the end (wish fulfilment will be gratified) but what exactly will be revealed isn't known (delayed fulfilment). If the words at the end are left out, the reader's expectations of a limerick's neat resolution is cheated and the reader wonders what is going on:

> There was a young lady called Harris
> That nothing could ever embarrass
> Till the bath salts, one day
> In the tub where she lay
> Turned out to be Plaster of Paris.

The limerick illustrates a cause and effect (the Plaster of Paris mistaken as bath salts causes Harris to be stuck naked in a bath), and it demonstrates another important ingredient in the effective construction of narrative: the 'raising of stakes'. There is more to lose or gain in the situation created. Our young lady Harris had more to lose, or 'further to fall', because she wasn't to be embarrassed. Frodo, the bearer of the ring in the *Lord of the Rings* trilogy (2001–03), didn't just have external powers of evil to deal with, he had inner demons to contend with because of the seductive power of the ring; therefore, the hurdles he had to overcome became higher. In other words, the cause-and-effect relationship is not inconsequential: by raising the stakes, the equilibrium of the situation, to use Tzvetan Todorov's (1981)[1] explanation of narrative, has been disrupted in a more heightened way.

This limerick also demonstrates the fabula and syuzhet at work when the reader finds out the bath salts are really Plaster of Paris. If the limerick were a film, the choice of when the Plaster of Paris was revealed would be integral to shaping audience expectations. What happens if the spectator finds out that the bath salts are Plaster of Paris before the character Harris does? In Hitchcockian terms, this scenario creates the dynamic engagement of *suspense* because the viewer can now anticipate what is going to happen but knows the character doesn't know. If the viewer, like the character, doesn't know what will happen next, *tension* is created by wondering what will occur. Consider, then, whether the spectator knows more than, less than or as much as the character, and how this contributes to the creation of tension or suspense. In addition, another element causing tension needs to be considered: conflict.

In causality terms, conflict causes problems and resolving those problems

Narrative, genre and film learning

generates tension. To 'raise the stakes' of the conflict doesn't mean increasing the action or violence of the conflict (although that could be a consequence); it means to increase the needs and desires of the characters or the situation. Quite simply, the man from Yuma in the first limerick 'needs' to befriend the puma to save his life, but the puma 'desires' to eat the man as retribution for the bad elephant joke and probably the puma 'needs' to eat because it is very hungry. Their respective 'needs' bring them into conflict, and so in creating narratives students must be clear about characters' motivations for actions that create a conflict. The conflict has to have a logic that is both internal and external in the causality of the chain of events, so meaning is coherent to the audience. Students need to know how to create and control tension through expectation and conflict to engage an audience effectively with their stories. However, narrative films do not always feature a state of high anxiety and constant tension, and this is when we step back to view the role of the beginning, middle and end of a story to see other principles and conventions of narrative at work.

Beginnings, middles and ends

Beginnings do not simply start a film; the spectator has to enter the world of the film through exposition devices. Sternberg (1978) explains that 'it is the function of the exposition to introduce the reader into an unfamiliar world, the fictive world of the story, by providing him with the general and specific antecedents indispensable to the understanding of what happens in it' (1978, p. 1). Exposition often includes description in a novel; in a film the images themselves are descriptive: 'It is not that cinema cannot describe; on the contrary, it cannot help describing, though usually it does so only tacitly. Its evocation of details is incessantly rich. Every screen "noun" is already, by virtue of the medium, totally saturated with visual "adjectives"' (Chatman, 1990, p. 40). Seymour Chapman in *Coming to Terms* (1990) discusses how films can use explicit as well as tacit description to contribute to narrative construction. The opening of *Rear Window* (1954) begins with a view into the courtyard of the apartment building. The camera moves around almost looking for something to happen, but no action of any apparent consequence does. The audience doesn't know with whom the camera is identifying, nor what it is looking for. The camera follows a cat up some steps, shows a couple who have slept on the balcony waking up, a dancer making her breakfast, and a milkman delivering milk in a passageway between the buildings and the street. No character is identified with from the perspective of what is seen (the point of view) and no characters we do see are close enough to identify with. *Rear Window* begins with a catalogue of New York apartment life, appearing to have no narrative cause and effect. However, it is a deliberately puzzling exposition that operates to serve the narrative by explicitly describing the details of the setting that become significant in the cause-and-effect chain of events about to unfold.

'Beginnings' highlight how exposition and tacit and explicit description in film are indispensable to understanding a story. 'Middles' develop audience expectations, and to return to E.M. Forster's (1927) example of 'The king died, and then the queen died of grief', Leitch (1986) points out that Forster's next example of the same story is more successful because it contains a middle: 'The queen died, no one knew why, until it was discovered that it was through grief at the death of the king' (1986, p. 86). The phrase 'no one knew why' is a middle, and Leitch explains that it 'gives the audience the opportunity to wonder in what way the expectations it arouses will be fulfilled' (1986, p. 11). Raising audience expectations determines the developments of narrative's middle, and in many ways it relates to character.

Characters' desires shape audience identification and expectations, and provide motivation and conflict. Characters are 'imagined' by what they look like, their actions, their relationships with other characters, what they say and what they don't say, and the setting and the landscape surrounding them. These aspects help to imagine and express the character, but they also function to serve the drama of the narrative as well. For example, in *The Lord of the Rings: Return of the King* (2003), when Gollum's brother (Deagol) finds the ring at the bottom of the lake, Gollum (aka Smeagol) is bewitched by the ring's power and kills his brother to keep it. In narrative terms, we learn how Gollum acquired the ring but through the scene the audience also gains insights into Gollum's schizoid nature from the transformation of the affable Smeagol into the selfish, possessed Gollum. Characters serve stories, but at the same time stories reveal identifiable and engaging characters interesting to audiences in their own right.

Beginnings, middles and ends infer a logical connection or unity between all the cause-and-effect events of the narrative, and it is useful for students to find a 'through line' in order to control the narrative form. For instance, the *Lord of the Rings* trilogy could be explained as: 'You must fight to protect what you hold dear' and *Babel* may be: 'People across the world must communicate with each other because ultimately all of humanity is connected to one another'. Films often have multiple meanings, but to explain a film in such a way demonstrates an understanding of all the logic and interrelated elements functioning to serve the idea behind a narrative pattern. Narrative meaning and engagement are created by audience perception and audience expectations, and beginnings and ends introduce and resolve those expectations. The manifestation of audience expectations, however, does not reside solely in the narrative form; it is very much at work in the concept of film genre.

The concept of film genre

Genre critics hotly debate the actual definition of 'genre', and dispute the actual boundaries defining particular genres (Neale, 2000). There may be disagreement, for example, about whether a film is a Western or not, or whether film noir is actually a genre. However, despite this, according to Jameson (1994), 'the idea is second nature to the movies and our awareness of them. Movies belong to genres much the way people belong to families, or ethnic groups' (1994, p. ix). Genre discourse provokes an analysis of classifying film types and a discussion of how genre types arouse audience expectations. Genre analysis allows students to understand how films are organised, categorised and consumed, and once again allows them to understand how meaning and engagement can be created by controlling what an audience anticipates seeing.

Genre recognises that there is a commonality in certain films because they use a similar style, narrative and structure. Films are categorised, for example, as crime films, musicals, comedies (screwball, romantic, gross out, spoofs), action, horror, war, gangster, Western, fantasy, melodrama, and so on. A genre's common elements become accepted codes and conventions because they are familiar to audiences through their repetitive use. As soon as an audience sees spats, a tommy gun and a 'sting', they expect a gangster movie with a moral universe governed by distrust, double-crossing, action and violence to drive the narrative. It is a genre's very preordained nature that is manipulated to affect audience expectations, just as the narrative pattern does. For Hollywood producers, genre can be used as an economic strategy to reduce the financial risk of a film, knowing it has audience appeal because of the audience's known expectations. At the same time, filmmakers and audiences can be excited by the experience of reworking expectations of a genre or blending of genres or creating new genres. *Thelma and Louise* (1991) gave the buddy movie and the road movie a feminist reworking, *The Matrix* (1999) blended martial arts with science fiction and *Un Chien Andalou* (1929) attempted to defy all expectations by being anti-genre and anti-narrative but became known as surrealism.

Genres can be viewed as 'ritualised' dramas, a concept derived from the anthropological theories of Claude Lévi-Strauss. This helps to explain the existence, appeal and social function of film genre or a genre film. Certain stories, themes, values and imagery in a number of films harmonise at one time as a reflection of public attitudes and values, such as film noir in response to the aftermath of the Second World War, science fiction films as a reflection of anxieties about the nuclear bomb in the late 1940s and early 1950s, and disaster movies as a reaction to the oil crisis of the 1970s. Genres and variations in genre development are cultural constructs, and their conventions validate social values in some way. Thomas Schatz (1981) goes so far as to say that 'as social ritual, genre films function to stop time, to portray our culture in a stable and invariable ideological position' (1981, p. 31). This helps to explain where genres come from and why certain stories are told in a certain way at a given time. So what actually constitutes a genre?

Defining genre

There is disagreement amongst theorists on defining genre, but as Steve Neale (2000) argues, there is common ground: 'All agree that genre is a multidimensional phenomenon and that its dimensions centrally include systems of expectation, categories, labels and names, discourses, texts and corpuses of texts, and the conventions that govern them all' (2000, pp. 25–6).

The difficulty is that genres are not different for the same reasons—that is, the definition for a particular genre can be made from differing criteria. Watson (2003) illustrates this with the following examples. A horror, thriller and comedy are determined by the criteria of their intended effect—that is, intended to horrify, to thrill and to generate laughter. Other genres are defined by their subject-matter, such as science fiction (futuristic technologies/future worlds), road movie (journey or road trip) and film noir (crime and institutional corruption). Genre can also be discerned by style, such as the blockbuster (spectacular effects) and film noir (chiaroscuro lighting and dark *mise en scène*). Postmodernist intertextuality (allusions to other films) and eclecticism (elements from other film texts, genres and media forms) in films place 'the question of genre squarely within the broader context of mass-mediated culture' (Watson, 2003, p. 153). Baz Luhrmann's *Moulin Rouge* (2001) illustrates the notion of genre hybridity and genre referencing, and redefines the film musical by 'hooking up with a range of other generic formations … the music video and MTV, but also Bollywood, television advertisements, computer animation and virtual reality' (Watson 2003, p. 161). Altman (1996) makes the distinction that 'not all films engage spectators' generic knowledge in the same way and to the same effect. While some films simply borrow devices from established genres, others foreground their generic characteristics to the point where the genre concept itself plays a major role in the film' (1996, p. 279).

According to Schatz (1981), genre ultimately depends upon one criterion:

> the determining identifying feature of a film genre is its cultural context, its community of interrelated character types whose attitudes, values, and actions flesh out dramatic conflicts inherent within that community. The generic community is less a specific place (although it may be, as with the Western and gangster genres) than a network of characters, actions, values, and attitudes (1981, pp. 21–2).

Genre learning

However genre may be defined, the significant aspect for students is twofold. First, in appreciation terms, genre recognition is a tool used to describe and evaluate a film's individual sensibility and its collective nature with other films. Genre is a reflection of audience appeal, expectations and experience, and it provides an insight into the social, historical and economic conditions shaping that appeal, expectations and experience. Genre analysis does this because it critically acknowledges collective patterns in the construction and consumption of films. Watson describes genre as the 'golden thread that knits the concerns of industry together with the desires of the audience' (2003, p. 151).

Second, understandings of genre conventions harness students' creative ability to control the possibility of using genre elements in their own films. This returns us once again to giving students the capacity to make meaning by recognising how to work with audience expectations—in this case, through genre. Neale (2000) overviews the discourse of genre criticism, and discusses how literary critic E.D. Hirsch places genre as fundamental to the interpretation of any work. Hirsch argues that the interpreter of meaning (the audience in film) always has genre expectations in order to ground meaning and understand details of what they are experiencing. They have expectations in order to be able to be surprised or thwarted by changes in expectations. This understanding of genre has an all-encompassing effect on audience engagement in terms of expectations, as narrative does. Neale applies the concept of genre widely when he says genres should be considered 'as ubiquitous, multifaceted phenomenon rather than as one-dimensional entities to be found only within the realms of Hollywood cinema or of commercial popular culture' (2000, p. 28). Before concluding this discussion on genre's application to film construction and consumption, another aspect of film discourse, auteur theory, must be examined in terms of its relevance to screen learning.

Auteur theory

Auteur theory in film is problematic, but it is important in our discussion of students and screen learning because it focuses on the authorship and impact of an individual on a film, although film is in fact a collaborative art form. The term 'auteur' was used in the 1950s by the French New Wave to 'refer to directors who infused their films with distinctive personal vision through the salient manipulation of film technique' (Watson, 2003, p. 131). Auteur theory locates the director rather than the screenplay writer or the producer as the creative centre of a film. Like genre criticism, auteur study is a means to create a structural approach to the analysis of a body of work from a particular director with a discernible style or vision. Directors like Howard Hawks, John Ford, Alfred Hitchcock, Federico Fellini, Jean Renoir, Jean-Luc Godard, Rainer Werner Fassbinder, Wim Wenders, Ingmar Bergman, Orson Welles, David Lynch and Martin Scorsese have been described as auteurs because they have infused their work with a personal vision and left a distinctive signature in the body of their work. Auteur study, then, provides another framework for students to examine the patterns of meaning created by individual directors by uncovering 'behind the superficial contrasts of subject and treatment a hard core of basic and often recondite motifs. The pattern formed by these motifs … is what gives an author's work its particular structure, both defining it internally and distinguishing one body of work from another' (Nowell-Smith, 1972, p. 80).

Bruce Kawin (1992) uses auteur theory to demonstrate how, in the collective work of a film, an individual's authorship can be accredited:

> Critically, the conventional test of an auteur is that a pattern emerges when all of his or her pictures are viewed together or are considered in relation to each other. But the real value of auteurism—once it is extended beyond directors

and as it may be critically applied to a single picture—is that it offers a reasonable explanation for a fact about cinema: that an often personal coherence *can* emerge from a collaborative project (1992, p. 294).

On the other hand, many film directors would say the success of a film is dependent on the collaboration of all the people involved. The iconic Spanish director Pedro Almodovar (2002) claims: 'I think that is important for a filmmaker to abandon the illusion he can—or even worse, *must*—control everything in relation to his film … it's hard to say what degree of control one can have over the film's basic idea' (2002, pp. 84–5). Recognising the role of other contributors to the art form of film is discussed by Watson (2003), who presents a practice-based model of art where the work of screenwriters, producers, directors, cinematographers, designers, actors, editors, sound engineers, composers, visual effects supervisors, and so on is recognised, with them seen as potential auteurs in relation to a film's authorship (2003, p. 141). He says it is useful to think of 'creativity as constitutive at every level of cinematic activity' and that authorship can be attributed to 'a range of labour, creative and commercial levels' (2003, p. 140). Watson also discusses how auteurism became usurped by the needs of film commerce so directors were marketed as auteur celebrities to sell the film as a commodity, so that director-as-auteur has become a commercial construct rather than an artistic one.

The questions raised by auteur theory do help to guide ideas in the development of screen learning for students. Auteur theory posits authorship as a means to understand the creative and sociocultural aspects of film as an art form. Appreciating the work of auteurs provides an understanding of an individual vision in filmmaking, but in its discourse it also brings into question the very existence of an individual vision when film is a collaborative art created by so many elements. The issues in auteur theory highlight how creativity and making in screen learning have the capacity to express the individual voice in different aspects of filmmaking (camera operator, sound operator, director, actor) as well as to author a group-constructed vision (screenplay, editing, post-production choices). In other words, in screen learning the director can be one role of many in collaborating to create a work of art as part of a joint vision or to shape a personal vision through collaboration with others.

We argue that screen, narrative, genre and auteur theory provide insights into film and ways to frame and organise the learning. They place the art form of film in an artistic, theoretical, cultural, political, economic and historical context that provokes critical discourse and engagement. A deep knowledge of the fundamentals of narrative and genre construction provides insights, understandings and directions for students creating film. In the next chapter, screen theory and practice will be blended with educational theory and practice to generate effective film learning through scaffolding the aesthetic.

5
Scaffolding learning in film aesthetics

> Film as dream, film as music. No form of art goes beyond ordinary consciousness as film does, straight to our emotions, deep into the twilight room of the soul.
>
> —Ingmar Bergman

The 'twilight room of the soul' is the space Ingmar Bergman (*Smiles of a Summer Night*, 1955; *The Seventh Seal*, 1957; *Persona*, 1966) inhabited when he experienced the magic of seeing and making a film. Somewhere 'beyond ordinary consciousness' is the space we want young people to experience when they work with film. We argue this happens when students engage with the aesthetic and process of filmmaking. It is achieved effectively through two pedagogical processes: learning scaffolds; and collaborative group learning (explored in Chapter 6). This chapter discusses how scaffolded learning structures, focuses and extends learning in the film aesthetic.

Student engagement with the film aesthetic: The Shostakovich Project

This chapter begins by referring to research from the Shostakovich Film Project (Jefferson, 2006). The project involved senior secondary school students from a city school and a regional, rural school making a collaborative, short film called *The Boy Who Loved Shostakovich*. It was a four-month extracurricular project conducted under the guidance of three teacher–researchers. Reflections from the students who participated in the project are used to illustrate how students experienced the film aesthetic and the filmmaking process.

Figure 5.1 An image from *The Boy Who Loved Shostakovich* (2006), a film project involving secondary school students.

The young people in the Shostakovich Film Project participated as screenplay writers, storyboarders, actors, directors, cinematographers, camera and sound operators, composers, location managers, designers and editors. After isolated workshops with teachers and students, the participants from the two schools came together in short, intensive shooting periods to create a 40-minute film about teenage apathy and bullying. The three protagonists in the film's story are inspired to combat these concerns through a 'revolution' of their imaginations and the making of a film inspired by two twentieth-century Russian artists, composer Shostakovich and filmmaker Eisenstein. The student Simon,[1] who plays the main role in the film as well as being involved in other roles such as screenplay writing, lighting and editing, said that working on the Shostokovich Film Project provided a 'fantastic opportunity to explore and experiment in the magical medium of film'. The intrinsic 'magic' of film that Simon refers to is what arts educator Elliot Eisner (2002) describes as an arts way of thinking, a way of transforming consciousness.

Eisner says that to experience the arts is to experience an aesthetic that touches and moves us. It is to experience the world in a more complex and subtle way. Like the great Swedish director Ingmar Bergman, the student Simon has become excited by exploring and experimenting with the film aesthetic and discovering the complexity and subtlety 'of its magic'. So by working with film, do students automatically get this experience or does the experience have to be harnessed or framed in some way? How do students experience the magic of film? How can they be introduced to the arts way of thinking that touches and moves them?

Ingmar Bergman (1988) gives us a hint about how to harness that 'magic' when he describes what the optical illusion of film movement created by 24 still frames a second means to him:

> A little twitch in our optic nerve, a shock effect: twenty-four illuminated frames in a second, darkness in between, the optic nerve incapable of registering darkness. At the editing table, when I run the strip of film through, frame by frame, I still feel that dizzy sense of magic of my childhood: in the darkness of the wardrobe, I slowly wind one frame after another, see almost imperceptible changes, wind faster—a movement (1988, pp. 73–4).

It is in understanding and controlling the art form of film 'frame by frame', or in other words at an essential level, that its magic can be appreciated and harnessed. 'Frame by frame' is a useful metaphor to explain that the magic of learning about film is in the detail. It is in discovering the parts to understand the whole, and engaging with the aesthetic in a fundamental way.

The parts of a whole aesthetic

Recognising the parts or elements of the filmmaking aesthetic was evident in student responses to the Shostakovich Film Project. The project was an extracurricular venture designed to extend and enrich students' interest in film. Some of the students had some experience with filmmaking, but most had none at all. Three teachers facilitated and collaborated with students in the learning of skills and knowledge in filmmaking through pre-production workshops and the process of shooting and editing. School camera, sound and computer resources were used, lighting boards were made, and a small tracking dolly and crane were hired for some shots. According to their interests, students were designated a number of filmmaking roles such as camera and sound operators, costume and prop sourcing, location and logistics management, catering and acting. Under the guidance of the teachers, a core group of eleven students was ultimately responsible for the shaping of the screenplay and the ideas for storyboarding, cinematography, directing, filming and editing. The project involved up to 50 students and adults as actors and extras. The city students travelled and stayed with students in a country town for an intensive five-day shoot, and later the rural students came to the city for a weekend shoot. At the completion of the project, students reflected on what they viewed as an intensive and memorable experience of the film aesthetic.

Simon, who was 'the boy who loved Shostakovich' in the film, said he had discovered that 'acting in the film was just a small part of a giant entity and that other parts such as lighting and sound were just as vital'. Another student, Jessica, likened their various roles such as screenplay writing, storyboarding, shot location, and organising the crew and equipment to being 'part of the one brain, connected and vital in their purpose'. Victoria, one of the camera operators, made a comment that was particularly intriguing. She articulated how the aesthetic purpose of all the parts of filmmaking should be 'connected to an internal emotion in the drama'. She said 'the landscape and the lighting had to stimulate a feeling and a mood that complemented the drama of the scene', and that the 'truth of the moment could only be captured by acting that expressed an intention as an internal emotion'. She felt that creating these internal emotions and moments in a film was like a 'memory that is slowed down and analysed'.

In the Shostakovich Project, the students had various roles for which they were responsible; however, they became very aware of how all the roles and components of filmmaking were vital to controlling what their film communicated. They were recognising the contribution of the parts to the whole, and conscious of working with an aesthetic that was challenging to learn and to control, but potentially powerful in communicating their imagined story. So deep was their engagement with the film aesthetic that camera operator Victoria had connected with an understanding of the art form of film at a profound and philosophical level. Victoria's reference to film as an experience of memory slowed down echoes Jones's (1941) description of motion pictures as 'thoughts made visible and audible' (1941, p. 17) and Susanne Langer's (1953) theory that film is 'the appearance of dream, a unified, continuously passing, significant apparition of culture' (1953, p. 413).

Collaborative, creative problem-solving in the aesthetic

Students were dealing at a fundamental level with the form and the function of the film narrative aesthetic. They were attempting to create and control the drama of the story they were telling through the aesthetic. In doing so, they were wrestling with choices and ideas, discovering and solving problems in a process they all had to manage together like one big brain—or, as another student described it, they were all 'gadgets in a machine where they all had to work individually for the machine to function and produce a final product'. In order for the collaboration to work on the Shostakovich Project, Harriet recognised during pre-production workshops and production shooting that part of the success of the team problem-solving was 'respecting the priorities of everyone else and knowing when or when not to interfere'. Camera operator Ben began to recognise when his shots were working or not working, and developed a confidence to make these aesthetic choices, but also realised the impact these choices had on the artistry of the whole project and the collaboration of the other students and teachers. Victoria best summed this up as 'learning to trust each other's decisions and actions', but most importantly she felt they had to trust themselves and their own learning and instincts. Although they all learnt the importance of organisation and planning as an index to the success of the project, they also discovered the value of expecting the unexpected and creatively problem-solving under pressure.

Learning continued when they edited their film, *The Boy Who Loved Shostakovich*. The reverberations of the students' choices in the shooting required further problem-solving and discovery learning in the editing process. Simon described the whole process of filmmaking as 'a trapeze act of trust' because he realised that 'the actors trust the camera to connect with and capture the drama. Then the editors rely on the actors and camera operators to produce the right material for the scene to edit together dramatically.' The choices made and problems solved under the pressure and constraints of production had repercussions in post-production editing, and required further problem-solving by a collaborative editing process.

Creative and artistic choices made in the pre-production and production stages have consequences for the post-production process and present a valuable tool for learning about the aesthetic. During editing, students realise what does or doesn't work. Lachlan's learning about acting for film on the Shostakovich Project is an example. He knew that 'acting in film should feel like life', but found it hard to trust that his own thoughts were enough to convey belief and truth on the screen. So in a particular chase scene where he had to slow down his actions, he decided to 'flag up' (heighten) his performance. While editing, he watched himself and felt he had made a mistake with his hammed-up acting choice, saying: 'I flagged it up and now I look like a complete idiot running away from who knows what. Boy, have I learnt my lesson!'

The aesthetic as process

The students in the Shostakovich Project had a rich learning experience from an immersion in a detailed 'frame by frame'-like experience of what film and filmmaking can be. They had what Eisner (2004) calls an aesthetic experience that resides not only in appreciating a work of art, but is embedded in the actual process of creating the art. The act of making, Eisner argues, is an aesthetic experience in itself. This is illustrated by Simon's memorable experience of the 'magical medium of film' and other student reactions to the film project, such as Jessica's surprise that 'a group of teenagers could mature, focus and thrive when placed in an intense environment', and Lachlan's response that it opened his eyes because he 'learnt so much' and now has an 'even greater passion for film and appreciation of shots and camera work'.

What principles of learning are being used to take students to the memorable intensity of an aesthetic experience? Is it purely the act of making art that leads to effective learning in the aesthetic, or are there pathways and strategies to arts learning that are more effective? From these student reflections of the Shostakovich Project, it is apparent that the learning was not haphazard. The core film group of eleven students, who had ultimate responsibility for creating the film, had to manage themselves and up to 50 other students and adults from their own metropolitan school and another rural school. How were these eleven students prepared for this considerable logistical challenge? How did they manage to organise themselves? How did they become so conscious about their learning? What did they know before they began? How did they learn about film aesthetics? How did they engage as a group with the many aspects of the film aesthetic? How much of the learning was student-centred? What was the role of the teachers? These questions are answered in part by a scaffolded approach to the learning of film aesthetics and the filmmaking process.

Theory and practice in scaffolded learning

Scaffolding in education as metaphor describes the instructional support a teacher provides for a student's construction of their own learning. The teacher provides processes, language and tasks to support students' abilities to develop cognitively. The construction of learning begins from the ground up, and therefore teachers scaffold new learning from a foundation of what is known and can be achieved to what is unknown by their students. These ideas are derived from a sociocultural model of education that has its historical and theoretical roots in Vygotsky, Bruner and Dewey. In this model, knowledge is socially and culturally constructed. Student learning is not natural, but rather dependent on what a teacher provides as well as the interaction the student has with more expert others. In the Shostakovich Project, Ben's response provides an illustration of how the process of scaffolding supported his learning and other students:

> I did not expect to have so much input into the creative aspects of the filming … I expected the camera operators to basically be told by the teachers what to do and how to film. This only occurred at the beginning. In the end, the camera crew seemed to be trusted to compose shots and run rehearsals of shots, etc.

To begin with, the students were supported and guided in fundamental understandings and control of the filmmaking aesthetic and processes. As the project progressed, they began to solve the problems of manipulating the aesthetic and organising the process themselves.

Jerome Bruner (1960) explains that the key to continued learning lies in providing the fundamental principles as well as a structure in which those principles can be applied: 'Mastery of the fundamental ideas of a field involves not only the grasping of general principles, but also the development of an attitude toward learning and inquiry, toward guessing and hunches, toward the possibility of solving problems on one's own' (1960, p. 20).

A teaching scaffold guides and supports the fostering of the students' own inquiry in learning through problem-solving. Problem-solving in the arts involves the mastery of communicating through an aesthetic. This was evident in the Shostakovich Project when Victoria questioned the purpose of her camera shots and solved the problem:

> What is the dramatic intent? What was I trying to achieve in this scene and how was I going to do this? … Behind the camera I discovered how we are just as much a part of the scene as the actors we are shooting—the same intentions are felt.

Bruner says a deep understanding of essential principles and fundamental structures help to explain complexity and make learning comprehensible. If students have the fundamentals, they can generalise from what they have learnt to what they will encounter later on.

Discovery learning

Scaffolded learning provides a structure for students to learn through discovery. What is new to the learner as found through the act of discovery engenders a sense of ownership of their own learning and a greater sense of engagement—possibly even excitement—with the learning. Victoria talks about her 'discovery' behind the camera and Simon remembers the Shostakovich Project experience as 'memorable because so much was discovered and learned, and such fun was had!' For film students to learn through discovery, it is necessary to do more than just give them a camera and let them go forth and create. As a practice, this may provide some learning outcomes; however, it is a hit and miss phenomenon. Some students may have success because they have a talent or disposition for film creativity and literacy, but the aim of education is to engage, extend and challenge all learners. In the 'go forth and create' scenario, learners will not necessarily know or understand what worked and why, or recognise what didn't work and why.

Bruner (1960) points out that the objective of teaching is not to produce self-confident fools but students who are informed, creative problem-solvers willing to make honest mistakes in the pursuit of, in our screen learning context, the aesthetic experience. Annabel, for instance—like Victoria—discovered that using the camera was like a live performance; however, she acknowledged that her learning involved mistakes because she realised when something didn't work:

> I discovered that using the camera was a lot more like performing than what I had previously expected; there was that same rush, excitement and nervousness to get it right but also disappointment and frustration when I felt I didn't.

Learning through controlling and understanding

As part of the Shostakovich Project, Annabel felt prepared and supported in the learning she was undertaking but was mindful at the same time that she was being challenged and constructing her own learning. As a camera operator, she talked about how, in trying to control the shots, she really understood and appreciated their purpose:

> Filming was nerve-racking, repetitive, frustrating, rewarding, hard to control, subtle and timed down to the millisecond. When I was doing my first tracking

shot I realised that in doing the camera movement in practice was where I really learnt what the shot was meant to achieve.

Annabel recognised that, by controlling the aesthetic in practice, she had greater understanding of the film aesthetic. Her learning process is exemplified through the pedagogical model (Teaching film) we outlined in Chapter 1. Learning to control the aesthetic contributes to aesthetic understanding, and in turn aesthetic appreciation informs her knowledge of how to control the aesthetic in practice. The two processes of making and appreciating inform and complement each other in developing student creativity and literacy in the film form. In our pedagogy for filmmaking and appreciation, the model is supported by scaffolded learning that develops skills and knowledge in the aesthetic control and aesthetic understanding of film language and film form.

Scaffolding the film learning

The example of scaffolded film learning shown in Figure 5.2 is directed towards classroom curriculum learning through a teaching program. The spiral structure illustrates how each module supports and builds on previous modules. Each module can take up 25 hours of curriculum teaching time (see the Appendix for further details on each module and its learning focus in making and appreciation). The first module of the program demonstrates what is fundamental or essential to the development of learning in the film aesthetic. The overall program from Modules 1 to 7 demonstrates a logical sequence in continued learning. Effective scaffolding builds from essential and comprehensible foundations. In turn, solid foundations determine and support the nature of the scaffold of future learning. A teaching scaffold sequences and supports the development of the learning like an upward spiral. If learning is like learning to juggle, you begin with one ball, then two balls, then three. Learning the subtleties of the film aesthetic has to be approached in the same way. Students need to learn to work with the complexity and sophistication of more filmic elements in a gradual or incremental way.

These modules are by no means comprehensive or prescriptive. They are merely an example of a sequenced learning program in film that begins from fundamentals and builds a logical structure for students to construct their own learning from the ground up. The last module on occupational health and safety is one that would be integrated throughout all the learning modules and designed to be appropriate for the processes and tasks for each module. Safety

86 TEACHING THE SCREEN

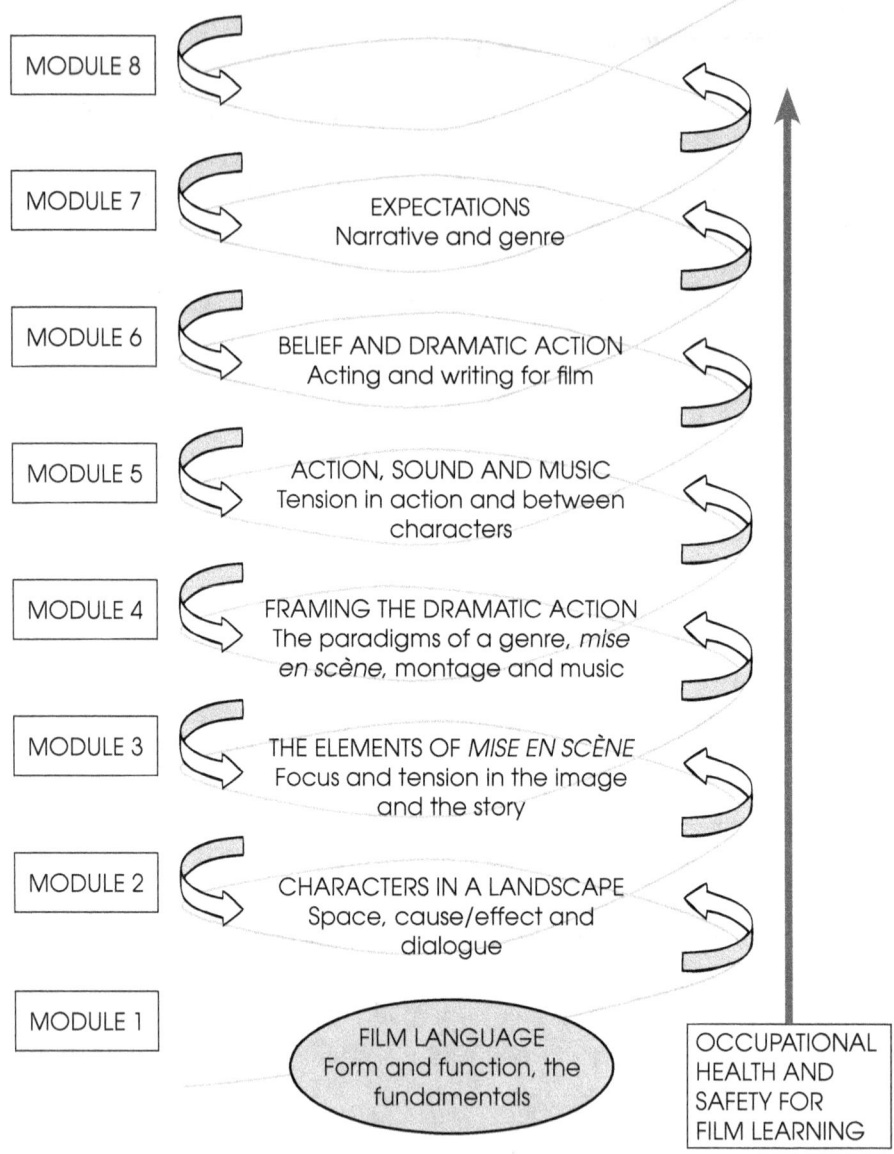

Figure 5.2 A teaching program based on a scaffolded sequence of consecutive learning modules.

concerns are applicable to the use of any equipment and collaborative group work inside and outside the classroom. Each module is designed to build from skills, knowledge and understandings of the previous module, and develop the level of sophistication of students' control and understanding of the film aesthetic.

The foundation of film learning

As mentioned previously, film is made up of visual images, sound, speech, music and graphics. These parts all contribute to the film aesthetic, and work together in an integrated way to create meaning for the spectator. The governing principle or foundation for the learning in all aspects of film is that all the parts of film have the function or purpose of creating meaning for the audience. Each part has developed codes and conventions, and requires specific skills and knowledge in the way it is controlled to communicate meaning on the screen. To address all these parts at the beginning of learning is to start juggling with too many elements.

The visual image is predominant over sound, speech, music and graphics. The starting point should be to control and understand the identification with, and tension within, the visual image. Therefore, the learning focus of the first foundation module is how the form of the image aesthetic alone communicates in film. Other components such as sound, speech, music and graphics are addressed and integrated into later learning modules in the program. This chapter focuses on the scaffolding of fundamentals in the first module. In the first module, students enter the engine of filmmaking and begin with the mechanics or semiotics of the image as a visual aesthetic experience on its own. The semiotics of visual imagery in film is referred to by theorists and practitioners as *film language*.

The first module of film learning: Film language

To begin screen learning is to introduce the fundamentals. Fundamental to teaching the film aesthetic is the relationship between the aesthetic form and its function. The first module begins with the predominant form of the visual image and the film language of shots, composition and montage. An overview of the first module, as an example of fundamentals and scaffolding, can also be presented as a spiral of learning (see Figure 5.3). This spiral supports, links and develops past, present and future learning.

The aim of this scaffolded learning framework is to support and guide students in controlling the film aesthetic at a fundamental level through problem-solving, making honest mistakes, discovering, creating and appreciating.

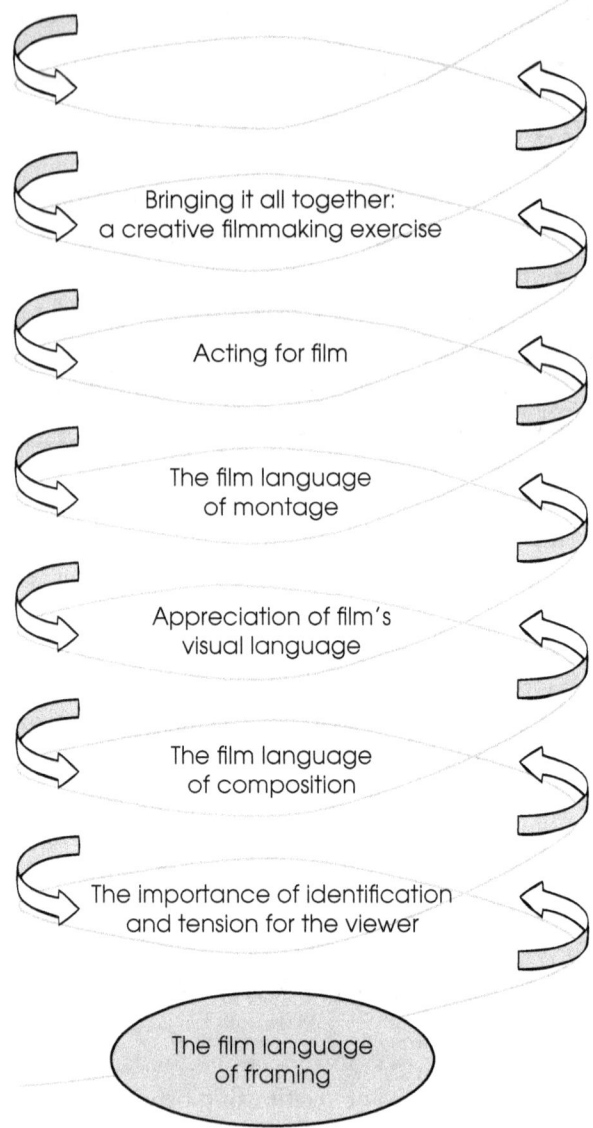

Figure 5.3 The spiral of learning: an approach to film learning fundamentals.

The film language of framing

To introduce film images as a language is an effective metaphor to begin with. Technically, visual images are not actually a language, as Metz (1974) points out. A language uses words to signify an image, idea or feeling, but in film the images are not signified or represented in another form; they are actualised and realised as they are. Although film is not a language *per se*, learning to make films is like learning a language. Learning a word from a foreign tongue doesn't mean you can create meaning or be understood by just saying the word. You have to understand what the word means and how it is used. In filmic terms, you must know how meaning is created through the denotative, connotative and paradigmatic associations made with an image.

For example, aesthetic control comes from knowing more than what a close-up of a character is; it lies in asking and being able to answer the following questions about the filmmaker's choice of using a close-up:

- What is its visual impact and effect on the audience?
- What is its dramatic purpose?
- When is it being used? Why is it being used?
- What is the audience's relationship with the character through the close-up?
- How do we identify with the character in the close-up?
- How should we identify with the character in a close-up?

These questions imply that the spectator engages with the close-up shot in a certain type of way. The spectator is being given a way to identify with the character.

The importance of identification and tension for the viewer

Viewing characters through particular shot frames (close-up, mid-shot, long-shot) can be understood as being like the relationships between people and the spaces they inhabit. Students need to imagine the proximity of the camera as being like the space we, as humans, inhabit with each other in determining how we engage with the world around us and with others. The principles of proxemics apply to the ways we engage through the lens with characters, the action and their landscape on the screen. In other words, how physically and therefore emotionally close should the spectator be with the characters on the screen? How should the viewer identify with the character?

For instance, in a close-up of a character, is the spectator identifying with the character's emotions? Or the character's relationship with other characters? Or the world or landscape which the characters inhabit? A close-up of the face really only satisfies one of these: the emotions of the character. That is how the spectator is meant to identify with the character in the close-up. In the mid-shot, the spectator identifies with the character and their relationships with other people. In the long-shot, the spectator identifies with the character and the context around them. With each type of shot, the spectator's identification with the character changes.

To merely capture what is happening in a scene with any shot is not to realise the aesthetic impact of the choice of framing of a shot and its effect on the audience for identification and the creation of tension. For instance, to say that the movement of a panning shot is used merely to reveal the rest of the world around a character is not to understand that it is the way it reveals the world that is significant. A long-shot in fact can do the same thing, but the pan creates a tension of discovery by not revealing the whole world immediately. The filmmaker has to know whether it is a string of tension that is appropriate in engaging the audience with the story they are telling. Or is the tension elsewhere? To manipulate the tension of the image can be likened to manipulating a puppet's strings. A puppeteer has to pull the right strings subtly in the right way to create the appropriate emotional affect with the marionette. So too does the filmmaker in choosing and using a certain type of shot.

Beginning to understand the fundamentals of film language involves students understanding the aesthetic purpose and aesthetic experience of the close-up, mid-shot, long-shot, high- and low-angle and point-of-view shot, and the moving lens shots of the pan, tilt, dolly and tracking. Simple and varied group and individual exercises involving dramatic role-playing, imagining, drawing or using the camera are necessary scaffolded activities for students to discover the purpose of the basic shot types and their aesthetic before embarking on a small filmmaking exercise. The creation of tension and identification with the viewer through the language of shot type is a crucial understanding for the learner.

Problem-solving activities relating to the dramatic purpose of shots can be accompanied by the viewing of a segment—for example, from *A Personal Journey with Martin Scorsese Through American Movies* (Scorsese, 1995). Scorsese illustrates how early filmmakers discovered the 'language' or 'grammar' of film. Students watching the footage of early films using close-ups, dolly shots, tracking and so on begin to realise how the aesthetic of film language was developed by discovering how the form of film's shots, composition and editing have a dramatic function in narrative engagement. Demonstrations and appreciation of film footage in this way help to consolidate students' own problem-solving in the aesthetic.

Scaffolding learning in film aesthetics 91

Figure 5.4 The early, 'raw' use of the camera in films like D.W. Griffith's *Intolerance* (1916) helps illustrate to students the dramatic function of shots.

The film language of composition

Shot types refer to the framing of the image. Film language, however, is not just determined by the framing of the image; it is also in the composition of the image. Arranging the image to engage the spectator's eye and control and heighten what is being 'read' means students have to solve these questions:

- What is the focus in the image?
- How is the eye being led or drawn into the image?
- Where are the vertical, horizontal and diagonal lines to balance and focus the image?
- How does the rule of thirds achieve this?
- How are balance, light, space and colour contributing to the balance, focus, mood and atmosphere in the image?
- How are diagonal lines and triangles in composition used to heighten interest and tension, and strengthen the point of focus?
- How has a three-dimensional perspective (depth) been created in a two-dimensional image?
- How do all these questions serve the visual impact and dramatic purpose of the image?

- Where is the movement in the shot?
- How is movement a focus in the shot?

As with shot size and type, students can explore the composition of images though group exercises in drawing, dramatic role-playing and using the camera. What is also effective in demonstrating the film language of framing and composition is the appreciation of brief extracts of films.

Appreciation of film's visual language

The use of carefully chosen film extracts for appreciation exercises is fundamental to our pedagogical model. Bordwell and Thompson (2004) mention that in their approach to analysing film they look at the whole film because audiences experience whole films, not snippets. Fabe (2004) argues that a shot-by-shot analysis is the best way to appreciate the filmmaker's art:

> I have learned that viewers trained in close analysis of single film sequences are better able to see and appreciate the rich visual and aural complexity of the film medium. Close analysis unlocks the secrets of how film images, combined with sound, can have a profound effect on our minds and emotions (2004, p. xv).

In our view, for learning purposes, featured extracts of films help to unlock the fundamentals. Extracts help to focus on an essence that explains a basic principle in the film aesthetic. Although the learning is focused, that doesn't mean interrelated concepts won't arise, nor does it mean they should be ignored. The focus on a basic principle usually demonstrates an understanding of those related phenomena. The following example of film appreciation in this first module will illustrate these ideas.

The eight-minute extract of the Odessa Steps massacre from Eisenstein's film *The Battleship Potemkin* (1925) can be viewed a number of times by students, first to describe the film language used, and second to analyse why it was used and to what effect. In the Odessa Steps scene, students are witnessing how an early, raw but highly effective and affecting film is both simple and sophisticated in controlling its visual imagery and meaning. A scene from a film like *The Battleship Potemkin* (freely available on YouTube) takes students to the essence of early developments in film language that they are experiencing themselves. An example of this film exercise in practice appears in Chapter 8.

Given the students' learning so far, they should recognise in the Odessa Steps scene of *The Battleship Potemkin* the use of shot types and composition to affect the audience's engagement and identification with the scene. The students will notice how the shot types, composition and editing serve to heighten the drama of the scene by identifying the viewer with the plight, fear and tension of the fleeing people during the massacre. The types of shots, composition and montage enhance the dramatic action and order of events, and increase the tension of and engagement with the scene.

Students might also comment on the role of the music, although it is not the focus of the learning in this module. They may discuss how the musical underscoring also contributes to the tension, dissonance and pathos of the scene through the music's rhythms, melodies, key and chord structures, and instrumentation. The music is related directly to the choices made in the dramatic aesthetic of the visual imagery. Students may also notice that the film time of the massacre is longer than the actual time of the massacre. Eisenstein has manipulated time and space (as film does) for a desired dramatic effect that is related to the intended dramatic tension, dissonance and pathos of the massacre scene.

Students might be perplexed by some of Eisenstein's imagery and juxtaposition of shots because they break certain filmic conventions. If students are then introduced to his ideas of intellectual or symbolic montage as a contrast to continuity and Hollywood montage, students are experiencing the idea that the art of film constructs its own conventions or rules. Eisenstein's convention of using intellectual symbolism in his films is determined by the political and social context of revolutionary Russia and his dialectical philosophical world-view. The shots and montage Eisenstein uses are chosen for more than telling a story for dramatic effect. His aesthetic is determined by his political world-view.

All these ideas are related to the fundamentals explored in this module—that is, form in the aesthetic is constructed to serve a function of engagement. Watching the film extract from *The Battleship Potemkin* can focus on shot choices, composition and conventions, but it also introduces students to fundamental ideas in montage or editing.

The film language of montage

Putting different shots together in the language of film is like structuring a sentence. A sentence is constructed from the choice, order, timing, flow and rhythm of the words. Montage, like a sentence, communicates meaning through the choice, order, timing, flow and rhythm of the images. When and how one shot changes to another is just as meaningful to the aesthetic experience of what is in the shot. There is another language to be explored in editing, but before doing so there is a fundamental principle to editing that needs to be understood. Breath allows speech; movement allows shots to be put together.

By examining an example of an extract from a film such as the opening sequence from *Rear Window* (1954), students can solve the following questions to begin an understanding of how movement works with editing:

- Where is action and movement in the shots?
- Are there any shots without movement?
- What is the eye focusing on and following in the shot and then in the following shots?
- In what way do action and movement connect one shot to the next?
- How does a moving shot (pan, tilt, dolly, etc.) connect to the next shot?
- How is the impression of a continuous flow created? What is the effect, both visually and dramatically?

Then students can explore the language of editing and consider choices that are made by the filmmaker to create meaning for the viewer:

- When do the shots change? Why do they change?
- How does the timing or pace of the action in the shot's *mise en scène* affect the timing of the editing?
- What is timing? How long do we need to read the image?
- How do we connect meaning in one image to that in the next?
- What is the effect of timing the editing of the shots?
- What is the effect of the pace, flow and rhythm of the editing on the viewer?
- What is the dramatic purpose and impact of the editing on the viewer's engagement?

These same questions can be applied to the film extract from *The Battleship Potemkin* and contrasted with the editing choices made in the *Rear Window* extract. In trying to answer the questions posed, students are problem-solving ways to explain the purpose of film language semiotics. What should be apparent to students from their deep semiotic analysis of framing, composition and montage is that they are beginning to see a narrative aesthetic where choices are made by the filmmaker for a desired dramatic effect. Students have to use the understanding they have discovered and put it into practice, but they also have to begin to explore the aesthetic of acting for film.

Acting for film

Essential to the development of the narrative film aesthetic in our pedagogical approach is an emphasis on acting for film. Acting is not only part of the aesthetic; it is a way to understand and develop the drama of a narrative. Acting explores the dramatic intent of a character in a scene and the dramatic purpose of the narrative's engagement with an audience. Exercises in acting for film give students the opportunity to physically and emotionally explore roles, characters and actions in a story as well as learn how to perform an acting role for film.

Students can undertake acting exercises to learn about how to be focused in role and bring belief to the playing of a dramatic intent. For example, focus can be explored in a drama game, where students go to hide in various parts of a room, and repeat the same action by being mindful of every moment and aware of others. For dramatic intent, pairs can be given a circumstance (the conditions of a situation such as a high-pressure exam) in which an individual commits an action (such as trying to cheat) to which the other reacts. Exercises in committing to an intention help students sustain focus and belief, establishes a relationship between characters, and develop the tension of a dramatic action and dramatic moment. These are basic and crucial elements in the aesthetic of acting. Acting allows students to explore dramatic narrative through the element of play in the created world of their film story. Students are now ready to create, control and perform their first film.

Bringing it all together

A scaffold has now been constructed for students to bring the fundamentals of film language together and learn though the creative filmmaking process. The creative task needs to be based on the fundamentals that have been the focus of the learning, and allow students to make further discoveries in both an informed and intuitive way. As long it is undertaken with integrity, the creative process—no matter how small the task—will always involve risk-taking and learning from successes and mistakes. Students now have an insight into the structure of their own screen learning. They know they are working with the basics of film language, and attempting to communicate and control an aesthetic.

Containing the task involves making the parameters of the exercise tight and the objective clear so that students can focus on what they are really trying to control in the film aesthetic. Although this appears limiting, it does in fact make the creative task more challenging and sophisticated because they have to attempt to control more precisely the aesthetic they are working with. At the same time, a creative task is always open to possibilities and discoveries because of the very nature of creating your own art work, no matter how small the work.

A creative task

A filmmaking exercise may be devised that is 30 to 45 seconds in length and explores how the visual language of framing, composition and montage serves to communicate the purpose of one dramatic action and engage an audience. The dramatic action could simply be one character being chased or a character seeking solitude or looking for assistance. No other aspects of story should be explored, just the dramatic action alone. No other aspects of *mise en scène* are used—for example, costumes or props; no other components of film such as sound, speech, music or graphics are used; and there is just one character. The problem students have to solve creatively is how to use the language of film at a very basic but sophisticated level to capture and control the visual impact and dramatic purpose of a scene of dramatic action. The problem-solving will entail grappling with these questions:

- What is the character's intent in the action?
- What does the character do and show to capture that intent? What moments are being created?
- How should the spectator identify with the character and the action?
- How should the spectator be engaged?
- Where (around the school) is a location that aids the dramatic purpose of the scene? Why is location important?
- What mood and atmosphere can be created through the location and the shots?
- What type of shots capture the dramatic purpose of the scene?
- What type of shots will be used to affect the audience's identification with the character?

- How will shots be composed? Where is the focus and tension in the image?
- How will the shots be edited? How will it flow? What is the pace and rhythm of the montage?
- How is movement being used for editing purposes?
- Why is continuity so important?

In the creative filming task, students have had scaffolded learning to guide them. Even with teacher support during the making process, the students will make mistakes and discoveries—but this makes the learning more effective and resonant with learners.

Scaffolding provides a structure within which students can learn the aesthetic of film through problem-solving in making and appreciating. Scaffolding is about finding comprehensible principles to use in setting up a logical framework for continued learning. This first module of scaffolded film learning in film language should lay the foundations for further learning. From the fundamentals of film language, a sequence or program of learning is built that spirals the learner along a structure that consolidates past learning. The scaffold should offer challenges for new learning in controlling and understanding the film aesthetic. From the basics, the learning focuses on other film elements and becomes more integrated, complex and sophisticated. Introducing the fundamentals and offering a sequence of learning and problem-solving that develops the learning provides a scaffolded, supportive learning framework, essential for the success of learning with film. The focus of the next chapter is the role and processes of collaborative learning inherent in a filmmaking pedagogy.

6
Collaborative learning processes in filmmaking

> I think making a film on your own is about as hard as playing tennis alone: if there isn't anyone on the other side to hit the ball back it just doesn't work.
>
> —*Jean-Luc Godard*

Jean-Luc Godard, François Truffaut, Eric Rohmer, Jacques Rivette and Louis Malle were the French New Wave who in the late 1950s developed the concept of the 'auteur' in the cinema, where the director is credited as the author of the film. The concept was a reaction to the prevailing convention of crediting writers as cinematic author, a legacy from the literary tradition. The New Wave argued that Hitchcock was as much an author as Tolstoy. Later, Godard (2002) qualified the concept of auteur in the cinema by saying 'the goal of this concept was not to show *who* makes a good film but to demonstrate *what* makes a good film' (2002, p. 214). What makes a good film is the way in which the aesthetic parts (screenplay writing, direction, acting, designing, cinematography, editing, etc.) are used to make the aesthetic whole of the art form. What brings the parts together in most cases (except perhaps for the lone animator) is a process of people collaborating.

This chapter is about how collaborative filmmaking is conducive to, and instructive in, a collaborative approach to learning. Vygotsky's ideas on learning through social interaction and scaffolds help to explain the benefits of a collaborative approach to film learning. However, the skills to collaborate and the understandings of teamwork and collective creativity have to be facilitated by teachers and learnt by students. The community of practice model (Lave and Wenger, 1991) demonstrates how filmmaking offers authentic learning experiences, socially active roles and responsibilities for students as well as conditions for self-directed learning. In film learning, trust and responsibility are essential for collaborative group learning and student management of film resources. Our approach to filmmaking offers students a shared experience in all parts of the filmmaking processes. Filmmaking has distinctive stages in its process, from pre-production to screening, and these stages provide a scaffolded structure for aesthetic and cognitive learning in the collaborative processes of making a film.

Collaborative learning theory: Vygotsky

Jean-Luc Godard (2002) recognises that the exchanging of ideas amongst a group of people can enrich the process of creating:

> I think it is of primary importance for a filmmaker to be able to gather around him a group of people with whom he can communicate and, most of all, exchange ideas. When Sartre wrote something, it was the result of endless conversations with forty or fifty people. He didn't come up with all this just sitting alone in his room (2002, p. 210).

Italian film director, Bernardo Bertolucci (2002) said he began making films thinking he was an auteur in the strictest sense, but then realised that by collaborating with others he was able to express far more:

> a director can express his fantasies even better if he is able to stimulate the creativity of everyone around him. A film is a sort of melting pot in which the talents of a crew must mingle. Film stock is much more sensitive than people think, and it records not only what is in front of the camera but everything around it (2002, p. 50).

A secondary school student who participated in the Shostakovich Film Project, discussed in Chapter 5, said he learnt 'how much people can achieve when they all put their minds together'. What processes, then, are at work to explain the benefits of collaboration in the creative process of making a film? How does a collaborative situation encourage a melting pot of ideas and skills, and serve learning? Vygotsky's ideas on the zone of proximal development help to explain how working with others, rather than being alone, furthers a student's capacity to learn.

A student's development, Vygotsky (1978) argues, is informed by a dynamic threshold of what the student is capable of learning through interaction with others, rather than the capability of what they can already achieve alone. In other words, students develop and learn more when 'they all put their minds together'. Vygotsky describes this dynamic threshold or ready potential in students as the *zone of proximal development*: 'It is the distance between the actual development level as determined by independent problem solving and the level of potential development as determined through problem solving under adult supervision or in collaboration with more capable peers' (1978, p. 86). Vygotsky likens students' internalised learning in the zone of proximal development to 'buds' of 'flowers' of development, rather than the 'fruits' of development. If a student can successfully complete a task alone, then according to Vygotsky there is no longer a zone of proximal development but the attainment of the actual development level. Therefore, 'learning which is oriented toward developmental levels that have already been reached is ineffective from the viewpoint of a child's overall development' (1978, p. 89).

Fundamental to Vygotsky's theory is the role of the social context to facilitate and consolidate learning. Learners are more capable of achieving their potential through the guidance of an expert teacher combined with the collective activity of working with more capable peers. External assistance from the teacher and participation in peer group work challenges, and hence facilitates, student learning in the proximal zone. As well, Vygotsky says social participation consolidates the learning. In Vygotskian terms, the process of social interaction with other students serves to internalise the learning: 'learning awakens a variety of internal developmental processes that are able to operate only when the child is interacting with people in his environment and in cooperation with his peers. Once these processes are internalised, they become part of the child's independent development achievement' (1978, p. 90).

In the classroom, the dynamic of social interaction (group work) within a sequenced learning structure (scaffolding) puts the student's learning process ahead of their developmental process. Teaching, then, is leading a student's development rather than responding to it. The idea is that this is achieved by both organising social interactions in the classroom between students in problem-solving tasks with teacher assistance, and designing a sequenced learning structure that 'provides the basis for the subsequent development of a variety of highly complex internal processes in children's thinking' (1978, p. 90). Scaffolded film learning exercises and filmmaking tasks aim to fulfil Vygotsky's principles and the qualities of collaborative learning.

The role of the teacher in collaborative film learning

Providing a scaffolded learning framework and organised group work requires active teacher facilitation in film learning. The teacher must have knowledge of the students and a deep knowledge of the film aesthetic and its pedagogy. If optimal learning occurs in Vygotsky's proximal zone of development, students need the help of the teacher to learn and be guided in scaffolded and collaborative learning. The idea is that students are taught fundamental understandings in an area of learning, and explore and consolidate these understandings through challenging task-oriented group work. The teacher leads students to develop their cognitive abilities by allowing them in groups to explore, experiment and solve problems. In short filmmaking tasks, students are attempting to create, control and communicate by using specific elements of the film aesthetic. The teaching scaffold is the instructional support that the teacher creates so that students may embark on these approaching tasks. The challenge in teaching is in providing a learning experience through tasks that are challenging for students, but also achievable.

Collaborative and creative work both challenges and consolidates student learning because the students in group work have to take mutual responsibility for their learning. Teachers in a collaborative learning environment must take mutual responsibility for student learning as well. Collaboration in itself is a process that teachers actively have to get students to learn.

Learning to collaborate

The aim of the Shostakovich Film Project was to include and challenge students in as many aspects of the filmmaking process as possible. In this large group project, students had to be focused on specific roles in the making process; for example, acting or cinematography. However, in the workshops before the shooting, the students quickly determined that the roles were inextricably linked. They realised they had to work together collaboratively to achieve their shared artistic vision for the film. On the shoot, the students voluntarily supported each other in their various responsibilities—for example, an actor when he was not needed would jump at the opportunity to hold a reflector board, or do the clapperboard, or work the sound boom. The students quickly recognised the benefits of teamwork inherent in successful filmmaking, especially when shooting under pressure. The student Ben realised the benefits of collaboration when he said he 'learnt how working effectively in a team utilised everyone's specific talents and produced a brilliant result'.

Filmmaking by the student group needs to be a valued enterprise for all the participants. Filmmaking means students must actively engage with each other for creation to work, and when it does it is part of the transcendental experience that Eisner (2002) describes as inherent not only in the product of the art's aesthetic but also in its process. Many of the students involved in the Shostakovich Project were effusive about how the bonds between everyone in the project led to a feeling of achievement. Ben commented:

> Everyone rejoiced in each other's success because it was a success for the whole team. It was an incredible atmosphere, difficult to describe. It's a special bond that builds between people of like mind all working together towards a high-quality result.

Although collaboration is inherent in filmmaking, working together successfully is something that has to be understood and learnt; successful and rewarding collaboration does not happen by accident or good fortune.

A teacher managing student group filmmaking work requires the same skills, as students need to collaborate effectively in a group. Both teachers and students have to listen, communicate, share, negotiate, encourage, organise and have mutual responsibility to achieve a common goal in learning. This is not easy to achieve if students haven't developed these skills. The only way the students will collaborate well is if collaborating is actively taught as part of their learning. Trust, listening and the ability to take risks are integral to the success of collaboration and creativity. Drama teachers actively develop this social culture of working through their experiential and creative activities and tasks in the classroom. Helen Nicholson (2002) argues that scaffolded drama learning helps students to 'recognise the implications of the task and, crucially for the establishment of trust, why they have been asked to work in these ways' (2002, p. 85). Students have to understand and learn the benefits of collaborating in the context of their learning.

When students recognise the value of collaborating in their shared enterprise or task, they develop a culture of mutual trust. Ben described the trust in the relationships developed during the Shostakovich Film Project:

The relationship changed from student and teacher to that of colleagues and equals trusting each other fully. This trust was reflected in the way that all of the students were willing to help in whatever way they could, and in the way they valued the opinions of everyone.

The paradigm of trust in the collaborative learning environment of drama education is relevant to film education, as is the concept of risk-taking and creative experimentation. They are the seeds for discovery learning (Bruner) and meeting the challenges of the zone of proximal development (Vygotsky). Nicholson (2002) explains how trust, debate and experimentation need to be inculcated in the drama classroom and this bears strong relevance to film collaborative learning:

> ... a productive and creative environment built on an ethic of care does not mean that there will be agreement between participants; on the contrary, a political theory of trust acknowledges that a caring environment may create a robust environment in which debate, dissent, generosity and artistic experimentation might be encouraged and valued (2002, p. 90).

Filmmaking: A community of practice in authentic learning

The richness of collaborative learning is a rationale for collective filmmaking as a process. Inherent in the filmmaking process is the collaboration of active social participation and social theories of learning. Wenger (1999) argues the necessity of 'social participation as a process of learning and of knowing' (1999, pp. 4–5) through active engagement with the world. These ideas of a community of practice were evident in the Shostakovich Film Project. For instance, Annabel said she learnt through the Project how 'important it was to be a participator as opposed to an observer in order to learn but also to grow as a person and develop lifelong skills'.

Authentic learning theory positions itself from the paradigm that learning is the way we relate what we learn to the real world (Brown, Collins and Duguid, 1989; Lave and Wenger, 1991). Authentic situations and activities are not just *useful* to learning, they are *essential* to learning. Students are not passive recipients of knowledge but actively engaged with experiences relevant to real life (Donovan, Bransford and Pellegrino, 1999). For example, film's capacity to be naturalistic and filmed on location takes students out of the classroom into the real world. Following are authentic experiences in student school filmmaking and the lifelike or real-world problems they may encounter to situate their learning.

Students may have to:

- film outside the classroom in the corridor of another school building, ask permission from teachers to do so, and politely ask others walking by to wait until they have finished their shot
- ask permission to film in a video store or the front of a court house and observe complex protocols relating to permission, courtesy and diplomacy when directing adults in their scenes
- get up at 4.00 a.m. to film a misty morning
- ask parents' permission to use the house as a set
- organise a shoot involving a number of people all coming together at the same time
- obtain permission to use a school out-of-bounds area
- organise a screening of their film for an audience.

In filmmaking, students often engage with real-world or lifelike situations beyond the culture of the classroom and the school. They are activities that have the potential to engage students with real-world concerns and authentic learning experiences.

Resource management and responsibility

Collaborative learning tasks require that students trust each other in order to take responsibility for the mutual undertaking of their task. In filmmaking, they also have responsibility for taking care of technical equipment such as cameras, tripods and sound equipment, and working outside the classroom in a location. Responsibilities for project resources must be integrated as an essential key learning area for students in film learning. Learning has to be explicit about the care of students, and the use and maintenance of equipment and computers. The students must be taught how to use the equipment safely, correctly and responsibly. This learning should be viewed as a responsibility and challenge for the students. Clear instructions on working with technical gear and clear consequences for the misuse of equipment are integral to the students' continued use of the technical resources and their success in using them.

Students need to understand the positive consequences and rewards of taking responsibility and being trusted. In the classroom, responsibility, trust and consequences can be supported by class rituals such as:

- groups signing equipment in and out, including the use of computers for editing
- filling in a time and location schedule each time they leave the classroom to film
- always charging batteries after any shooting
- maintaining a fixed class set of mounts and leads
- returning equipment to its storage areas before the bell.

Maintaining equipment and technology in teaching film demonstrates the necessity for energy and time to be spent scaffolding responsibility into film learning, just as trust is built in drama education. Learning to be responsible should be part of a student's cognitive development and it is the teacher's responsibility to facilitate that learning.

In a curriculum teaching situation, each small group in a film class will have specific filming requirements such as locations, and inevitably each group will be at slightly different stages in the filmmaking process. Some may still be in pre-production while some have begun filming, or others have begun editing while others are still filming. These issues are best addressed by imposing time constraints for each part of the making process, but some groups will have their own particular difficulties to address. This is the nature of creative, problem-solving tasks, but time constraints and pressure do focus the problem-solving, as they do in the professional world of filmmaking, and will help students to manage their time.

Self-directed collaborative learning

Like trust, responsibility is learnt through focusing on what has to be achieved through the learning task. Adolescents characteristically yearn for their own liberty, but have to learn that it comes with responsibility. Filmmaking involves using equipment and working in locations outside the classroom without constant teacher supervision. In this way, filmmaking provides an opportunity for students to be autonomous learners. Self-directed learning 'is a basic human competence—the ability to learn on one's own' (Knowles, 1975, p. 17), but it is usually associated with independent adult learners. Brockett and Heimstra (1991) argue that accepting personal responsibility for learning should be promoted and fostered in schooling so that students develop the skills to be lifelong learners. The idea is that education should encourage each student to be 'a continuing, "inner-directed" self-operating learner' (Kidd, 1973, p. 47).

A model of self-directed learning by Garrison (1997) is useful in understanding how motivation, responsibility and self-monitoring are vital for achieving task outcomes and learning:

> ... self-directed learning must go beyond task control and include the process of accepting responsibility to construct meaning and cognitively monitor the learning process itself (i.e. metacognition awareness). Furthermore, motivational states should be included, given their mediating effect on both task management and cognitive monitoring (1997, p. 21).

To achieve this, teachers have to provide students with support, direction and expectations for the achievement of educational outcomes indicated by clear criteria. Students' responsibility for their own learning means a greater construction of the meaning of the learning. Critical reflection and feedback from the teacher about the process and product of the filmmaking task will focus students on self-monitoring, which is fundamental to self-directed learning. Responsibility and ownership of the learning are also inextricably linked to motivation. On the Shostakovich Project, Jessica at first found the challenges and responsibility overwhelming, but it also became a motivating force:

> At the beginning of the project I did not feel like I would enjoy being a part of it—although it was this that made me want to step up and try to get the most out of it. I was attracted to the fact it was out of my comfort zone.

For some students the concept of responsibility is, as Annabel described on the Shostakovich Project, 'basic commonsense and compassion'. But Annabel did feel that the experience of making a film in such a cooperative way taught her that she, and all the students, had the potential to be more responsible. Jessica felt she 'matured more because of these responsibilities and seeing them through'. For many of the students on the project, responsibility was a large part of the challenge of the film production. Success at assuming responsibility and achieving trust contributed to the reward of their learning achievements. Harriet realised this when reflecting on the film project. She said: 'I learnt so much about cooperation, patience and people. It was not only a learning experience with filmmaking but about myself and what I can achieve.'

Collaborative filmmaking provides an active, authentic and self-directed community of practice model where students can explore 'who they are, who they are not, who they could be' (Wenger, 1998, p. 272). This can be achieved through a collaborative learning process and the opportunity for students to share multiple roles in the process.

Shared learning roles

The roles played by drama students when they create drama help to illustrate how film students can take on multiple and shared roles in their group work in the classroom situation. Seminal to the underlying theory of drama in education are Dorothy Heathcote's ideas from the 1970s and 1980s. The Brechtian[1] notions that theatrical processes can be an ensemble construction by the participants creating the drama influenced Heathcote. Rather than viewing the practice of theatre in a hierarchical structure with the director or writer at the top having the most power, the ensemble process of theatre acknowledges that making theatre is fundamentally a collaborative and interactive act between the actors, designers, writers, directors, crew and audience.

In film, a director like Oliver Stone (2002) (*Platoon*, 1986; *JFK*, 1991; *Natural Born Killers*, 1994) says making a movie is a collective effort but that 'you have to have a person in charge, a person whose vision makes it all coherent. Otherwise, the collective won't add up' (2002, p. 137). The same can be said of the director in the theatre, but in an educational context the inherently collaborative nature of theatre making and filmmaking is conducive to collaborative learning practices and the negotiation and creation of a group vision.

Drama educator John O'Toole (1992) explains how the functions of playwright, performer, audience and director in Western theatre are performed by separate people with discrete tasks and responsibilities, but says that in drama education these 'functions are subsumed in other functions and roles and another network of relationships—the real roles and purposes of people in school' (1992, p. 4). In the drama classroom, for example, students creating drama through improvisation together are all performers, playwrights, directors and audience at the same time. In the film classroom, students can be writers, directors, cinematographers, editors and audience at the same time.

The capacity for and recognition of theatre as a collaborative art form inform drama pedagogical practices and concepts of shared roles in the creation of the live dramatic form. At the forefront of drama learning processes is experiential 'doing' or 'making' learning, where ideas and skills are explored through communication, negotiation and collaboration between students in small groups or whole-class groups. The process of communal collaboration in drama education is learning that is valued in itself as well as being a conduit for other learning in drama. Drama in education does not dismiss the creative force of the director in theatre practice, but pedagogically in the classroom, drama learning involves students in group collaborative learning, coming together as shared participant creators of the drama. They do this by negotiating and exchanging ideas and roles in order to create, explore, challenge and solve. The potential of the ensemble and the communal of theatre theory and practice underpin the social interaction and students' roles in drama pedagogy. So too can the collaborative and communal nature of filmmaking inform a collaborative pedagogy for the film classroom with multiple, shared roles and responsibilities throughout the stages of a film creation.

The stages of the filmmaking process

The process of making films is colourfully described by French director Robert Bresson (1977) (*The Man Escaped*, 1956; *Pickpocket*, 1959; *Lancelot of the Lake*, 1974) in the following way: 'My movie is born first in my head, dies on paper; is resuscitated by the living persons and real objects I use, which are killed on film but, placed in a certain order and projected onto a screen, come to life again like flowers in water' (1977, p. 7). Bresson's creative journey from the seed of an idea to the flowering of the screened film is a path that provides sequential stages and challenges for students in their filmmaking and their learning. The filmmaking process can be used to underpin a pedagogy, just as improvisation or rehearsal or role-playing does in the drama classroom. The filmmaking process is a creative metamorphosis. It begins with conceptualising and visualising ideas. The ideas are developed and organised by describing them in words and images. The ideas continue to develop when they are filmed, edited and screened.

Filming as an art form has a sequential structure to its aesthetic creation, no matter how small the film. It requires the following three stages:

- *pre-production*: the preparation before filming
- *production*: filming, recording images and sound
- *post-production*: editing, graphics, music, sound, effects.

Success in one phase is an index to the success of the following phases, and each stage provides different skills in developing and controlling the film aesthetic. The sequential stages involve components of the film aesthetic that develop and contribute to the whole creative result.

Controlling the aesthetic is primarily concerned with decisions involving:

- what to shoot
- how to shoot it, and
- how to present it.

However, these three aspects of controlling the film aesthetic do not neatly align themselves with the three stages of the making process. These three aspects of film's semiotics have to be developed in theory to some degree in the pre-production stage, and then they are further developed as they undergo the practice and circumstances of the production and post-production processes. Learning how to control the aesthetic throughout the pre-production, production and post-production processes creates a film as an artistic product, but there is equal value in educational outcomes in the working processes themselves. In the making process, there is the capacity for students to develop their learning to imagine, communicate, negotiate, solve, organise and collaborate.

The pre-production process

The making film task for the first module on film language presented in Chapter 5, for example, requires students to collaborate in small groups of around four members and create a 30-second to 45-second scene without dialogue, sound and music. The scene has to focus on and explore how the visual language of framing, composition and montage serves to communicate one character's dramatic action and engage an audience with tension and identification. The dramatic action can simply be a character being chased (like Roger Thornhill in Hitchcock's *North by Northwest*, 1959) or a character seeking solitude (like Ada in Jane Campion's *The Piano*, 1993) or a character needing assistance (like Manuela in Almodovar's *All About My Mother*, 1999). No other aspects of story are to be explored—just one character and one dramatic action. A digital camera and tripod are all that are used for filming, and computer software for editing.

In the making task, students problem-solve how a dramatic action can be expressed through the visual aesthetic of film language. Prior learning for the task constitutes the scaffolded exercises and activities described in Chapter 5, and students then embark on this creative task. In the pre-production stage of this filmmaking exercise, students have to conceptualise an idea that will meet the criteria of the task. The idea, as with all aspects of the exercise, has to be negotiated and agreed upon by all the group members. A dramatic action needs to be chosen, the character's intent and actions decided, and the appropriate location for the scene chosen. Students need to reconnoitre the location and develop their ideas by using the camera and practising shots. The idea can be workshopped through kinaesthetic storyboarding, where students explore their scene and shots by acting it; they then can develop and consolidate the ideas further through the creation of a visual storyboard.

Figure 6.1 An example of a visual storyboard created after choosing a location and kinaesthetically workshopping a scene with students involved in the Shostakovich Film Project (2006).

The kinaesthetic storyboard is a moving and embodied storyboard that explains the shots and what is happening in them, and the visual storyboard is a sequence of comic-strip-like representations of the edited shots in a scene. The shot choices and their order in the scene reveal the dramatic intent of the action and its effect on the audience. The visual storyboard can be sketches or photos of the students' ideas for the scene. The storyboard is a draft of what they have to capture during the camera shoot. Storyboards in the film industry are not a pre-production requisite. Some directors only storyboard scenes with action or complicated camera work. However, for educational purposes the kinaesthetic and visual storyboard represents a way for students to develop, discuss, communicate and draft their ideas conceptually, kinaesthetically and visually. The storyboard is also a representation of the students' pre-production process that can be communicated and discussed with the teacher for feedback and assessment before commencing the second production stage.

In the pre-production phase, students have to organise their shoot. This entails deciding what roles the students will take during the shooting. All the members of the group are equally responsible as the conceivers, directors and cinematographers of the film exercise, but someone has to be the actor, and the others have to direct the actor, and direct and operate the camera. Pre-production is a time for the group to workshop the acting for the dramatic action. The organisation of the group for the date and time of the shoot, even in lesson time, must be thoroughly prepared for. Anything that may impact on the shoot must be considered, particularly continuity issues. Continuity is the consistency of the look from shot to shot, such as the appearance of the actor, the lighting and the weather. If this changes in the scene, a lack of visual continuity disrupts the viewer's belief or engagement with what is going on in the film. This can happen, for example, when in the same scene a bright, sunny day inexplicably becomes flat and overcast.

The negotiation, conceptualisation, visualisation and organisation in the pre-production stage lead to a greater likelihood of success in the production and post-production stages. On the Shostakovich Film Project, Victoria recognised the necessity for pre-production preparation before undertaking the pressured intensity of the shooting process:

> I realised more than ever over the filming period how important preparation is. Each day filming we knew what we wanted and how it was going to be achieved. Details such as camera position and shots were refined during the shoot but the storyboard acted as a great guideline.

However, what does Victoria mean when she said the camera position and shots were 'refined' during the shoot? The next step in film is another creative and problem-solving situation because, in the reality of shooting, ideas may be developed, refined and even change.

The production shooting process

Film director Martin Scorsese (2002) feels he must be thoroughly prepared before a shoot, but recognises the tension between the preparation and the actuality of the location shooting:

> I need to have my shots decided in advance, even if it's theoretical … You need to know where you're going, and you need to have it on paper … it's a tension between knowing exactly what you want and being able to change it according to circumstances, or taking advantage of something more interesting (2002, pp. 61–2).

The something more interesting may be that the location is different to the way you imagined it would be. Scorsese asks: 'Do you try to get a new location, or do you change your shots?' Director Tim Burton (2002) (*Edward Scissorhands*, 1990; *Sleepy Hollow*, 1999; *Sweeney Todd*, 2007) describes the shooting process as an 'experiment' and, although his approach is intuitive, he says: 'You can improvise only if you have decided on a very strict set of parameters beforehand. Otherwise you end up with chaos' (2002, pp. 96–7). Spanish director Pedro Almodovar (2002) (*Women on the Verge of a Nervous Breakdown*, 1988; *All About My Mother*, 1999; *Volver*, 2006) finds shooting on set and location 'the most concrete and the most unstable part of making a film' because there is always the possibility for intuitive, improvised and accidental decisions that can create something 'magical' (2002, pp. 86–7). Jean-Pierre Jeunet (2002) (*Delicatessen*, 1991; *Amelie*, 2001; *A Very Long Engagement*, 2004) does detailed storyboards because his films are very visual, but he recognises that 'a storyboard isn't made to be respected but to be transcended' (2002, p. 116).

The tension between the decisions made in the first stage of pre-production and the second stage of production is remarkable in an educational sense. Filming in stage two requires putting the theory of the students' imagined ideas into the practice of a real-world setting. The transition from theory to practice generates constraints, variables and possibilities that impact on and further the creative process and creation of the art form. Scorsese (2002) describes this process in shooting: 'the whole problem is being able to know what is essential, what you absolutely cannot change, mustn't change, and what you can be more flexible on … Sometimes an accident or a last-minute change can create something unexpected and magical' (2002, pp. 62–3).

Victoria also discovered on the Shostakovich Project that she needed to 'expect the unexpected—sometimes the greatest moments can come from this'.

The pre-production process does not make the shooting process a mere technicality. It is a process for further creative problem-solving and improvised spontaneity to be negotiated by the group in a time-pressured environment. There are a number of variables that can affect filming, such as the availability of the group members, availability and accessibility of locations, the state of the weather and the time of day. The teacher making a deadline is also a time pressure to achieve a task, and heightens the necessity of a group working efficiently and effectively, but also creatively. The amount of recorded film needs to be essential, not excessive or extraneous. Preparation before filming dictates how much has to be filmed. There are also practical consequences and constraints on the amount of recording done in terms of the amount of time available to edit and the amount of memory available on computers in the school situation.

Once the camera is recording and 'Action!' is called, the commitment, focus and energy of the directors, actors and camera operators must come together instantly as one for the scene to work. This is integral to the success of the collaborative, creative process of filmmaking. A student, Jessica, noticed that filming involved a focus and energy that she had never experienced before, and she described every shot as 'a performance not only for the actors but also for the crew, who all had to be 150 per cent aware of their intentions and actions'.

The post-production process

Editing, like all the roles in the previous stages of making, should be a shared responsibility between all the members of the group. It is a negotiated group process like every aspect of the filmmaking exercise. Taking it in turn, students control the computer editing software while the others in the group sit with them making decisions and trying to solve the problems of montage. Editing is the stage when all the previous decisions are seen to have consequences. Everyone in the group sees the results of the pre-production and production processes and has to determine what will work in the edited form. Editing involves more skills to be learnt in the semiotics of the film aesthetic. It is an inextricable part of a film's form that is linked fundamentally to the function of the scene. This was suggested by the student Simon's response to editing the film *The Boy Who Loved Shostakovich*:

Editing seems like constructing a tower and the way in which you assemble each piece affects the way people can and will enter the building. The editing must flow with the drama of the scene and capture the scene's essence and purpose.

Editing is not just a simple process of putting together the shots; it has a myriad of aesthetic elements of its own that need to be scaffolded into the theory and practice of the film learning. By focusing on small exercises and the building blocks of film language, students become aware of the difficulties, complexities and rewards of controlling all aspects of the film aesthetic.

Screening

Joel and Ethan Coen (2002) (*Raising Arizona*, 1987; *O Brother, Where Art Thou?*, 2000; *No Country for Old Men*, 2007) explain how, when making their films, they imagine an abstract, generic audience: 'When we're on set making decisions, we're always wondering whether a scene works or not, whether it's going to play or not, and really, we're wondering that in regard to the audience, not for us specifically. But it has to work for us too' (2002, p. 159). Lars von Trier (2002), Danish director and creator of the Dogme 95 film charter,[2] feels 'that you must have some desire to communicate to others', but that your motivation to make a film is for yourself (2002, p. 187). Even in a collaborative approach, making a film is a form of self-expression for students, and this is explored in the next chapter. The role of the audience in the educational setting is a valuable evaluative and reflective tool for learning. All the film exercises should be screened for a class viewing. It is an opportunity for students to learn how to evaluate each group's work. How each film meets the objectives and criteria of the exercise should be the discussion focus of peer and teacher feedback and assessment. In the filmmaking exercise for Module 1 on film language, the focal questions would be concerned with the group's success capturing a dramatic intent through their chosen actions, shots and montage and how well they engage the audience with tension and identification. Other learning such as an individual student's collaborative skills in responsibility, motivation and contribution can be assessed as process. Assessment for film learning is discussed in Chapter 9.

The making process of film learning in the three stages of pre-production, production and post-production, and then the appreciation process of screening, provides a challenging creative journey for students to communicate their ideas by controlling the film aesthetic. It is a process that offers a rich experience in collaborative and authentic learning. When Bernardo Bertolucci (2002) (*The Conformist*, 1971; *1900*, 1977; *The Last Emperor*, 1987) speaks of what filmmaking means to him, we gain an insight into the creative and explorative process that students can experience when making their own films:

> Seemingly a film is the setting of an idea to images. But, more secretly for me, it has always been a way of exploring something more personal and more abstract. My films are always very different in the end from what I actually imagined. Therefore it's a progressive process. I often compare a film to a pirate ship. It's impossible to know where it will land when you leave it free to follow the winds of creativity (2002, p. 54).

The next chapter discusses how students can explore the 'personal and the abstract' through the imagining and creating of dramatic action and storytelling in filmmaking.

7
Learning from imagining and being in film stories

> There are two main reasons why I make movies. First, because I always had trouble communicating with people, so films are a way to create a bridge between myself and the rest of the world. And second, because I like to explore, to discover things about people and myself.
>
> —John Woo

This chapter examines why filmmakers tell stories and why students in schools need to tell stories. John Woo (*A Better Tomorrow*, 1986; *Face/Off*, 1997; *Mission Impossible II*, 2000) is one of the great action film directors of all time, yet filmmaking for him is about discovering and exploring something very personal. Woo's attraction to filmmaking highlights the potential of the film learning process for students in education as a way to communicate with others and a means to explore themselves and others. Films, although made for an abstract audience, are also an intimate exploration of self. This exploration of self is achieved not only through the collaborative process of working with others in a filmmaking endeavour, but also takes place in the way film stories are conceived and created.

In film learning, students not only have to learn how to create film stories, they have to embody the story by acting it out. This is the same process of imaginary role or character playing as in drama education, but in film learning the performing role can be defined more broadly to include camera, sound operators and editors as 'technical actors'. The film learning in this book uses narrative creation to explore an intimacy and perception of self with a connectedness to others. To do this, students must learn how to imagine, construct and communicate film stories.

Why do filmmakers tell stories?

Personal expression and commercial imperatives are often at loggerheads in the film industry; however despite this tug of war, Hollywood director Martin Scorsese (1997) still views film as a means of self-expression. Scorsese (2002) argues that the main imperative to be a filmmaker is to have something to say. For John Woo (2002), a film begins from the heart and must be your truth. Takeshi Kitano (2002) (*Fireworks*, 1997; *Zatoichi*, 2003; *Takeshis*, 2005) says he makes a film first and foremost for himself and that a film is like 'a wonderful toy box that I play with' (2002, p. 169). There are two reasons for making a film, says Wim Wenders (2002), and he is torn between the two. One is to express a clear idea and the other is to make the film to discover what you are attempting to say. The personal journeys of discovery these directors have in the professional world of filmmaking are explorations that are profoundly applicable to young people and their film learning. To make a film is an expression of a personal vision, but it is also a means to explore and refine a personal understanding of the world.

For students, the creation of film stories is not just a tool to learn about film and the pervasively visual world surrounding them; it is a way for students to learn about themselves and others by telling stories. The film story created for the Shostakovich Project, for example, was the students' imagined story of their real-life story. The film was about how the arts in their lives enriched them, opened up possibilities and challenged orthodoxies. In the fiction of

Figure 7.1 The students' personal concerns with apathy, bullying and the role of the arts were realised in their imaginative film story in *The Boy Who Loved Shostakovich* (2006).

the film story, it was the music of Dimitri Shostakovich and films of Sergei Eisenstein that fired the characters' imaginations to stage a revolution against prevailing attitudes of teenage apathy and bullying. In the world of the film, the apathetic teenagers became zombies and the bullies were Soviet agents. The magical realism of the film story was based on a truth in the students' own lives. They had transformed and explored their reality through an imagined fiction. Film stories give students the capacity to understand, explain and further their experience, providing what Wim Wenders (1988) calls a route on the map of life:

> When I look at a map, it turns into an allegory for the whole of life. The only thing that makes it bearable is to try to mark out a route, and follow it through the city or country. Stories do just that: they become your roads in a strange land, where but for them, you might go to thousands of places without arriving anywhere (1988, p. 54).

The creation of film stories as a process is a way for students to navigate understandings of their lives and those of others. As well, the collaborative creation and screening of film stories are ways to publicly test and communicate those personal understandings.

Personal and public expression

In class, students' exercises in film learning must ultimately be screened to an audience of others in the class. As an exercise, screening is a vital aspect of film learning because the medium of film is about personal expression becoming public. The narrative aesthetic endeavours to dramatically engage an audience. Chapter 6 discusses how screening is a valuable tool for reflection and evaluation of the learning that has already been undertaken. However, in film learning—like drama education learning—students are involved in the communal act of creating an art form together. In group filmmaking, they are exploring and refining ideas and feelings as a shared experience. This social interaction of collaboration in a creative process is also an interface between the private self and a public voice. Drama education has expressed these ideas in the practice of creating and improvising as a group dramatic activity. Bolton (1984) explains that: 'Because it is a group enterprise, there is a natural striving towards "finding a public voice", towards having one's feelings and thoughts publicly tested, towards collaborative meaning' (1984, p. 163).

The dynamic of self-expression and the negotiation of that expression within the group in a collaborative, creative task is a rich environment for students to discover ideas, to challenge those ideas or to be challenged by them. Students' self-expression is facilitated and consolidated by the social, 'public' process of the collaborative enterprise of making. In educational terms, testing personal ideas in the social sphere is probably more intense in the group process of making than in the public act of screening the film. Therefore, the conceptualisation, shooting and editing of film stories during the stages of pre-production, production and post-production are spaces and processes where personal visions and their public expression interact and shape each other. But why do students need to test and explore their personal ideas through the collaborative creation and public expression of telling stories? And why is narrative so valuable and intrinsic to education?

Why is there a need to tell stories?

The presumption is that stories are everywhere: we tell them, we are in them, we live them and they will always be there. Following on from Roland Barthes' famous assertion that narrative is 'simply there, like life itself' (1977, p. 79), literary theorists, Bennett and Royle (2004) discuss narrative in the following terms:

1. Stories are everywhere.
2. Not only do we tell stories, but stories tell us: if stories are everywhere, we are also in stories.
3. The telling of a story is always bound up with power, property and domination.
4. Stories are multiple: there is always more than one story.
5. Stories always have something to tell us about stories themselves: they always involve self-reflexive and metafictional dimensions (2004, p. 41).

Stories surround us and define us, they are a tool and they are ideological, political and complex. Arguably, for these reasons, students must understand how stories are made, and make their own stories. Stories define who we are for 'as long as human beings retain an idea of time which presupposes a past, present and future there will always be stories because stories report the past in terms of the present for a future audience' (McQuillan, 2000, p. 3).

Bruner (1986) argues that narrative is a way of thinking, a way of organising experience and constructing a reality. Imagining a narrative, he says, leads to 'good stories, gripping drama, believable (though not necessarily "true") historical accounts. It deals in human and human-like intention and action and the vicissitudes and consequences that mark their course' (1986, p. 13). We engage fundamentally with stories because they deal with the changing fortunes of human intentions. Bruner links narrative construction to an understanding of our perceptual experience of self and others:

> Insofar as we account for our own actions and for the human events that occur around us principally in terms of narrative, story, drama, it is conceivable that our sensitivity to narrative provides the major link between our own self and our sense of others in the social world around us. The common coin may be provided by the forms of narrative that the culture offers us (1986, p. 69).

Bruner's (1987) view is that our telling of our own life as a narrative is shaped by culturally shaped cognitive and linguistic processes. In other words, our ability or means to tell stories shapes the stories we tell of ourselves to construct our identity. The stories we receive, and the way in which we receive stories, shapes both our understanding of them and the way we perceive ourselves. The film director Kitano's image of filmmaking as a toy box with which to play is a model for how students can construct and deconstruct narratives that are defining their perception of themselves and the world around them. What is particular to filmmaking and drama-making is how students experience storytelling through a sense of kinaesthetic, imaginary 'play'.

Students 'playing' their stories

Playing in an imaginary world is normally associated with small children and pleasure, and is viewed as crucial to the child's development. Erik Erikson (1976) went further, arguing that child play is 'an infinite resource of what is potential in man' (1976, p. 689) to 'settle the past and anticipate the future' (1976, p. 702). According to Vygotsky (1976), play does not die away at school age but permeates our attitude towards reality. The essence of play, he argues, defines the relationship between 'the semantic and visible fields—that is, between situations in thought and real situations' (1976, p. 544). The imagined world of film stories is a 'play-space' or make-believe world where students can explore ideas, thoughts and feelings, testing what Erikson calls the potential of 'reality' beyond 'actuality'. According to Eisner (2002), all manifestations of the arts 'are close in attitude to play' and allow us to pursue 'qualitative experience in the constructive exploration of what the imaginative process may engender' (2002, p. 4). To play is to imagine possibilities and potential.

Many areas of arts curriculum learning encourage students to learn through the imagination. But students doing filmmaking, like students doing drama-making, experience story by creating and being in the imagined drama as a performative, physical act. Gavin Bolton (1984) argues that drama education 'articulates inventing, anticipating, recollecting, hypothesising, creating, musing and day-dreaming or any other mode of imagining through the medium of concrete action' (1984, p. 142). The concrete action involves the actor or participant playing a role and imagining they are someone else. The audience watching the actor or participant playing a role imagines that person to be someone else. At the same time, actor and audience know the imagined world is not real. In drama education, the 'metaxis'[1] of holding two worlds in mind as an interplay and tension between the real and the fictitious is a potent form of consciousness for learning (Bolton, 1984; O'Toole, 1992):

> This dual consciousness invites in the role player both submission and detachment. He is able to see his experiencing as an object to be reflected upon. Further than that, like all imaginative states, it can free the individual from his habits of perception and conception. For this reason, I have argued, enactment of any kind, whether functionally or aesthetically attended to, is a powerfully effective tool for the teacher. For education is about change in conception and perception (Bolton, 1984, pp. 147–8).

Bolton's 'epistemological purpose' for drama in education (1984, p. 148) is relevant to film in education. When students act out their stories for film, they inhabit a dual consciousness of being themselves and being a character in a story that can change how they conceive and perceive the world. It is not only in creating a story in film that students have to interpret the world, but it is also explored through the kinaesthetic embodiment of acting a role. To act for film is a form of 'play' and concrete action. It is an experience of Stanislavsky's[2] 'magic if' at a 'felt' level of consciousness.

Acting and the 'magic if'

Stanislavsky's 'magic if' is like a child's capacity to believe in a make-believe world where their actions, reactions and interactions are 'as if' the imagined world is real and 'as if' the role or character they are imagining they are is real. To act in a film story requires total belief and commitment in the 'magic if' of the make-believe world being created. Acting or playing a role is a process that allows students to slip the bonds of their identities and participate in other forms of existence (O'Neill, 1995, p. 151). Although acting requires complicit and complete belief in the fictional world, there is always awareness of the 'real context', so that students move between the parallel worlds of the imagination and the actuality of their surroundings. Inhabiting the 'magic if' of a make-believe world is a vital part of the narrative film aesthetic. To act or play a role is to control and refine how thoughts, emotions, dialogue and actions are communicated with belief and dramatic intent through the lens of a camera to an audience.

The 'technical actor'

Too easily, film learning can be characterised as technical knowledge and technical skill. Learning how to use technology is required knowledge in the expression of the art form, but it is not at the heart of the aesthetic or the learning. We have already discussed in Chapter 3 how film aesthetic choices made with the camera, sound, music and editing are all related to the dramatic purpose of the scene being communicated. Connecting with the drama of the story is vital for all the creative choices made with the film aesthetic. Emir Kusturica (2002) (*When Father Was Away on Business*, 1985; *Time of the Gypsies*, 1989; *Underground*, 1995) says the worst mistake young filmmakers can make is to believe that film is an objective art. He believes expression in the art form must be personal at every level. Bertolucci (2002) talks about how the camera for him 'enters and leaves the scene like an invisible character in the story' (2002, p. 52). It is this connection with the drama of the characters in the story that determines how the camera is used, where the sound microphone is placed, how the lighting is designed, what location is chosen and where the action is placed. In this sense, students who are collaboratively directors, designers, operators and actors in a group learning film task are 'performing' or 'acting' the scene through the directing, the camera, the microphone and the lighting when a scene is being captured by the technology.

Every element of the shooting of a scene must come together at the one moment when 'Action!' is called. During the debriefing of the Shostakovich Film Project, Jessica noticed that the connection between the actors and the crew was different from what she had experienced when performing for the stage. During technical rehearsals in the theatre, Jessica said she knew the theatre technical crew was making dramatic choices for the lighting and the sound. However, she said she never felt a connection with the crew in the theatre when she performed but she did when acting a scene for film. Students operating the cameras, holding the sound boom and even holding the lighting reflector boards felt a similar connection with the actors in the scene. One student remarked, 'behind the camera I discovered how we are just as much of the scene as the actors we are shooting, the same intentions are felt'. All the students acknowledged that their focus during filming was 'intense' and that this contributed to the heightening of their dramatic involvement with the scene.

For an actor in a scene, their perception of 'performance' in front of the camera when shooting can be a revelation:

> I anticipated being slightly thrown by the presence of a crew crowded behind the camera; however, the crew seemed invisible as if they served as a camouflaged audience for the world of the film. They almost felt like an additional actor in the scene (Simon).

If the camera and sound operators, and other crew, are viewed as additional actors who we call 'technical actors' and directors of the drama, then editing must be considered in the same way. Editing is not a technical eventuality of the production process, but another stage in the creativity of the film process. When a group of students sits together editing their film, the choices made are once again derived from the dramatic purpose of the scene, and how the plot (the syuzhet)[3] of the story (the fabula)[4] is manipulated in its telling for the audience (see Chapter 4). When editing, students are creators and audience at the same time; they notice how the ordering and choice of their shots create and change the meaning of their film. Editing continues to control the dramatic elements of tension, time, space, pace, rhythm, mood and atmosphere in the scene. When putting the shots together, the students editing are still experiencing and controlling the drama. They decide what goes in and what goes out, and through their 'choice and arrangement of images and sounds, will create new, though not necessarily unforeseen, patterns, rhythms and emphases' (Perkins, 1972, p. 159). Editing has been described as 'directing the film for the second time. To gauge the psychological moment—to know exactly where to cut—requires the same intuitive skill as that needed by a director' (Brownlow, 1968, p. 280). It is this psychological connection with the drama to create the final 'performance' of the film through editing that enables the students as editors to be called technical performers as well.

Inhabiting, embodying and feeling the story and its drama are essential to understanding and making the film aesthetic. But without the form or structure of a narrative, there is no story to be felt. Students need the implements and materials to build their own stories. They must learn the fundamentals of narrative construction as they learn to control and understand the film aesthetic.

Learning how to construct film narratives

In previous chapters, we have explained how scaffolding the learning begins with finding the fundamentals in the learning area. This provides a base and direction for future learning. Finding fundamentals means distilling skills and knowledge to the 'essential oils' to explain how potentially sophisticated and complex ideas work. Stories, although always around us, are difficult, complex and unwieldy to create in their construction and their effectiveness to engage an audience. Narrative construction requires the learning and control of a complicated and challenging aesthetic structure. The reward in this learning is to be able to create and communicate stories more expressively. Being able to shape form to create expressive content is what causes us to be touched or moved by a work of art (Eisner, 2002, p. 81). Aiming for and achieving the moving qualities of an aesthetic is the payoff and delight for both the creator and spectator of the film story. To aim for and accomplish control of the film narrative aesthetic is to acquire and use the essentials of story construction and build from there.

The example of a first teaching module for a film program in Chapter 5 introduces the basic unit of film narrative as 'dramatic action'. Dramatic action is a base ingredient for film storytelling. Moments and scenes of a narrative cannot be told without dramatic action. Through dramatic action, all aspects of the story are revealed and the audience is engaged. For example, to show a person running is not necessarily dramatic action, but to see someone being chased is. The second scenario suggests a relation to other events that we expect will be revealed to us. The audience wants to know why the person is being chased. Who is chasing them? In the small narrative unit of dramatic action, an element of tension is being created to engage the audience to know more about the action or the event and connect it with an aspect of story. Going simply for a run to keep fit is not dramatic action unless it contributes to the telling of a story. Students must have this understanding of dramatic action at an entry level of working with film language. When students are being introduced to the fundamentals of film language, they can only control the aesthetic if they have a dramatic understanding of the effect of the shots and composition within the framing. Dramatic understanding lies in knowing how an action furthers the drama of the story's structure and knowing how to engage an audience with a specific dramatic purpose. Does the audience, for example, identify with the runner being chased (dramatic action) and experience an adrenaline rush of fear through the action and the filming (dramatic purpose)?

When students are introduced to the basics of film language, dramatic action and dramatic purpose, they are also learning about an initial building block in narrative construction. In a teaching program, an understanding and control of film narrative should be scaffolded into the development of film learning. For instance, the small narrative unit of dramatic action can be followed by the idea that film narrative is defined as a cause-and-effect chain of events occurring over time and space.

Cause and effect in narrative

To control film storytelling is to understand how there must be a cause and effect for the creation of dramatic action and ultimately a larger encompassing narrative. Introducing students to the concept of cause and effect provides them with another essential tool in film storytelling that they can explore in small, incrementally developing film exercises. Learning about the causality between a chain of events helps students to understand how a story is catapulted forward with its own momentum. A story is thrust forward because a cause has an effect and then the effect is a cause for another effect, and so on. Cause and effect do not have to be presented in a linear fashion, but through cause and effect the story is connected, makes sense and is gradually unveiled and revealed to the audience.

To understand narrative development, cause and effect can be placed under the microscope to examine further how stories can be controlled and manipulated. The way cause and effect are dealt with heightens the dramatic action, tension and engagement for an audience. For instance, if the needs and desires of a character's intent for a dramatic action are heightened, then the stakes are raised. The consequence is that the cause and effect in the narrative become greater and hold more tension for the viewer. In heightening the needs and raising the stakes, the universe of the story is less stable—or, in Todorov's[5] terms, there is less equilibrium and so the story must be told in the hope that equilibrium will be restored or resolved in some way. Quite simply, if our chased runner holds a secret and so has a dire need to get away, the stakes are raised. The effect of being chased is greater if the runner is either caught or gets away because of their need to keep a secret. Whoever is chasing the runner can have their needs heightened as well, by raising the stakes of causality. They need to know the secret because it will give them power. Obstacles in the dramatic action also increase the stakes and the need of the characters. If the chased runner has a wall in front of them, their hurdle to escape is even harder, their need to escape from the chase ever greater. If filmmaking students recognise, create and control the nature of dramatic action and the necessity of cause and effect, they have at a foundation level elemental tools in building a narrative.

The audience and narrative

Fundamental to story construction is to know why, how and what an audience expects and engages with. An audience expects narrative to have an established, perceptual, structural pattern of a beginning, middle and end. It is this audience consciousness of knowing what to expect of a story that begins their engagement. The audience anticipates that connected events will be revealed to them in a way that aims to develop their interest in the story, and transport them to the world of the film story:

> We assume that there will be characters and some action that will involve them with one another. We expect a series of incidents that will be connected in some way. We also probably expect that the problems or conflicts arising in the course of the action will achieve some final state ... As the viewer watches the film, she or he picks up cues, recalls information, anticipates what will follow, and generally participates in the film's form. The film shapes particular expectations by summoning up curiosity, suspense, and surprise (Bordwell and Thompson, 2004, pp. 68–9).

When watching movie stories, we as spectators learn a lot about narratives, particularly in terms of expectations and conventions, but the elements that construct the narratives are invisible inner workings. It is these invisible workings of which students have to be cognisant and aware to manipulate and control their stories effectively in film.

Filmmaking students have to identify and manage the audience's expectations of film stories. Filmmakers as storytellers invite, engage and frustrate the audience by delaying, gratifying or cheating their expectations, and in doing so create the audience's tension of engagement with the narrative. Understanding how a story (the fabula) is told in terms of plot (the syuzhet) is crucial to filmmaking students' ability to create a narrative that takes the audience on a particular journey with a specific dramatic purpose. For instance, should the spectator know why the runner is being chased before, during or after the chase? The choice is a plot (syuzhet) device. Although the story stays the same, the way in which the story is told affects the engagement or journey of the spectator with the story. Bordwell and Thompson (2004, p. 73) illustrate this with the following example of the detective film.

(a) Crime conceived.
(b) Crime planned.
(c) Crime committed.
(d) Crime discovered.
(e) Detective investigates.
(f) Detective reveals a, b, and c.

The story in reality happens (a) to (f), but the plot can begin at (d) when the crime is discovered. The way the story is revealed through plot changes audience expectations and the dynamic of their engagement with the story and the characters. The Agatha Christie murder mystery form of Robert Altman's *Gosford Park* (2001) unleashes a narrative from the discovery of a crime, and in solving the crime it also unearths and examines the complexity of relationships and the tensions of the British class system. If the plot begins with the conceiving of the crime, such as in Steven Soderbergh's remake of *Ocean's Eleven* (2001), it helps the audience to identify with the characters hatching the planned crime and their hopes in carrying out the elaborate heist despite the obstacles in their way.

The inner workings of story construction can be learnt by students in small tasks in a scaffolded, pedagogical approach to filmmaking with a narrative focus. Understanding narrative construction begins by understanding and controlling dramatic action and the need for cause and effect. Student filmmakers will then realise how a narrative's chain of events can be ordered to manipulate the audience's expectations and their reception of the story. Students learn there is a structure they have to build to tell their stories effectively. At the beginning of film narrative learning, students don't necessarily have the skills to build a whole narrative but they are introduced to the essential foundations to develop their capacity to tell complete and longer film stories later.

Where do students' stories come from?

As much as students need to understand how to control the aesthetic of the film art form, they have to be able to have 'an idea worth expressing and the imaginative ability to conceive of how' (Eisner, 2002, p. 81). To conceive dramatic stories in part or in full requires the ability to imagine. Learning in film has to encourage and develop a student's capacity to imagine and create something that is an expression of their own that they share, negotiate and shape in a collaborative filmmaking endeavour. Good teaching in all the arts, according to Eisner, has to foster diversity, originality, individuality and surprise in students' thinking (2002, p. 236). To do this, students must enter and explore an imaginative space that is their own so that creativity may be learnt and developed. These imaginative spaces need to be scaffolded into the exercises and activities in film learning, beginning simply and building with greater complexity. The boundaries of these imaginative spaces are defined by the creative learning tasks provided by the teacher.

A filmmaking task, for instance, may be defined by the boundaries of exploring the dramatic intent of a person hiding from someone else in a 30-second film. Although the task has a given dramatic intent, the imaginative space for students is to create the scenario or given circumstances for who the person may be and why that person needs to hide. Another more complex task may explore the dramatic purpose of an interaction involving a threat between two people. In less than a minute, students need to create a cause and effect relationship and raise the stakes of the interaction in order to create tension and a sense of continuous story. The task is prescriptive, limited and clear in one way, but open to the development of the imagination in another. The interaction of a threat leads students to imagine: Why is there a threat and where does the threat lead? Does the threat involve a stalker? Does it involve a breach of trust? Who does the audience identity with? Why is there danger? These decisions are in the realm of the imagination, and students in a collaborative endeavour are able to test their imaginative ideas with each other in the creating process. After making the film, the group's imaginative ideas are then shared with the class in a screening. Student and teacher feedback after the screening continues to shape and encourage the students' abilities to release and develop their imaginative and creative capacities.

Unlocking the imagination

Maxine Greene (1995) eloquently describes the freeing dynamic of the imaginative space for the individual: 'A space of freedom opens before the person moved to choose in the light of possibility; she or he feels what it signifies to be an initiator and an agent, existing among others but with the power to choose for herself or himself' (1995, p. 22). Greene argues that the role of the imagination is to awaken the mind and the senses and open up possibilities rather than find definitive answers. When the imagination is awakened, she says, our bodies are brought into play, our feelings excited, and the doors of perception have been opened (1995, p. 28).

The obstacle to imaginative and creative thinking is derivative, formulaic, unoriginal, banal thought. To encourage students to think beyond the obvious and the routine is to heighten their awareness of what they are doing by encouraging them to explore, to search and to ask why they are doing what they are doing. Developing a culture of questioning and searching, and gaining more control of the aesthetic, helps students to discover uncertainties, revelations, nuances, subtleties and the unexpected to express greater layers of meaning in the art of film. Teachers in their questioning, the scaffolded tasks they provide and the films used in appreciation viewing should challenge students to go beyond the mundane.

An imaginative space for students is offered when they are given problem-solving exercises that involve prescribed boundaries. These exercises require creative solutions, so in solving these problems students are extended and exposed to something new. If the film exercise involves a character in a landscape, for instance, students have to determine how the landscape enhances the dramatic action of the character, and the dramatic purpose of the scene. They also have to find a real location of the landscape to film. The problem-solving involved in this task asks for tangential, lateral, reflective and creative thinking.

The model of making and appreciating as a learning dichotomy allows students in appreciation to be exposed to small parts of films that can take them beyond their experience and what they know of films. For example, when focusing on how sound can be used in a film, parts of the following eclectic range of films are useful: *400 Blows* (1959), *The Seven Samurai* (1954), *Babel* (2006),

Sunset Boulevard (1950) and *Gosford Park* (2001). The learning focus is to discover how sound can be used to different effect, such as the raw reality audio of Truffaut's *400 Blows*, the overlapping sometimes indiscernible dialogue sound in Altman's *Gosford Park*, the use of no sound in González Iñárritu's *Babel*, the sounds and silences of landscapes and battles in Kurosawa's *The Seven Samurai* and the use of the voiceover in Wilder's *Sunset Boulevard*. But students are also being exposed to footage of narrative films that are varied in their style and their cultural and historical context. This appreciation exercise opens students to creative possibilities and avenues in the making of their own films.

As well, students can be extended by creative activities such as using limericks for kinaesthetic storyboarding. Limericks can be used, for example, to illustrate narrative and plot construction as a classroom exercise; however, students' imaginations are also 'freed' by the nonsense of the limericks' content when they present a kinaesthetic storyboard of their envisioned film. A 'kinaesthetic storyboard' rather than a visual one is when students can explain their dramatic action and shots by presenting it through acting it out. The imagined film does not necessarily have to be made, but the content of a nonsense limerick in itself releases student thinking from the routine and banal. Although the imagination may be released by the nonsense of the limerick, the imagined film still has to have the inner logic of story construction and belief for it to work for the spectator. All creative exercises and activities such as these in the film classroom have to encourage a situation where students' imaginations are engaged and developed beyond the mundane, 'to awaken, to disclose the ordinarily unseen, unheard, and unexpected' (Greene, 1995, p. 28).

The imaginative space for the film student is not only in the mind; it is embodied in the concrete form of acting out imagined persons in imagined circumstances. We have argued in this chapter that the camera and sound operators, directors and editors experience that embodiment as 'technical actors' in the filmmaking process. It is essential that film learning involves the learning of dramatic embodiment in a make-believe world. This is learning in the aesthetic art of acting, and more specifically acting for film.

How do students learn to act their stories?

The pedagogical approach in this book is focused on narrative and developing students' capacities to construct and deconstruct stories in the film form. Film narrative is a form of dramatic storytelling that is acted out physically and observed by the camera for the audience to experience. The dramatic purpose of a scene and the dramatic intent of the characters inform the acting of a scene. Conversely, the process of acting out can inform the dramatic purpose and intent of characters, their actions and the film language used to communicate the dramatic action. Acting or playing an imaginary role in an imagined situation must be viewed as integral to the teaching of film narrative, as it provides an understanding and exploration of the drama in a narrative. Students must be introduced to this pedagogical approach in role-playing, workshopping and film acting throughout the film learning. Much can be imagined, but the concrete physicalisation of human action is a vital conduit for exploring the psychology of human behaviour. To act is to connect the mind and the body.

Activities such as kinaesthetic storyboarding (referred to in Chapter 6) invite students to workshop scenes physically in role to explore and communicate their ideas for an imagined film. The process of acting or playing a role is used to explore and develop ideas, but it also develops students' abilities to sustain a role. Physically workshopping ideas and scenes before shooting has the dual purpose of allowing students to play with their imaginations while at the same time learning how to act for the camera. Specific exercises in acting with belief, dramatic intent and action refine the students' skills in film acting and fuel their understanding of dramatic intent and action.

It is essential for students to learn that what the actor is doing in a film entails the actor knowing and being committed to the imagined 'given circumstances' of the character or role they are playing. The commitment of the actor to the imagined world in the film is the same as that required towards the real world:

> In life, everything is specific. Nothing is generalised. When you talk, you are flashing up pictures of who you are talking about, where you've been, what you want. Your scripted imaginative life must be just as vivid, just as precise, just as specific. No millisecond must pass you by, without you completely being in the moment of thinking and reacting as that character (Churcher, 2003, p. 57).

The playing of role or character is a fundamental in teaching drama in education, and it is essential for film learning as well. However, the style or aesthetic of the acting for film is different to the acting of live stage drama. Acting for film is shaped by the camera capturing what the audience will see.

The distance and closeness of the frame and the ability of the camera to be a third eye in a scene or the eye of a character in the scene shape the nature of acting in film. Film acting is characterised by a more internalised approach as a technique of communicating emotions and actions compared with stage acting because the spectator, through the camera, can be so close to and intimate with the characters. Film acting is also shaped by the semiotics and proxemics of three dimensions becoming two-dimensional moving images. Like all the other aspects of film learning, the aesthetics of acting can be scaffolded into activities and filmmaking exercises and become more complex, layered and sophisticated as students progress.

The focus on learning about acting for film begins when students determine a character's dramatic intent for an action. Finding the motive for the action becomes not only the dramatic catalyst for an event in the film story, it is the internal motivation or intention for the actor. Director and actor Sydney Pollack (2002) sums this up by simply saying that the actor 'only needs to understand what he needs to live truthfully in an imaginary set of circumstances … all acting comes from wanting something. It's what you want that makes you do something, not what you think' (2002, p. 22). To develop the students' understanding of acting is to scaffold into the learning exercises a way to see the given circumstances of the character through the character's eyes. Students creating and inhabiting their film stories need to ask themselves Stanislavsky[6]-type acting questions such as:

- Who am I?
- Where and when am I?
- What are my relationships?
- What do I want?
- How do I get what I want?
- How do I react?
- How do I change?

To focus on and be committed to what the character wants as a compelling 'need' raises the stakes and tension of the drama, but it also helps the actor to be real and to find a belief that is convincing for both the actor and the viewer. To achieve this, students, through acting exercises and filmmaking tasks, have to develop focused concentration and a heightened awareness of what they are doing that is not self-conscious. The truth of what they are doing in the film must have a belief and focus that is evident in the actor's eyes. Students, like

Simon on the Shostakovich Film Project, have to discover that: 'You don't ever "play" a character, you "are" a person. You've got thoughts and feelings and a whole universe in which you live.'

Film's need for continuity requires the actor to repeat dramatic action in a very precise way. Rather than constrain and deaden the film performance, continuity can heighten and focus the actor's awareness of their actions. The realness of the location or set helps the actors to believe in their character's given circumstances. Students in film acting have to realise the power of a 'moment' or a 'beat' on film. When something in the character changes, the audience senses this with a 'moment'. In a chase scene, this 'moment' may be to register the fear on the character's face as they look back and see the person closing in on them. Film acting has a very different energy and means of transmission from live stage drama. As Churcher (2003) points out, the difference between the two is best compared with the changing physical relationship of the director to the actors. In the theatre, the director works in close proximity with the actors in rehearsal. As the performance nears its opening night, the director pulls away into the more distant proximity of the audience. In film, the shooting usually starts with the long-shot, moving to the mid-shot, finishing with the intimacy of the close-up. The camera has the potential to explore acting that captures the subtlety and nuance of a look and make it a resonating 'moment'.

Learning from acting and stories

Acting as a form of play and communication should be viewed as a powerful tool for learning in film. Acting and telling stories in film allows students the opportunity to experience and express a sense of self and a sense beyond self. To act or play roles in filmmaking is a concrete manifestation of what Greene (1995) describes as imaging and seeing oneself on a strange island, poking around that world, paying attention to it and thinking about it (1995, p. 24). The arts in education aim to extend students' perception of themselves and the world around them. In film learning, the creating and acting of stories is a lens through which to explore different perspectives of reality. David Lynch (2002) (*Eraserhead*, 1978; *Blue Velvet*, 1986; *Mulholland Drive*, 2001) describes how film creates a reality of the imagination:

> To me, the power of film goes beyond the simple task of telling a story. It has to do with the *way* you tell that story and how you manage to create a world

of your own. Film has the power to depict invisible things. It works like a window through which you enter a different world, something close to a dream (2002, p. 127).

Film learning requires an embodiment of role, belief and dramatic action that encompasses and extends from the actors in front of the camera to the production crew unseen behind the camera. To *act* in our model for film learning is to connect and contribute to the telling and embodiment of the story through the conceiving, directing, acting, camera, sound and editing in a collaborative and shared process. Everyone in our filmmaking model for education *acts* because they have to connect in a feeling way with the *magic if* of the drama of narrative film. It is then that all the parts of filmmaking are unified with a dramatic purpose and intent, and the creativity and imagination of students are utilised and developed. Using the performative, physical act of *acting* is also a way to develop an understanding of dramatic intent and purpose in the construction of narrative and film language for all film students.

Eisner says to experience an aesthetic brings joy to the creator and the receiver of an art form. We have argued that this is the delight that students should experience with film learning and the telling of their stories. That is not to say there won't be trials and tribulations in the learning of the aesthetic and the experience of the creative arts process. Film stories are complex constructions, and creativity and imagining challenge the expression of our thoughts, feelings and ideas. Filmmaking and film stories are the personal made public and the public made personal: 'it's something that you do for others but which will only work if you're convinced that it's solely for you' (Almodovar, 2002, p. 86). Our premise is that film learning is a means for students to explore a perception of self with a connectedness to others through the creation of a shared narrative.

Narrative, according to Barbara Hardy (1977), is a 'primary act of mind transferred to art from life' (1977, p. 12). We think in stories and we shape our thinking by the stories with which our culture surrounds us. Film learning allows students to engage with film stories as more than passive recipients; they become active participators in their creation. They learn to construct stories, inhabit stories and communicate stories, as well as to be challenged by these creative processes. The storytelling potential of film learning presents an opportunity for students to imagine, explore and embody the narrative of human consciousness. The artistic creation of film stories offers valuable and meaningful learning for young people because: 'Art offers life; it offers hope; it offers the prospect of discovery; it offers light' (Greene, 1995, p. 133). A student on the Shostakovich Film Project reminds us of this potential when she says:

> It was probably the most amazing experience of my life so far … it has sparked my love for drama and film, as well as taught me skills that I will have for the rest of my life. I was inspired to the point that I realised I have so much more to learn and want to learn (Victoria).

The next chapter examines how film learning can be introduced across the curriculum in schools.

8
Developing a film curriculum

> It is easier to change the location of a cemetery, than to change the school curriculum.
> —*Woodrow T. Wilson (former US president)*

Innovation and the curriculum

Those striving for change in the curriculum may well acknowledge Wilson's frustration. The reality in the enlightened twenty-first century seems little different, even for a learning area with immense student interest such as film. For those who would like to integrate film learning into their classrooms, there are some natural advantages. Our students already have a comprehensive and thorough exposure to (if not understanding of) film. They also come to class with more experience of the key technologies that are the basis of film learning: the computer and the camera. You might be excused for thinking that, given these conditions, schools would be encouraging film learning. This assumption under-estimates the politics of curriculum development. Screen learning sits in curriculum terms in several different areas. It occupies space in media, English, drama, visual arts, design and technology, amongst other areas. Film is rarely studied in its own right, although there are celebrated exceptions. Halpin et al. (2004) comment on the difficulties of implementing a responsive and inclusive curriculum in an education system that values 'high stakes testing'. They argue that, in these settings, tension between reality and rhetoric emerges:

> while government exhortations to 'raise standards', 'innovate' and 'promote social inclusion' clearly served an important rhetorical function, they may

have underestimated the challenges involved and overestimated the capacity of schools within disadvantaged areas to 'make a difference' (2004, p. 205).

As Halpin (2004, p. 205) argues, there are significant ongoing competing agendas in schools that make the emergence of new curriculum areas that do not conform to these agendas difficult at best. In response, schools have attempted to do more, expanding their curriculum, introducing student welfare programs as well as concentrating on testing. All this crowding has left little space for innovations in curriculum—even curriculum that has become a standard part of every child's life, such as film and television.

While educators could be forgiven for shrugging their shoulders at this gap between the lives of young people and schooling, there is a more pressing issue here. If one of the purposes of schooling is to prepare young people to face the challenges of the world they are entering, we are failing if they do not know how to critically respond to and create media—in our case, with film. It locks these young people out (Carroll, Anderson and Cameron, 2006) of the opportunity to express themselves skilfully in the pervasive media, and does not support their critical engagement with those same media. If teachers believe that they must equip young people for a future that we cannot even imagine yet, they must strive to close the gap between their schooling and their lived experience.

This chapter imagines (perhaps a little hopefully) that in the near future the obstacles that have emerged from curriculum politics and schooling generally will give way to the logic of including film in the curriculum in its own right. In this chapter, we argue for a comprehensive and sustainable approach to film learning that takes account of the recent innovations in film technologies. There is ample evidence in the practices of film learning that it can constitute a viable and worthwhile subject for study. We examine how this might occur on a whole of schooling basis, and look at how film learning occurs now in two schools. The case studies offered in this chapter are a way of comparing our aspirations with the realities of modern schooling. We begin by discussing how the continuum of film learning begins and how linkages can be made from primary to secondary and post-compulsory schooling, then discuss some of the various practices of film learning in schools through our two case studies.

Developing a continuum of film learning

The development of a learning continuum illustrates what might be possible if we were able to overcome some of the obstacles in the way of film in the curriculum. Our discussion of a continuum is drawn from practice and our understanding of what is possible for children in screen learning from the early years of their education. The continuum presented here provides a discussion of the foundations of film learning and indicates the bases for the development of film curriculum. The descriptions indicate what students can achieve at the upper end of the age range indicated. These statements are no substitute for a full discussion of the different stages of film learning. They are not designed to be comprehensive treatments of learning in each stage; these can be found in many other places. Our intent here is to sketch out briefly the kind of experiences that are age-appropriate and that build a comprehensive and thorough understanding of film. We begin with a discussion of the potential for film learning for three- to five-year-olds.

Film learning in the early years

It is not possible to consider a comprehensive film learning curriculum without discussing the foundation experiences of the early years. The Kaiser Family Foundation found that by age six children spent two hours a day with screen media—the same amount of time as they spent reading or being read to (Kaiser Family Foundation, 2006, p. 7). These figures are often quoted as a shock statistic about the screen's role in the imminent moral decline of our children. Notwithstanding these concerns, the figures do indicate that young people have experience of the screen from a very early age. The British Film Institute argues that:

> ... film, television, video and an increasing number of web sites and computer games—are important and valuable parts of our culture. It follows that children have a basic right to learn about these media in school ... Our message here is a positive one: that the moving image media provide us with a distinctive and vital means of expression, are a dominant and global source of stories, ideas and opinions, and are an increasingly important part of our cultural heritage (BFI Education, 2003, p. 1).

Even in early childhood, there is a responsibility on us to develop ways for young people to interpret and make their own media. Teaching screen literacy to the very young is an important step in providing access to cultural codes and languages that are pervasive in the lives of young children. Table 8.1 outlines some of the possibilities for learning for students aged from three to five. The learning statement outlines the learning expectations, and details the kinds of learning experiences with which children might engage across age ranges.

Table 8.1 Film learning in early childhood

Age	Learning statement	Aesthetic understanding	Aesthetic Control
3–5	Students in the early years of learning have broad experience in screen media. They should be able to identify characters they like, discuss storylines and make predictions about plot. At this age, children identify basic genres such as cartoons. They can respond to colours, shapes and sound in film and express preferences.	<ul><li>Identify films that they like</li><li>Discuss the characters in films that they like</li><li>Retell basic storylines and plots of films</li></ul>	<ul><li>Describe stories they would like to see their favourite characters enact</li><li>Make choices about sounds and characters to put in short movies and create one or two storyboard frames</li><li>Improvise scenes that can be filmed by others</li></ul>

Film learning in primary school

The imagination is central to learning in the early years, and the maintenance of the role of the imagination and play is crucial as children grow older. As children can name the different genres and identify the different features of written text (literature), they are then able to begin developing their own short film projects. While this is more likely to happen to its fullest extent toward the end of the primary years, there are learning experiences in the earlier years of primary schooling that can prepare students to film, edit and direct their own work in small groups.

Table 8.2 Film learning in primary schooling

Age	Learning statement	Aesthetic understanding	Aesthetic control
5–12	Students in the primary years have seen many hours of diverse screen-mediated media. This experience allows them to discuss their preferences and provide some justifications for them. If they have undertaken film learning in the early years, they should be able to script short scenes and film them. They can assemble, edit and add titles in the later years of primary schooling, using computer-based editing software.	• Identify different genres of films • Discuss the way the characters interact and the way the characters create a plot • Discuss the way the different elements of the films create the tension and the mood of the film	• Develop a series of shots to make a basic storyline in an identified genre • Shoot scenes based on the storyboard with assistance from the teacher • Act for the camera and create dramatic roles for the screen • Use basic video editing software to create scenes and manipulate the sound to create mood and tension

Film learning in junior secondary school

As students enter secondary school, they are becoming more aware of audience. The adolescent's sensitivity to the views of others is often constructed as an impediment to their learning. In film learning, the obsession with performance and audience may be a distinct advantage. A growing sense of what affects and moves an audience can be put to great use in the development and execution of a film project. By high school, most students will have seen many movies and will have made choices about the kinds of movies they like and why. Some children, by this age, will be tempted to mimic their favourite genres and this can be problematic for those teaching these students. There are opportunities for young people to move from imitation to original creations by understanding and implementing the aesthetics of film to create their own work.

Table 8.3 Film learning in junior secondary schooling

Age	Learning statement	Aesthetic understanding	Aesthetic control
12–15	Students in secondary school have had exposure to a vast amount of film in many different genres. Depending on their prior learning, they can identify and describe a genre and discuss how the elements of film are used to create the distinctive features of that genre. They are beginning to understand the ways the filmmaker can use different approaches to manipulate the audience. They are able to use some of these techniques in their films to engage an audience.	<ul><li>Analyse how the different elements of film contribute to the development of film narrative</li><li>Analyse the development of characters and their function in film narrative</li><li>Discuss the influence of cinematic movements on the growth and development of film as an art form</li></ul>	<ul><li>Develop a script and storyboard to develop a film project to pre-production stage</li><li>Direct the camera and the actor/s to create meaning and support the dramatic intention of the script</li><li>Work with others in different roles to realise a self-devised film project</li><li>Edit a film to final-cut stage to support the dramatic meaning of the film through the skilful use of mood and tension</li></ul>

Film learning in senior secondary school

By the time students have reached post-compulsory schooling, they have been exposed to a variety of making and appreciation experiences that help them to analyse film and synthesise much of that learning into their own work. By this stage, students have chosen to continue in film learning, and that choice should be rewarded with greater autonomy and a greater reliance on self-directed learning. By this stage, students should be able to understand the features of multiple genres and create films that fit within those genres. They should have the opportunity to script, plan and implement their own films and direct others taking on other roles. They should be able to negotiate and organise the pre-production, production and post-production phases of their filmmaking.

Table 8.4 Film learning in post-compulsory schooling

Age	Learning statement	Aesthetic understanding	Aesthetic control
15–18	Students have analysed a diverse and large body of filmed media. They are able at this stage to nominate influential artists in cinema and discuss how their work has changed the art form. They are able to create their own aesthetically informed vision, drawing on these artists without being derivative of their work. They can develop a project with the collaboration of others and create a film that engages and affects an audience.	• Identify different film artists and analyse their impact on the art form • Discuss the way different artists manipulate the elements of film, including camera direction, direction of actors, editing and sound to create a unique contribution to the aesthetic • Analyse and respond to discussion about films, using evidence in their responses	• Script and storyboard a short film (five to seven minutes) of high quality • Use the elements of film, such as camera direction, acting, lighting and sound, to create a distinctive short film narrative • Synthesise the innovations of other filmmakers while retaining an original vision in their own work • Develop a film by negotiating and directing the multiple roles in the process

Film learning in practice: Case studies from the real world

The development of a rational and methodical continuum of learning is useful, but is perhaps a little utopian. To counterbalance these aspirations, the next part of this chapter outlines how schools are dealing with film learning. The approaches detailed in the case studies here have been chosen to indicate some of the diversity of film learning that already exists. These cases demonstrate that film learning is possible when teachers, school administrators and students develop an enthusiasm for the art form. In the face of at least some systemic apathy and disinterest, the two case studies presented here demonstrate different systemic contexts for student learning. The case from Cambridge in the United Kingdom (Parkside Community College)[1] examines what is possible when a system integrates film learning in the context of a media studies course. The second case, from Newtown High School of the Performing Arts in Sydney, Australia, examines what happens in film learning when it sits on the margins of the curriculum.

Case Study 1: Integrated film curricula—Parkside Community College, Cambridge

Context

Parkside is a school in Cambridge, United Kingdom for young people aged eleven to sixteen. Cambridge has a system where Sixth Form students (senior secondary, ages sixteen to eighteen) go to separate Sixth Form Colleges, or Further Education Colleges. Parkside became the first media arts college in 1997, and there are now about 40 of these media arts colleges in the United Kingdom. James Durran has taught at Parkside for many years, and has published widely on film learning in addition to developing and delivering professional development for teachers. He also teaches film with primary-age children in the feeder schools around Cambridge. The following discussion of film learning at Parkside is based on an interview with James in June 2007. He begins here with a discussion of how he sees himself as a teacher of film.

Teaching film

I still consider myself an English teacher. I don't make a distinction: I am a teacher of literacy in its broad sense and I work with children and texts. That might be a novel or poetry, or it might be a television program. There's a perception that somehow media arts is a distraction from the more serious business of teaching children to read, write and be numerate. There's also a perception that it's easy, and that it's a soft option. Serious media education is finding itself always to be in tension with those sorts of forces. We regard media literacy as preparing people to interact with a media-rich culture in this technological age in a pleasurable, creative and critical way.

I employ the same sorts of pedagogies and discourses in whatever subject I am teaching. In an ideal world, I would be teaching a curriculum that saw working with texts as much more integrated, which is what we try to do here at Parkside. We have a fairly integrated curriculum; children are working with the same teachers, in the same rooms, in the same ways and for the same assessments; the same practices are used, working with film one day, poetry the next.

The critical and the creative

The critical and the creative are always interlinked in practice. A lot of weight here is given to a critical appreciation of texts; we are perhaps erring on the side of an analytic deconstructive approach, which looks at codes, the languages of media texts. We enjoy that, and the children enjoy that, taking things to pieces, learning a language with which to describe those things, acquiring the tools and resources to decode.

We always do try to tie in critical work with production work. We have a strong commitment to production work, partly because of the belief that the best way to understand something is to create it, to work in a hands-on way with the form. We also want children to be producers as well as consumers, to take an ownership of media forms, which only comes through a hands-on approach to production.

Film learning in Key Stage 2 (ages seven to eleven)

We do a lot of work with primary children working with narrative animation. At the Key Stage 2 level, we're engaging children in ideas about narrative, about how moving images tell stories, and the grammar of moving images—shot types, and so on. We use animation to give student an exposure to a variety of filmic approaches and partly because it strongly connects with popular media forms for children at that age. They're using stop motion animation, and it's nicely contained in the school; we don't have to go out filming. We did quite a lot in the past with 2D computer animation with primary children.

Film learning in Key Stage 3 (ages eleven to fourteen)

In Key Stage 3, we have a project in Year 7, when they first come in, on a short film called *Patterns*. The film is part of the English and Media Centre Key Stage 3 book and video media pack, although we do our own things with it. It's a seventeen-minute film about an autistic child, which they look at and talk about. There's a lot about narrative and storytelling. They look at specific scenes very closely, almost a shot-by-shot analysis, and they do storyboarding out of that. This is all done on paper and they have not used a camera yet.

Romeo and Juliet *remixed*

In Year 8, they study Baz Luhrmann's *Romeo and Juliet* with subtitles on and look at elements of language. At this stage, they look at *Romeo and Juliet* as a complete work of art on film. The students do some sequencing work with camera shots. They do a close analysis of film grammar, shot choices and how following a shot with another shot creates meanings. They make discoveries about how a different choice would tell a different story. They re-edit a sequence of the film using Adobe Premiere. They come out of this exercise thinking that the filmmaker is masterful and wonderful, but that they are masterful and wonderful too.

When they are repurposing Baz Luhrmann's material, they often change the mood. They take the scene at the end where Romeo is being pursued across Verona with a helicopter and police cars, and put it into a different order—add slow motion, put a different soundtrack on it. They often create something that is melancholic, rather than thrilling.

While they are doing this, they are learning editing techniques, they're deploying the kind of understandings they've gained by doing the analysis. They're thinking about continuity, such as, 'if I follow this shot of the helicopter in the sky with the shot of Romeo looking up, we create the illusion that he is looking at the helicopter'. They are also thinking that if it is slowed down, it changes the mood. If we insert a transparent shot of Juliet laughing, we create a sad and reflective mood. It's about meaning making in complex ways. You'll have some kids talking at a high level about very subtle things, and others just banging bits together, and being pleased with the result.

The hospital drama

The other thing they do in Year 8 is a course on hospital dramas, looking at genre, and they do a little bit of in-camera editing. They produce a sequence; it may only be ten to sixteen seconds long. It's meant to be a typical hospital drama sequence, perhaps the build-up to an accident. They look at examples like *ER* and *Casualty*. Coming out of this they also do a treatment for a new hospital drama.

They are commissioned to do a treatment for a hospital drama for children, bringing together the genre of early evening kids' drama with the more peak-time (popular) hospital genre, and come up with a hospital drama, maybe called something like 'Children's Ward' or 'Sticks and Stones'. It has a kids' angle and they decide what kind of narratives and what kind of regular characters they will put in their show. They have fun with that, and what they do is an in-camera editing production exercise, so they shoot a short sequence, in sequence, with no post-production editing. It really is set up, shoot it, take it, move the camera, next shot, next shot, which is really hard to do. That's great fun. Results are very mixed: some of it falls to pieces, while some of it looks fantastic.

Film learning in Key Stage 4 (Years 9 and 10)— filming drama and genre learning: Horror

In Year 9, students learn about the particular demands of acting for film and television. They then learn about how a single camera drama is filmed and edited for continuity. This leads into a group project, in which they prepare a short piece of drama and film it repeatedly from different angles. They then edit this footage, using Adobe Premiere, to tell the same story from different viewpoints.

They do a course in horror, looking at *Psycho* (1960). We look at horror as a genre that involves a lot of analysis, thinking about fear and film. That leads to an exercise where they produce a presentation, very analytically, on a part of the film. The students are given the whole of *Psycho* in Moviemaker, so they can find their way around, and can find bits to use. They use simple editing software to assemble moving clips and stills, which they can then put into PowerPoint. When they need to explain something in their presentation, they use the excerpt from the film to demonstrate their point. It is like an essay analysis exercise that uses actual pieces of film to provide evidence for their argument. For example, one girl used individual stills to make a storyboard, and then moving clips. When they analyse the film, they quote from it as they would from a novel or poem. You get a curious hybrid of discourses. Watching and discussing horror films is a familiar teenage event that we are just formalising as a film learning activity. In the classroom, rather than the lounge room, they watch the film repeatedly, looking at excerpts and using the language of form media discourse.

Year 10: Producing a film trailer

The main production work is making a film trailer. They look at examples, and then they have to make one. They do that in a fairly concentrated chunk of time. They spend a solid two days making it. They don't storyboard for a real film. So they're just re-editing what they've got, they have the whole film on Premiere, and make a two-minute trailer from that, and what they come up with isn't bad. The films we use for this learning activity are *Shrek* (2001),

Spiderman (2002) and *Minority Report* (2002), which is a very difficult film to make a trailer for.

Case Study 2: Film in the curriculum margins—Newtown High School of the Performing Arts, Sydney

This case study emerges from Ula George's experience as a teacher of film in Sydney, Australia. Ula is a visual arts teacher who began teaching film around five years ago at Newtown, an inner-city suburb of Sydney. Newtown High School of the Performing Arts is a state school and has a focus on the performing arts—mostly drama, music and dance—but visual arts also is prominent in the school and there are crossovers between all the arts. The performing arts are very well supported and, because of the school's reputation for excellence, students come from all over the state to attend. Seventy-five per cent of the students gain entrance through audition (in dance, drama or music) and 25 per cent come from the local area. Film curriculum in the New South Wales system is taught in several other subject areas, and does not have a course devoted to film study in its own right. In that sense, the work reflected in this case study is on the margins of the formal curriculum. The case study begins with a discussion of Ula's attitudes to film and then describes how film has been integrated into the curriculum at her school.

Teaching film: One teacher's perspective

I just want to talk about how the students are getting more and more excited about film. There's a real demand for it from students and parents. I've had a lot of parents who come here, to see if they want to put their student into the school. They are most excited that we are giving kids the opportunity to learn about film in such a comprehensive way. They think it's a pity it isn't done in Year 7.

As a teacher, I don't want film to get lost in other subjects. I don't want it to become just an adjunct to drama, English or visual arts. The curriculum authorities say film is already in visual arts but we don't have time to teach filmmaking properly in art. Nor is what we teach in our film course like what we teach in art. In film, I have a wonderful opportunity as a visual arts teacher to work with drama teachers who understand the dramatic creation of narrative. What I bring as a visual arts teacher is an understanding of the visual aesthetic, the imagery, textures, colour, light and perspective.

Art and narrative

Often the older students want to make 'arty' films with no narrative. We [the film teaching team] have realised we haven't paid enough attention to narrative in film. A narrative film allows the audience to ask more questions, it takes the audience somewhere; art films leave their audiences disconnected. This is crucial in teaching because it distinguishes this course from film done elsewhere (in visual arts, drama, media and English). We are teaching children how to tell a story, usually a two-minute filmed story. We are trying to get them to tell better stories. I am still learning about teaching good storytelling. It starts by teaching them film language and then it builds from there. So, the hard thing in this course is the stuff that people don't think is hard.

Context

I think our students do film at this school because for them it's a form of communication and a form of entertainment that's pervasive. A lot of them say they love it; they love watching films because it takes them somewhere else. They love the experience of going and seeing a film. When the lights go down, they're immersed in the illusion of the film.

Film in the Newtown curriculum

The students here are usually very focused, committed and passionate about what they want to do. They really want to be here. Our students can choose film as an option in Years 9 and 10 and it's very popular. They do two 80-minute periods a week. Around 65 per cent of our students take it as an elective for the two years. This year we have three classes of 25 students. In Years 7 and 8, our students get a very small taste of film in visual arts, where we take them into the film room, show films that their fellow students are doing and get them to talk about their engagement with those films. At this stage, it is not practical to do filmmaking with Years 7 and 8 because the logistics of that many junior students in a small timeframe with equipment makes it too difficult.

Years 9 and 10: Some examples of film learning

In Year 9, we teach them about the elements of film, in the same way we would in visual arts or drama. We start with the language of film and ascertain how much they understand. We show them a few films and explore how much film language they recognise. We start off with language, and then we look at the Odessa Steps scene in Sergei Eisenstein's *Battleship Potemkin* (1925) and begin exploring intellectual montage, which is quite a high level for Year 9, but they really get it. They are so intrigued by this scene; it's a contrast to what they usually watch.

We discuss dramatic purpose, intent and audience engagement in the scene, and look at how in editing film you create illusion and make something look as though it can go on forever and ever. We teach them about shot sizes and the purpose of different shot sizes. Once they have done this and go and make something and look through the camera, they really understand composition and shot sizes. We are teaching appreciation so that they start to understand how filmmakers use and manipulate the language; it helps them in their own filmmaking.

Their first practical filming exercise is to actually film somebody coming down or going down the stairs with some dramatic intent (the character could be running away from something) for 30 seconds with no sound. All of the technical stuff they get easily but it's telling a story simply that is the most difficult. For example, in the stairs exercise using *Potemkin* we originally had murders, falling down stairs with blood, but now we've limited them, so they just have the steps and a character and intent. By limiting this exercise we are teaching them that that they can tell a story without embellishing it in that way.

In Year 10 we teach them fight sequences as a way of acting for the camera, which they love. The students create a fight, and put in sound to heighten the sense of drama. They learn it as choreography so we never have accidents. They learn when they perform a kick, they have to manipulate the camera so it looks like someone is actually kicking them and learn how to pull their head away at exactly the right moment. And they come up with sounds to put in at that point—for example, the crunching of paper.

Years 11 and 12: Some examples of film learning

We only have three periods a fortnight, that's two hours a week. I've had up to two classes of twenty. They're all fantastically keen, seeing they are not doing it for a university entrance mark. They make a six-minute film. The students put imagery and sound together for a dramatic purpose because they understand what a narrative looks like on screen. They don't make surreal films that leave the audience grasping for meaning. We've all seen those kind of films where we come out thinking it's the director's indulgence.

In Year 11 they do two exercises. The first is an appreciation, because there are some kids who are new to that year. So we look at film language again, and we look at montage and exposition. We watch the opening sequence of Orson

Welles' *Citizen Kane* (1941). They write about the dramatic purpose and effect of that sequence. They start to appreciate the film through close analysis, even though at first it looks old-fashioned to them.

Next we do an exercise about the school. They have two minutes to put a little montage together, showing what a unique place of learning the school is. That's their first exercise; they can put any type of music to it, but I tell them not to make a music video. The music is not what will drive the audience; the imagery is what will drive you and create the intended mood. Through the years, we've had totally different moods created through this exercise, some nostalgic and quite beautiful at times.

In Year 12, they make their film. The problem is that all this time they've been working in a collaborative situation where everyone has responsibility for a role, and has had a chance to take on many different roles. When it comes to Year 12, some people want to work together, but some want to make their 'own film'. They work with a crew, but they don't want to make a committee film.

Reflecting on the cases

These cases demonstrate that focused and systematic film learning can take place in schools, given sufficient will, energy and the opportunity. In Newtown and Cambridge, there is an enthusiasm that emerges from the school community to engage with film learning. In Cambridge, James Durran and his team have developed a film learning curriculum by connecting the critical and creative approach of film learning. His desire to make his students creators as well as consumers is reflected in the methodical development of aesthetic control and understanding in his learning programs that seem to be continually informed and supported by popular film. One of the exciting innovations in his program is the distinctly postmodern way he asks students to recut a director's work for different filmic effect. For students to be successful in this exercise, the aesthetic understanding and control must be interdependent.

At Newtown High School of the Performing Arts, there is pioneering work going on in the face of systemic indifference. The school and the teachers have created film learning that taps the potential engagement of students and creates learning by prizing narrative in the development of film learning. One of the striking features of this case study is the emphasis that narrative has in the film learning. The Newtown case represents a move away from a media arts curriculum and toward a filmed narrative approach. In this approach as well, there is a strong focus on the integration of making and appreciating in the development of film learning.

The key differences in these cases relate to the curriculum history of both contexts. At Newtown, the history of film curriculum has been dominated by its marginality. Film's piecemeal presence in English, drama and visual arts in the New South Wales syllabus has limited its expansion into a mature and sustainable curriculum area. What has emerged is a film curriculum at Newtown that focuses on student making. This differs in emphasis slightly from the Parkside model, which works within genre to develop a keen appreciation of filmmakers and filmmaking traditions. Parkside owes some of its development to the media studies and English curriculum roots.

Concluding reflections: Towards a sustainable film learning and teaching culture

Ultimately these cases indicate that film learning is achievable in a range of school contexts. What they also demonstrate is the emergence of a pedagogic model of film learning removed from an industry model and focused on fostering young people who appreciate film form and are able to create within that form. The aspirations of the continuum of film learning presented at the beginning of this chapter seem achievable in the light of these cases. What is required from schooling systems, schools and individual teachers is an engagement with film learning as a sustainable learning area in an already crowded curriculum. We have presented here a continuum and cases of effective practice that have engaged and supported student learning. What is required now is the political will to support film's rightful place in the curriculum so it does not become the captive of other subject areas.

In Chapter 9, we examine approaches to assessing film learning that are authentic and support students in their development of skills and understanding in screen learning.

9
Assessing the screen

> I was thrown out of college for cheating on the metaphysics exam; I looked into the soul of the boy next to me.
> —*Woody Allen*, Annie Hall *(1977)*

In the opening chapters of this book, we called for a model of film learning that sought an interaction between making and appreciation. Perhaps one of the last bastions of this arbitrary separation is seen in the ways film learning in particular, and learning in the arts in general, is assessed. For mostly pragmatic reasons, appreciation is confined to pen and paper essay responses, and if there is assessment of student filmmaking it often assesses an individual's making skills in what is essentially a collaborative, interactive learning experience. Assessment of film is about nuance and subtlety, and so the traditional high stakes testing regimes that seem to be all the rage currently will not suffice. As Posner (2004) argues, for assessing complexity and subtlety found in the real-world tasks of film learning it may be necessary to seek more sensitive approaches to assessment than standardised testing:

> For real problems, the appropriate methods of attack are not immediately obvious and may well vary greatly from those that apply to problems that seem similar. In contrast, on a standardised test, where there is no time for subtlety or deep analysis, problems are by necessity formulaic. Could an education driven standardised test scores leave students unable to understand such subtleties? (Posner, 2004, p. 749).

While standardised testing does have its place, it is by its very nature a reductionist approach, and not particularly useful for many areas of the arts that rely on ambiguity and subtlety rather than binary responses. In film learning, where subtlety and nuance are at the heart of the learning, this is especially true. When students learn to edit film, they are learning to control nuance and subtlety to create meaning for an audience. When students edit, they are using the subtle intercutting of scenes, the skilful use of pace and the manipulation of sound to connect with their audience's emotions, imagination, memory and so on. Pen and paper examinations have their uses (which we will discuss later in this chapter), but they cannot teach the embodied yet intellectual skill of film editing, to take one example. Film editing can be taught and assessed in a mechanistic way or in a manner that takes account of aesthetic control (editing for narrative, pace, etc.) and how that affects an audience. What is required for film learning is assessment that mirrors the requirements of the learning rather than narrow reporting imperatives that so often drive learning measurement strategies.

We are not claiming for one moment that we should be backing away from assessing film learning—far from it. We are arguing that many of the traditional, and to some extent enduring, models of assessment that place a reliance on pen and paper testing are not appropriate for film learning. What is required is a new approach to assessment that engages authentically with the art form. This approach mirrors the skills and knowledge of film learning rather than relying solely on assessment practices of the pre-digital era. We also believe strongly that there is a place in a balanced approach to film learning for written responses. Student understanding of appreciation in many cases must be expressed through an academic critical mode, and a written response allows these kinds of responses to be assessed efficiently.

We now have the opportunity using screen-based technologies to assess students' appreciation and making skills in an authentic way. Our argument here is that learning must drive assessment, and with this objective we suggest in this chapter some approaches to the assessment of film learning that are founded on innovations drawn from arts education and authentic assessment approaches. This is no small task, but we feel it is crucial that the engine of assessment that so often drives learning is suitable for film learning.

This chapter first explores the issues that relate to assessment in the arts and then focuses more specifically on issues that relate to assessing short film. Our argument is that we should approach film assessment with that guided subjectivity (Eisner, 1993) we all apply to the teaching we do. The chapter presents some different approaches to assessment in film learning and provides some suggested principles that can be applied to the assessment of learning in film.

We are not suggesting here that there are definitive models, but rather that a set of principles exists that can be applied to film learning to make it fair and productive for our students. We would like to turn to the wider context of assessment in the arts before focusing on our aspirations for assessment suited to film learning.

Assessment in the arts

There has been much, often fruitless, discussion about how the arts can be assessed. On the one hand, the subjectivists argue that arts learning cannot be assessed—this is the 'beauty is in the eye of the beholder' argument. Others push for objective summative testing, as seen in national literacy and numeracy testing. This kind of approach asks students to fit their art work into rigid criteria. Both of these extremes present great difficulties for film education. There is an approach that is tried and tested in the arts that allows a trained subjectivity to be applied to the assessment of art works and, for our purposes, short film. 'Trained subjectivity' (Thompson, 1991, p. 77) accepts that film teachers (and assessors) come with an understanding and experience of film from their lives as teachers, film audiences and filmmakers. Rather than seeing this as some kind of inhibition to effective assessment, this subjectivity or experience is prized. The next step is to train those assessing film through discussion and moderation practices to ensure valid criteria can frame effectively the subjectivity of the teacher. We are not arguing here that any of us can claim objectivity in any of our assessment practices, but rather that we should prize our subjectivity (which comprises knowledge and experience) and strive with others skilled in assessment to come to a common understanding using common but flexible criteria. We have devised the following principles as a way to frame the development of assessment in film.

Five principles for effective film assessment

Later in this chapter, we will discuss specific approaches to assessment in film learning. There are, however, some principles that emerge from best-practice arts assessment, which we believe underpin an effective approach to assessment in film learning. We have identified here five principles that support an approach to film learning that interrelates appreciation and making processes in the learning. This perspective draws from a broad spectrum of assessment and learning theory to construct an approach that provides authentic assessment constructively aligned to the learning.

1. Film learning assessment should be authentic and relevant to the art form

Unlike other areas of education, film learning not only has an aesthetic to measure itself against but also has an active and pervasive industry to consider. Assessment in this area should in this sense have one eye on that relationship with the industry and the innovations occurring there and one eye on the aesthetic of film. This provides a wonderful opportunity for film educators to develop film learning assessments that borrow from the film industry in authentic forms that Wiggins (1993, p. 229) says engage students in 'worthy problems or questions of importance, in which students must use knowledge to fashion performances effectively and creatively. The tasks are either replicas of or analogous to the kinds of problems faced by adult citizens and professionals in the field.' While there is nothing particularly new about authentic assessment, it does allow teachers of film to make a case for their learning area based on its relationship to the most pervasive of cultural industries: film and television. The necessary caveat here is that film education is not, and can never be, the same as the film industry. As Carroll (2008) argues:

> A professional craft-based model produces a particular form of film, which cannot be reproduced in classroom environments because its very nature demands time, energy and skill to the exclusion of any other curriculum concern ... the expense in time and effort is often too high for secondary curriculum-based schools to sustain (2008, p. 182).

When designing a film assessment approach, teachers should always be guided by the learning needs of the students, not just the nature of the industry. Schools do not have the resources to make, nor can they justify making, classrooms into film training centres. Rather, film learning should be a place where the best of the craft-based model can be employed to support the learning and assessment aims of the film classroom.

While there is much in the industrial filmmaking processes that teachers can borrow to create film learning, we do not need to slavishly follow the industrial model. Borrowing of industrial or professional arts form practices and adapting them for learning is commonplace in drama, music and design-based curricula where the precedents exist. The implications for film learning are that we must strive to align the learning with the skill or understanding being taught. If we want to assess a critical response to a film, a written essay response is appropriate.

Authentic assessment in film must align with film practice, so instead of an essay response about editing, an actual film-editing task is assessed. Rather than writing about the editing of film, students actually edit film, and that task is assessed against a series of criteria that align with the outcomes and are known to the students before they begin the task. Writing about film also has a strong place in our conception of film learning. The critical analysis elements of this approach are best suited to critical written responses that allow reflection on the aesthetic, personal experience and the craft of filmmaking. This is a departure from an objectivist literature criticism approach, and recognises the value of personal reflections on filmmaking and appreciating processes. In this approach, teachers recognise that students have their own skills in critical analysis since film learning encourages students to be critically engaged and informed in their viewing

As we will discuss later in this chapter, screen learning is not only about individual response but also about collaborative development of film projects. Film learning requires much of students in collaborative group contexts as well as individually. Creating authentic learning in a collaborative setting requires planning, but there are many cases where this kind of assessment has proved robust and successful in arts education.[1]

2. Assessment should be about learning and not only about measurement

The overwhelming legacy of the assessment for learning movement has been the shift away from a narrowly based conception of assessment for learning to incorporating assessment as a learning rather than just a measurement tool. One of the strongest proponents of this approach has been Paul Black, who has long argued the case for the centrality of formative assessment in the development of student learning. His studies in 1988 and 2004 explored the links between assessment and learning. He found that there was overwhelming evidence that formative assessment practices are central to the growth and development of student learning. There was, however, some ambiguity about how formative assessment might be optimised to make learning even more effective for students. Table 9.1 summarises the findings of his 2004 study (Black et al., 2004) that makes recommendations for improving assessment practices to enhance learning and notes the implications for film learning.

These implications mean a wholesale reorientation of the way learning takes place. For many arts educators, this will make sense, while for others the

Table 9.1 Implications for assessment of film learning

Assessment for learning in the classroom	Implications for film learning
- Change the 'classroom contract' so all expect that teacher and students will work together for the same end: the improvement of everyone's learning. - Empower students to become active learners, thus taking responsibility for their own learning. - Incorporate changes in the teacher's role one step at a time, as they seem appropriate. Move from 'instructor' to 'facilitator'. - Pay attention to and reflect on ways in which assessment can support learning.	- Learning in film should focus on continuous assessment that relies on the process and product of film. The expectations here are for group rather than individual learning. Students are responsible for their peers' learning as well as their own. - An environment of intellectual and aesthetic curiosity should be established to promote active and responsible learning as the tasks become more learner centred. - As the teacher is able, they should hand over the aesthetic responsibility to the students so they become less directive in their teaching and more of a support for the learning. - Learning should follow the skills or understanding being taught. For instance, film acting should be assessed on the ability of students to act for the camera.

approach will be new. It is an expectation of many drama, music and visual arts classrooms that students will take responsibility for each other and their own learning.

3. Film learning should assess the making and appreciation of film as an interaction rather than a bifurcation

We have argued throughout this book that the bifurcation of making and appreciation has done the arts a major disservice. The implications for assessment are that we must develop assessment that reflects the interconnectedness of appreciation and making in film learning. We would like to provide an example to demonstrate how this might be possible.

The chase scene is perhaps one of the best-known narrative devices. When students are learning how to create their own chase scene, the most logical approach is to analyse some of the great chase scenes. Watching chase scenes from *The Blues Brothers* (1980) and *The Fugitive* (1963) provides a strong basis for the development of their own chase scene. After students have analysed and discussed how the chase scene is being created cinematically, they can then begin the process of developing their own chase scenes. The intention in this learning scenario is that the appreciation of these excerpts is supporting their developing understanding of how they might make their own scene. In the making phase, they storyboard and shoot their own short (30- to 45-second) chase scene. The assessment here must tie the analysis in with the making in the same way the learning activities take place. Our approach is to ask students to develop a portfolio with screenshots of their chase scene annotated with how their analysis of other chase scenes helped them to develop their own. Perhaps the most effective way to do this currently is to use movie software that allows spoken or written commentary as the film plays. Alternatively, it can be presented as a seminar with the students explaining how their analysis of other chase scenes has informed their own filmmaking. The assessment criteria then focus on the process (portfolio) and the product (finished chase scene) to align the learning to assessment and make the link between appreciation and making in film. There are potential pitfalls here. There will be students who are not able to create their own filmic vision, and who create derivative or poor imitations of the original. In any approach that relies on the appreciation of a filmmaker's practice, this is a potential danger. A key expectation of this approach is that students develop their own approach that is influenced by, but not a copy of, the work of other filmmakers. The soundest response to this potential threat is to devise criteria that ask the student to be innovative in their approach while using some of the established techniques.

4. The assessment of film learning should be achieved through some group assessment

A focus on collaborative processes is hardly new, and for decades collaborative learning has largely been uncontroversial. The main instrument is formative assessment; this is also now largely uncontroversial, but does sit at odds with some of the high-stakes testing schemes in place for students of all ages in large Western education systems. In the first chapter, we characterised learning in film as a group enterprise, as a community of practice that relies on interaction and cooperative learning. While these are not new pedagogies, they do demand a reconceptualisation of the often-individualistic approaches to assessment found in secondary schooling. The most common complaint about these approaches from our experience is that they lack integrity because individual achievement is dependent on the interactions of others. This view of collaborative assessment is superficial. It misunderstands the reorientation that arts education demands for learning and consequently assessment. This view is also based on the premise that you cannot assess an individual's contribution to the whole effectively without other students 'contaminating' the individual's contribution. The evidence for the effectiveness can be seen in high-stakes testing regimes[2] that include group assessment forms. The New South Wales Higher School Certificate is the matriculation examination for students in that state. In the drama examination, more than 6000 students are annually examined on their ability to devise and perform a group performance, eight to twelve minutes in length, with three to six performers. Students are assessed formatively through classroom-based assessment and summatively on their performances before two or three external examiners. These examiners mark against a set of defined criteria and established standards. This process has been in place since 1993. This is one small example, but many others abound demonstrating how cooperative learning can be rigorously and uncontroversially assessed and can be incorporated into high-stakes examinations for university entrance if required.

Given these significant precedents, there is ample scope for those involved in film learning to develop a similar approach. Our approach to assessing collaborative learning has a similar flavour to this example. Students are assessed on the development of a short film on the basis of the role they take in the process. So, for instance, a student undertaking sound design in a collaborative film project has a set of formative and summative criteria applied to her work. The formative assessment may take the form of a portfolio or a seminar on how she plans to develop and use sound to create the film she is making. The summative phase of the assessment is the finished product, and this has two components. One component provides a mark for the completed film based on a set of summative criteria, while the other half of this mark relates to the sound design specifically, which has its own set of criteria. The assessment schedule is reflected in Table 9.2.

This approach underscores the importance of both the collaboration and each individual contribution. In addition, each individual student's contribution to the whole is assessed. What emerges is an assessment approach that

Table 9.2 Assessment schedule for collaborative film task

Assessment type	Individual role (lighting design director, sound design, etc.)	Completed film
Formative weighting	25	25
Summative weighting	25	25

more closely reflects the responsibilities of each individual but does not diminish the importance of the collaboration.

We have not discussed the other learning that is taking place here, which may be considered non-film learning. This includes team skills, the development of negotiation skills, problem-solving, project management, and so on. We have not separated these competencies out from film learning, as they *are* film learning. Film learning is learning about negotiation, problem-solving, and much more. Like the other arts, very few teachers believe that all of our students will one day enter the profession. We do believe, however, that involvement in collaborative learning such as film learning contributes significantly to developing significant life skills such as negotiation and teamwork. Film learning is the content, while these 'social competencies' are the method. As such, they must be an integral and obvious part of the learning. As we consider the complexities of film learning, it may be worth discussing the place of process and product in that assessment process.

5. Assessment in film learning should avoid dichotomies

The long-running and ultimately futile argument about the place of process and product in learning and assessment in drama education (Anderson, 2004), and to a lesser extent other areas of the arts, has no place in film learning. This discussion is roughly analogous to the questions that permeate educational assessment relating to whether summative or formative assessment is more appropriate.

The evidence of a meta-study of over 250 other studies by Black and William (1998) is that formative assessment does raise student achievement from early childhood to adulthood. Gillies (2007) argues that 'there is strong evidence that that the use of formative assessment or assessment for learning leads to higher quality learning and enhanced learning outcomes'.

This is another ultimately futile dichotomy that has had its day. You will have noticed that through this chapter our examples have been drawn from summative and formative assessment approaches. Our message is that there is importance in process and product, formative and summative, and appreciation and making. While at times one will and must outweigh the other, the tendency toward a balance is likely to be more effective. The distortions that emerge in curriculum and assessment can be seen everywhere when product-based assessment is allowed to override formative assessment of processes. The insidious over-testing of students in the United States, the United Kingdom and Australia demonstrates a system out of balance, where learning has become subservient to sometimes meaningless diagnostics. The challenge for the teacher of film is to cope with the issues that arise in the assessment of process. While assessing product in film learning is no simple matter, there is significant skill required for the teacher attempting to assess the subtleties of a collaborative process and to provide a rigorous and perceptive assessment task that supports learning. For example, if we set our senior students in a collaborative filming team the task of producing a three-minute film adapted from a short story, we need to assess the following in the filmmaking process of a collaborative group:

- How has the 'directorial vision' developed, and what contribution does each student make to the completed film?
- How does each role contribute to the effectiveness of the whole film? For example, how does the lighting designer or the director of photography contribute to the process and the final product of the film?
- How does each student's role demonstrate aesthetic control? For example, how does the sound designer use sound to support and enhance the dramatic meaning of the film?

This is not a checklist; rather, it indicates the processes and product that need to be discussed and engaged with as part of the filmmaker's process. The balance between formative and summative assessment reflects well the demands of film learning, which draws on the process and the product to create a film.

These principles provide the underpinnings of what we argue is a sound and authentic approach to film assessment. In the next section of this chapter, we put some tangible strategies around these principles by suggesting a coherent assessment strategy that can be used to assess film learning in the classroom. Following is a scheme for developing film learning in the classroom. There are two approaches to assessment suggested here. The first is suited to junior high school students and the second supports assessments in the senior years of schooling. The assessments are a mixture of approaches, including:

- a graded collaborative project (all members receive the same mark for the completed film)
- an individual grade based on the student's contribution to the collaborative project
- an individual project with an individual mark.

These examples attempt to balance formative and summative assessment of process and product.

Creating a genre-based trailer—age level twelve to fourteen years

Outcomes
The student:

- uses filmmaking skills to develop a trailer for a genre-based film using existing footage
- understands the conventions of specific genres and styles, and is able to demonstrate them in a trailer
- appreciates the features of each genre, and is able to analyse these features in their own work and the work of others
- values and understands elements of the film aesthetic
- appreciates some of the basic processes of filmmaking
- organises and presents relevant material relating to genre in a coherent and informed manner.

Content
Genre is an important part of understanding the different narrative styles in films. Choose a genre and the associated film from the following list:

- fantasy (*Lord of the Rings*, 2001)
- film noir (*Double Indemnity*, 1944)
- history (*Braveheart*, 1995)
- science fiction (*Star Wars IV: A New Hope*, 1977)

- western (*The Wild Bunch*, 1969)
- romantic comedy (*When Harry Met Sally*, 1989).

Genre discussion

Choose a genre and a film, and look closely at the features of that film. You will need to identify what sets this film apart from other films. Write a short response using examples of films to describe the features of your chosen genre. This is worth 20 per cent of the final mark.

Building a trailer

Using the footage from any of these films, create a trailer for that movie. You should use the features of the genre you have identified to build your own scene in groups. The trailer should last no longer than 60 seconds and should conform to the conventions of a film trailer. Your final product should include:

- a discussion of genre
- a storyboard for your trailer (30 per cent)
- your scene (no longer than 60 seconds) (30 per cent)
- an explanation of how your scene meets the requirements of the genre (no more than 500 words) (20 per cent).

Table 9.3 Assessment task 1

Assessment task	Description	Weighting /100
Genre discussion	Individually identify a genre using examples from film.	20
Storyboard	Each group produces a storyboard of their genre scene.	30
Film: Scene	Develop a short scene in groups.	30
Genre explanation	Individually explain how your scene reflects the genre you have chosen.	20

As students become more confident and experienced with collaborative approaches to learning and making, the teacher can allow more autonomous learning to take place. The shift here is from the teacher as director to students devising and producing their own film. This will not be feasible if they have no experience of the making and appreciation of this art form.

Collaborative film project—age level fifteen to seventeen years

Outcomes

The student:

- uses filmmaking skills to communicate a story
- uses knowledge and experience of film to support the development of their own films
- cooperates in the development of the film project
- reflects on the development of the filmmaking process
- collaborates respectfully with others in the project
- values and understands the film aesthetic
- engages an audience through an understanding of filmmaking
- appreciates the processes of filmmaking
- synthesises, organises and analyses knowledge, experience and opinion in coherent, informed filmed, oral and written responses
- understands the different roles and responsibilities involved in the film-making process
- works effectively in their specific role in the development of the film while supporting the overall directorial vision of the film.

Content

Filmmaking is a cooperative art form. In this collaborative project, students will develop an original short film (seven to ten minutes). All students are expected to negotiate and discuss the project to develop a coherent and effective short film. Each collaborative film project will have a minimum of three and a maximum of five students taking on different roles. Each student will take on one of the following roles in the development of the short film:

- director
- sound designer/sound recordist
- director of photography (DOP)/camera operator
- designer sets/props and costume
- editor
- actor/s.

All groups will be assessed in the process of developing their film on three occasions:

- pre-production
- production
- post-production.

In addition, all groups will submit a completed short film that is seven to ten minutes long, including titles.

The collaborative film project

The project will be an original film that:

- is a complete narrative that creates dramatic meaning and engagement for an audience
- allows each member of the team to contribute to the finished film
- is seven to ten minutes in total.

The collaborative film project will be assessed as shown in Table 9.4.

Table 9.4 Assessment task 2

Assessment task	Description	Weighting /100
Pre-production pitch	The whole group describes in detail the idea for their film and then each individual describes their approach depending on their role.	25
Production portfolio	Each student produces a portfolio describing the process of developing their film, focusing on their specific role.	25
Film: Individual role	Each student is assessed on how their role contributes to the effectiveness of the final cut of the film.	25
Film*	The completed film is assessed.	25

* Each student's individual mark may be moderated against the completed film.

The teacher will facilitate and support the development of each film project as required. At no time will the teacher or any other outsider (non-student) direct, write or edit any group's work.

This approach is a starting point for those who are interested in integrating a collaborative approach to filmmaking but feel unsure about the assessment process. It recognises that filmmaking is an essentially collaborative endeavour, and values process and product in the production of a short film. The balance between process and product reflects the value of formative assessment and recognises that a finished product (the film) is an essential part of learning in filmmaking. It also values the individual roles/skills as they contribute to the process and product of the completed film.

Some may consider the approach to assessment in film learning presented here to be radical. Our approach moves away from a concentration on appreciation for its own sake and integrates it with the making process so students are assessed on the ways their appreciation supports their making. We believe this learning has been implicit in arts education for decades. The approaches here attempt to strike a balance between making and appreciation, and formative and summative assessment. Our approach looks first to the film learning objective and then aligns the assessment to it.

We are not pretending that assessment approaches such as these will be popular with all teachers, and they will need to be tailored and changed depending on each school's context. The intent of this approach is to authentically reflect the processes of filmmaking and adapt those processes to schools. There is significant further work to do in developing assessment processes in this area of learning, but these ideas are offered as a way of enlisting assessment in the service of film learning rather than the other way around. In the next chapter, we consider how the teacher–researcher can extend their understanding of film learning through classroom-based research.

10
Researching screen learning in the classroom

> Together our stories may begin a process of unearthing assumptions that lead to rediscovering truths about ourselves and that lead to making culture, particularly in schools, that is relevant to our lives.
>
> —*Brunner (1994, p. 31)*

When we do research, we are telling a story about our past, reflecting our present and imagining our possible futures. A large part of our imagined future for film education can only come to pass if we establish and maintain a reflective, viable research base. We envisage a future for film education that does not separate practice from research. The future we envisage engages research with classroom practice as praxis. For Paulo Freire (1973), praxis is at the base of our development as a community. He says: 'Liberation is a praxis: the action and reflection of men upon their world in order to transform it ... Men are not built in silence, but in words, in work, in action-reflection' (1973, pp. 75–6). Friere is calling for the development of a research base that is transformative, liberating, action-based and reflective. In film learning, this takes place as educators join together to collaborate on their practice and the learning of their students. Our ambitious aspiration for learning in film and in schools generally is the same as Friere's—that through reflection and action we might transform our schooling structures to make them more effective and engaging for the young people they serve.

There is another reason teachers involve themselves in research. They are curious about what they have seen in their classrooms. In our opinion, curiosity is the essential precondition for research. Curiosity, creativity and research are linked concepts. As Walt Disney said (Disney Institute, 2001, p. 111): 'We keep moving forward, opening up new doors and doing new things ... and curiosity keeps leading us down new paths.' Curiosity motivates our students and spurs us to seek responses to those questions that have arisen for us as educators. Sadly, many educators, due to lack of resources, time, energy or support, feel unable to go any further than curiosity. We must find ways to overcome these challenges to justify film learning's place in a crowded curriculum. In the midst of rapid social and technological change, research provides a way for us to reform our practices at a micro level (in our own classroom) and gives us some evidence and theory to use at a systemic level. Our fervent hope is that this chapter might dispel some of the myths about research and provide strategies that are classroom relevant and rigorous, that satisfy initial practitioner curiosities and create new questions.

Teachers as researchers

You will notice that we have made an assumption that if you are reading this chapter you are interested in researching the screen. We have addressed 'you' throughout the chapter as a beginning, probably classroom-based researcher. Where we have referred to 'the researcher', we are referring to issues for researchers in education more generally. There are many other sites of film learning research. Most of the discussion here will address film learning in classrooms, but much of the discussion will be relevant to learning film in other settings. We have also dotted examples of studies of film learning research throughout the chapter to provide examples of how other people have researched the area. This will hopefully inspire you, the beginning researcher.

This chapter is not the last word on educational research. There are plenty of in-depth texts that will give you more detail than we could hope to provide in one chapter. Our intention in this chapter is to demonstrate that film learning can and should be researched by classroom practitioners. The approaches contained in this chapter will hopefully whet your appetite for greater detail that can be found in several books that are devoted solely to doing research (see Denzin and Lincoln, 2005; Cohen and Manion, 2000; Freebody, 2003; O'Toole, 2006). We suggest strategies for film education researchers who would like to deepen their understanding of screen learning by researching their practice and the learning of their students. The chapter suggests some effective and accessible methodologies for collecting data, discusses ethical issues in this area and suggests some innovative approaches for developing a sustainable culture of reflective practitioner research in this area.

Doing education research

In John O'Toole's (2006) excellent book *Doing Drama Research*, he nominates four motives for doing education research:

- to create knowledge for its own sake
- to create knowledge in context
- to create knowledge for a particular context
- to create knowledge in the social context for social reform.

As you can see, there are strong research questions that emerge from each of these motives for film learning. For example, film learning research can examine how young people read the meaning of editing in modern films (create knowledge for its own sake). Researchers might also be interested in discovering whether providing film learning for disenfranchised young people gives them access to cultural capital (create knowledge in the social context for social reform). The nature of the research is formed through the curiosity of the researcher and their access to resources to support that research. Before we discuss approaches to film learning, we would like to contextualise film learning within arts education research.

Arts education research: The context

For perhaps the first time in the history of arts education, there are international and national calls for a renewed examination of the role and benefits of arts education in the lives of young people (Fiske, 1999). There has been a stream of policy, research and advocacy documents that relate to arts and education such as *Champions of Change* (1999) and *Critical Links* (2003) from the Arts Education Partnership, and the Department of Education, Science and Training's *Evaluation of School-Based Arts Education Programmes in Australian Schools* (2004). Internationally, UNESCO is developing strategies to support arts education. In its 'Road Map: Aims and Reflections' (UNESCO, 2003), it nominates the following aims for the future of arts education:

- recognition of arts education as a concern of education
- consolidation of discussions between the sector of education and culture
- strategies from the governmental organisms to improve the quality of arts education

- designing national and regional policies of research in connection with the specific necessities in the field of arts education
- possibilities to enhance access to arts education (UNESCO, 2006).

These documents, and others like them, outline the areas where significant research might be undertaken. A new generation of arts education scholars is engaged in exploring these exciting questions in diverse settings. The time is ripe for arts researchers to examine our past research heritage and plan for the future in partnership with other educators in schools, hospitals or youth outreach centres throughout our nations and the world. Film learning can be part of that resurgence. Film learning has the inherent advantage of being the 'new kid on the block', with its strong relationships with technology and popular culture. Young people are already engaging with these technologies, and film learning acts as a site to examine the interplay between technology, aesthetics and youth culture.

The research need

The difficulty of working in arts education is that we seem to be forever justifying our existence. We have been arguing for our place in the curriculum through advocating our usefulness and importance to schooling as a whole. If arts education faces difficulties anyway, film learning faces an even more challenging battle for recognition. In other words, if arts education is on the fringe of schooling (O'Toole, 2004), film learning is on the fringe of the fringe. This does present practical problems, but it also provides green fields for researchers where there is so much to do and so little done so far. We are not suggesting that no one has been involved in examining this area. On the contrary, the fields of media studies, drama education, English curriculum and film studies itself have made strong research contributions. There are, however, several unexplored territories in the vast landscape of film learning ready for research attention.

Film learning research is also an exciting field, as it is arguably the art form that is most affected by changes in technology and popular culture. While institutions such as schools and universities may not necessarily be engaging in research in this area, young people are involving themselves with these technologies as a part of their lives (Prensky, 2005; Gee, 2005). The American Arts Education Partnership also senses the possibilities in the intersections between the arts and technology. It argues that: 'New technologies—notably computers, digital sound and visual image recording, and the Internet—are changing both the nature of the arts and the nature of arts education ... From a methodological perspective, this is an exciting area of research. The new technologies themselves provide intriguing ways of capturing student work, student reflections and critical appraisal ...' (Deasy, 2004, p. 19). Their identification of the unique qualities of this medium provides a strong reason for research in film learning. In the remainder of this chapter, we examine the practicalities of doing research in film learning. The first step in any research process is to identify what you want to research. In this sense, you are beginning to define your 'inquiry space', or more specifically your research questions. With so much choice, the challenge is perhaps to locate a logical achievable question that will sustain the research and not overwhelm you and your available resources.

Finding the research question

Often, potential researchers approach research with a nagging curiosity that manifests itself in the form of a question. The question might be something like 'What do students get from film learning?' While on the face of it this sounds a reasonable question, it betrays a lack of research experience. Without doubt, the question is serious, well intentioned and interesting; however, it is difficult to manage as research since the question is too vague and too broad. There are several 100,000-word dissertations in this one little question alone. And it contains myriad sub-questions. While it is necessary to have sub-questions, they should not be of such a multitude that they overwhelm the initial question.

When you are developing a research question, it is worth remembering that the questions you arrive at have involved you in a process of choice. One way to formalise these choices is to set out in a three-column table the different questions you are considering. In the first column, write all the questions you are considering. In the second, write all the sub-questions that emerge from the questions. And in the third, record some of the methodologies and strategies you think might be useful. The final stage of this process is analysing which of your questions is the most 'researchable'—which of the questions can be tackled feasibly by you with the resources you have available.

In research, you choose to open doors to some questions and close the door on others. These closed doors represent other opportunities, other research questions to be pursued later. It is better to put these opportunities on hold rather than bloat your initial question to the point where the research cannot be managed. When you do make these choices, it is important to acknowledge the limitations of your research in the publications that emerge. Acknowledging research limitations indicates to those reviewing or examining your research that you know you have made logical and deliberate choices about the range and the scope of your research.

> ### Box 10.1 Kate Early
>
> Kate Early (Faculty of Education and Social Work, The University of Sydney) was interested in understanding whether using Wenger's (1998b) concept of a community of practice in film learning enhanced student and teacher experiences. In her Masters level study, called 'Video as a Learning Medium: A Case Study of Film Video Learning as a Community of Practice for Secondary Drama Students', she interviewed four students and one teacher. She found that for the teachers and students involved in the film learning, the community of practice model provided an enriching and challenging framework for film learning in an authentic real-world setting.

Refining the research question

To begin with, you need a question that will 'sit in the palm of your hand'—it will be self-contained and self-explanatory. The question should be specific enough so that the way you examine the question seems logical. Instead of asking 'What do students get from film learning?' you might ask 'Do students have improved literacy scores after undertaking film learning?' or 'Do students become more critically literate when they undertake film learning?' or 'Does film learning create social cohesion in the classroom?' Table 10.1 outlines these questions and some of the sub-questions that arise, and suggests some of the research strategies that could be used to explore these areas.

Table 10.1 is not intended to provide in-depth methodological responses to questions. Rather, it makes the point that methodology is often inherent within the question. The question should be specific enough to support a clear, well-defined and deliberate examination of a 'research problem'. As you delve deeper into your inquiry space, the evidence may lead you to change the question in some way. Changing the question is usually part of the research process. The researcher must be allowed to alter the course slightly so long as the

Table 10.1 Organising the research question

Research question	Research sub-questions	Research methodology and strategies
Do students have improved literacy scores after undertaking film learning?	• Does film learning affect students' literacy differently at different ages/stages of schooling? • What kind of literacy does it improve (oracy, reading, writing, etc.)?	• Collect student literacy scores from tests in the targeted class. • Teach an intensive film learning course to these students (intervention). • Test students after the course and compare the results with other students who have not undertaken film learning.
Do students become more critically literate when they undertake film learning?	• Does film learning help students critically analyse other media (advertisements, etc.)? • Does film learning help students critically analyse other art forms (novels. etc.)? • Do the skills of critical literacy transfer into other areas of learning?	• Ask students to analyse a piece of film before learning skills for critical literacy. • Provide students with critical literacy skills that relate to the analysis of the film. • Ask students to analyse a different piece of the same film and record the difference in language used and its application to the analysis process.
Does film learning create social cohesion in the classroom?	• What elements of film learning (if any) create social cohesion? • Does film learning create social cohesion for students from disadvantaged backgrounds? • Does this social cohesion manifest in other areas of schooling?	• Interview students prior to being involved in a film learning project about teamwork and collaboration. • Undertake a filmmaking project with these students. As this project progresses, ask them to keep a journal or a blog that relates to teamwork and team-building. • Interview the students after the project, specifically asking them about their learning about teamwork and collaboration.

integrity of the area is maintained. When you have decided on the question/questions, the next step is to read around the areas in which you are interested with the ultimate aim of constructing a literature review. The literature review will help to refine, and perhaps will even change, your research question.

Managing the written reflection: First steps

As a beginning researcher, your written research reflection (thesis, dissertation, etc.) may only be 10,000 to 20,000 words. This may seem like a great many words, but once the structural parts of the written research reflection (literature review, methodology, conclusions, etc.) are accounted for, there is not much space left for the discussion of a broad topic. A good starting point when you have settled on a question is to find a thesis of the same length (which may or may not be related to your question), and read it. This will give you a feel for the length of the work and what length each of your chapters might be. The next step is to plan out your chapters and allocate a 'word budget' to them. A word budget expresses how long you think each area might be. For instance, you might decide that the literature review is to be 5000 words. The effect of this in a 20 000 word thesis is that you have 15 000 words remaining. It also allows you to keep track of where you have overwritten.

Finding the literature

The literature search/review should outline the supporting evidence for the research question and the gap in the literature that the research question is addressing. If, during the literature search, you discover the specifics of your question have been addressed, you might need to recast the question so that your approach is addressing a gap in the literature. The question must be original in the sense that your specific question has not been asked in this way before. Thankfully, technology has made the construction of the research review pyramid much more sustainable.

Academic web-based search engines technologies such as Google scholar, A+ Education and Endnote have radically changed the process of a literature search. Five years ago, a researcher might have sat isolated in a library poring over journals and edited books for citations that they would then pursue through journals, taking weeks and often months to get what they needed. Today, researchers associated with universities have instantaneous access to research materials that can be brought directly to their desktop and used as part of their literature review. Apart from the obvious saving in time, this approach also allows researchers to see further than their own disciplines and survey the literature from other fields. For instance, in film learning the disciplines of education, aesthetics, performance studies, computer–human interaction, organisational psychology and others may be relevant to a research question. While researchers might know their own field in depth, it is unlikely that they would know these other areas in the same detail. These search technologies provide massive amounts of irrelevant material, but they also uncover valuable areas of research in sometimes quite unrelated areas. For example, drama educators have recently connected with researchers making video games for learning (Carroll, Anderson and Cameron, 2006). In both drama education and video games research, protocols that relate to role and simulation have been the subject of research attention. This has led to some exciting opportunities for researchers in both areas to collaborate and examine real-life questions that are not restricted to disciplinary borders. In the twenty-first century, the convergence of technologies and disciplines will require researchers to skip nimbly between their home discipline and other areas of research. Present and emerging technologies make this possible.

Crafting your literature review

The aim of a literature review is to identify the research and scholarship that are most pertinent to your research question. The best way we have found to explain this approach is to liken it to a set of radiating circles (see Figure 10.1). At the centre of the circle is the research question. As this question addresses a gap in the research literature, there should be nothing that covers exactly the same ground as your question. For instance, your question might be 'Does film learning provide students from inner-city London with creative skills that can assist them to find work when they leave school?' While there will be no specific studies on this, because this is your focus question, there will be studies that relate to students from inner-city areas finding work after school. There will also be studies on the link between schooling and work, and so on. The radiating circles relate to the relevance of the research literature as it addresses your research question. As your literature review continues, you will find literature that supports the basis of your research and other research that might represent the outer circles, which are not as relevant. The research on the outer circles may be useful to file as background but probably will not become a central part of your research question. When you have arrived at a question, you will then need to determine which research methodology will serve the needs of your question.

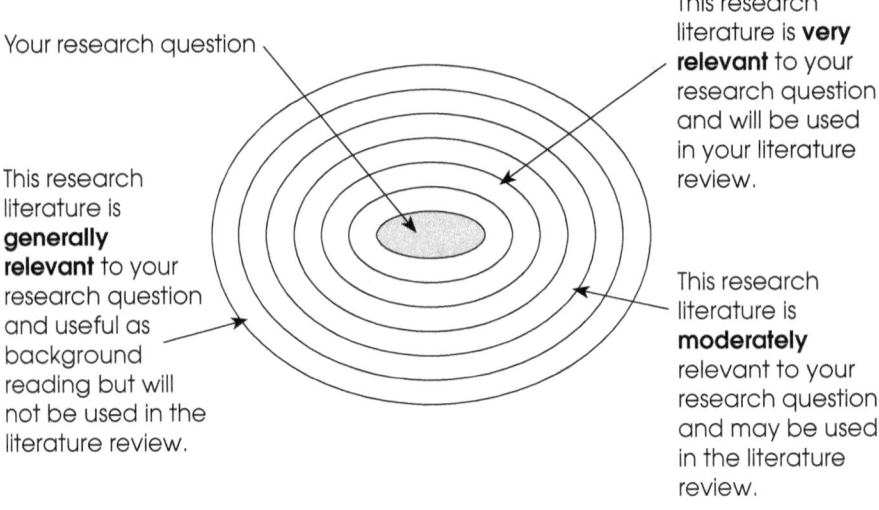

Figure 10.1 The radiating circles of research literature.

Finding methodology: Rejecting the dichotomy

There has been a strong and useful discussion in education about how we should examine research questions. Habitually, the arguments have usually fallen into a dichotomy: the qualitative versus the quantitative. As Carroll (1996, p. 74) argues, we should be mindful that all methodologies are human constructions and therefore have inherent political, historical and gender biases. Having accepted that objectivity is a myth, we can then discuss the more important question: what methodology will suit the needs of the question? In some cases, it will suffice to run a quantitative analysis; in other cases, a more complex design will be necessary. Sometimes both will be required to explore an issue adequately. The approaches discussed here might be implemented over a series of lessons as a short-term or cross-sectional study that allows researchers to examine many cases over a short period of time. Other research projects may take a number of years in a longitudinal study. Longitudinal studies examine 'features of people or other units at more than one time' (Newman, 2006). The longitudinal design is relevant to film learning as it allows examination of the possibility and significance of change (or no change) over time. Time allows consequences to take place. The length of the study usually corresponds with the nature of the question, the available resources and the space available to report the outcomes of the question. Some of the approaches discussed below are useful strategies in researching film learning.

Quantitative research: Findings with 'hard edges'

In film learning, quantitative methodology does have its place. It can give an overall summary of simple information such as 'How many students undertake film learning?' or 'Does film learning improve literacy scores?' When delving into the complexities of the learning experience, qualitative methodology is a natural choice. As Elliot Eisner (1978, p. 201) points out, in exploring the complexities of educational research there is little to be gained in reducing the 'human mind to a single score'. Conversely, the qualitative method attempts to 'adumbrate its complexities, its potential, and its idiosyncrasies' (1978, p. 201).

Within the double-speak that sometimes passes for discussion in bureaucracies, there is often a call for findings with 'hard edges'. What we think this means is findings that can show significance in a statistical way—for instance, 'X% of students achieve higher numeracy scores as a result of film learning.' There is, of course, an inbuilt discrimination in a call for 'hard-edged data', as it presupposes that anything important can be demonstrated in a quantitative way. Most educators agree that the complexity of classroom learning is difficult to reflect with quantitative methodologies. The collaboration and interactions of film learning make this interaction potentially more complex. Our praxis is so based in experience, intuition and human interactions that much of our research depends on understanding and interpreting the lived classroom experiences of students and teachers.

This kind of research does not always come with hard edges. We should continue to qualitatively examine and report the depth of what goes on in learning, and particularly film learning, by searching for new methodologies that represent the complexity of learning film. Whichever methodologies we choose to use, we must be aware of the audience we are attempting to persuade. If our aim is to advocate our case to policy-makers, perhaps we will need to speak the language of statistics to make our point. If we are striving to describe the complexities inherent in film learning, we could continue using existing and new methodologies where they suit our research question and are able to describe the multidimensional nature of film learning. Many questions that teachers are exploring in the classroom are too complex to be examined through quantitative methods alone.

Mixed-methods approaches

Mixed-methods approaches can examine a large set of questions in the middle ground between qualitative and quantitative methods (Johnson and Onwuegbuzie, 2004, p. 15). Johnson and Onwuegbuzie argue that mixed-method research occurs 'where the researcher mixes or combines quantitative and qualitative research techniques, methods, approaches, concepts or language into a single study. Philosophically, it is the "third wave" or third research movement, a movement that moves past the paradigm wars by offering a logical and practical alternative' (2004, p. 17). For example, this approach could allow a researcher to use a survey to examine why certain demographic groups do not engage with film learning. The results of this survey may lead to some interesting correlations that suggest further analysis. In the analysis of these survey results, you might undertake a cluster analysis that groups variables. Maybe your variables are student access to technology, student literacy scores and engagement in film learning. Perhaps for the sake of this example, the survey found a group of students with low literacy scores and high access to technology did not engage with film learning. This is a potentially very interesting finding. The problem, however, is that the quantitative analysis tells us that the correlation exists but does not tell us why. To examine why, the researcher would need to use a qualitative approach such as interview or case study of those within this group. This approach has the potential to provide the quantitative measurement that policy-makers crave and the qualitative responses that many educators require to explain the complexity of learning in the classroom. Johnson and Onwuegbuzie (2004) argue that this method has the potential to unify elements of educational research and examine research questions that cannot be examined by qualitative or quantitative research alone: 'By narrowing the divide between quantitative and qualitative researchers, mixed methods research has a great potential to promote a shared responsibility in the quest for attaining accountability for educational quality' (2004, p. 24). There are, however, some questions that are suited to qualitative methods alone. We will spend the remainder of the chapter discussing qualitative methods, as we believe they have the most relevance to those researching film learning in the classroom.

Qualitative research

Qualitative research has had a 'distinguished place in the human disciplines' since the 1920s and 1930s (Denzin and Lincoln, 1994, p. 1). The growth and development of qualitative research paralleled the need for a more powerful and naturalistic research method than positivism (Eisner, 1978, p. 202). Bruner (1990, p. 130) says that 'neither the empiricist's tested knowledge nor the rationalist's self-evident truths describe the ground on which ordinary people go about making sense of their experiences'. Qualitative research allows researchers to delve into the complexity and layers of lived human experience. Research into film learning requires methodology that allows for the complexity and idiosyncrasies that are inherent in a process of group creativity. The depth of analysis possible in qualitative research is not available in more reductionist methodologies. As Grady (1996) argues, to deal with the complexity of human experience, research should be undertaken from an informed position, which allows the researcher to 'choose challenging rhetorical and methodological tools that allow us to focus on the complexities of the practice of theory in practice' (Grady, 1996, p. 70).

Eisner (1978) defines qualitative methodology as 'that form of inquiry that seeks the creation of qualities that are expressively patterned, that seeks the explication of wholes as the primary aim, that emphasises the study of configurations rather than isolated entities, that regards expressive narratives and visuals as appropriate vehicles for communication' (1978, p. 198). This definition identifies several key elements of film learning. His identification of the 'creation of qualities that are expressively patterned' (1978, p. 198) reflects the importance of identifying the quality of the learning experience through its features. Even though film learning is context specific, the research findings from one place will have resonances for other teachers in other settings. This approach seeks to analyse each specific context to create broader understanding of the film learning experience of teachers and students. Denzin and Lincoln (2005, p. 3) also argue this kind of research has power to transform because it has immediate relevance to its community—in our case, the film learning classroom. They argue that qualitative research is 'a situated activity that locates the observer in the world … qualitative research involves an interpretive, naturalistic approach to the world. This means that qualitative researchers study things in their natural settings, attempting to make sense of, or to interpret, phenomena in terms of the meanings people bring to them'. Qualitative approaches fit well with research that seeks to transform learning rather than just depict or reflect current practice.

> **Box 10.2 Isabelle Kim**
>
> Toronto (Canada)-based Isabelle Kim is a recent PhD graduate from the Ontario Institute for Studies in Education at the University of Toronto (OISE/UT). Her dissertation, Youth Videomaking Projects: A Spoken Word Study (2007), reported on work done in publicly funded, community-based youth video-making projects (YVPs), the conditions and spaces in which it occurs, and what it means to the young people and others involved with YVPs. Isabelle is a former YVP coordinator and emerging video-maker. She conducted and recorded (video and audio) nineteen in-depth individual interviews with past and present youth participants, organisers and funders involved with YVPs over the last twelve months in Ontario. The video-making process enables youth to make critical statements about issues they care about, tell their stories, and comment on their world. YVP work can potentially reframe the way dominant discourses about young people have been produced as 'passive'/'active'; 'at risk'/'a risk'; media-'savvy'/'vulnerable'; cultural-'producers'/'consumers'. This doctoral research advocates for YVPs while bringing into sharp focus critical questions about these projects, including the ethical implications of using video to show and tell 'youth stories'—and recorded interview data. Isabelle's study contributes to the growing body of work on digital storytelling and multimodality by theorising the semiotic work and radical potential of YVPs. She also examines the pedagogical implications of media education implicit within YVP work for schools. This 'spoken word' study makes a methodological contribution through its use of new media to both present and analyse qualitative research data.

Creating a research *bricolage*

The research task is made less onerous by the inherent flexibility of many qualitative methodologies. Denzin and Lincoln (1994) call the qualitative researcher a *Bricoleur*, or one who produces a *bricolage*—that is, a pieced-together, close-knit set of practices that provide solutions to a problem in a concrete situation (1994, p. 2). As the *Bricoleur* analogy suggests, qualitative methodology is 'multi method in focus' (Denzin and Lincoln, 1994, p. 2). When you have decided on your chosen question, you can then begin to construct a *bricolage* of approaches that will help you collect the data to examine it. Some of these strategies/methods/approaches may be of assistance to you when you are designing your research project in film learning.

Developing case studies

A case study is defined as 'the study of the particularity of and complexity of a single case, coming to understand its activity within important circumstances.' (Stake, 1995, p. xi). The case study of the teachers' experience of teaching filmmaking and film literacy is a rich, deep and complex picture to analyse, and although generalisations are unable to be made as a result of that analysis, it is an insight into a process at a 'close-up' (to use a film metaphor) context of the teacher in the classroom and the 'mid-shot' context of teacher and their school, that may illuminate the 'long-shot' concerns of film teaching in the context of the curriculum:

> They [the research participants] may be similar or dissimilar, redundancy and variety each having voice. They are chosen because it is believed that understanding them will lead to a better understanding, perhaps better theorizing, about a still larger set of cases (Stake, 2000, p. 437).

Participants in film research are specific and unique 'cases' who have their own constructed realities. Having several 'cases' affords this study the opportunity of making comparisons and contrasts that may lead to a better understanding of the wider world of film learning, and learning more generally. The information drawn for comment from these cases will obviously reflect the research question—or, as Stake (1994) argues: 'My choice would be to take from the case from which we feel we can learn the most' (1994, p. 243). Consequently, when material is chosen from the interview transcripts and developed into narratives, it should be selected because it is most appropriate to the themes and sub-themes of the research.

Interviews

Interviews provide a way to discover the participants' attitudes, recollections and understandings about a certain research topic in some depth. The aim of the interviews is to engage in a conversation that creates mutually constructed meaning. The most useful research interview in our view is the semi-structured interview. In the semi-structured interview, the participant and the researcher both have input into the process. This type of interview is more honest, morally sound and reliable, as it treats the respondent as an equal, allows them to express personal feelings and therefore presents a more 'realistic' picture than can be uncovered using traditional methods. As Fontana and Frey (1994) argue: 'Forgetting the rules [of traditional interviewing] ... allows research subjects to express themselves more freely, and thus to have greater voice both in research process and in the research report' (1994, p. 368).

Often, these types of interviews begin with a discussion about the process that encourages the participants to negotiate the interview as it progresses. The participants have the right not to answer the questions, to ask questions of the researcher and to add their own observations of the process. At any stage, they can terminate the interview. Video can be used to record the interview that captures the non-verbal features of the discussion (Fontana and Frey, 1994, p. 371) that may be important in the data-analysis process.

There are still problems with this more informal style of interviewing, however. This approach supports the idea of a discussion, although the interviewer's first task is to listen. As Ely (1991, p. 67) comments: 'LISTEN, LISTEN and LISTEN MORE.' Even though there is a collaborative element, the first priority is to listen to the story. To do otherwise is to reinstate the hierarchy of the researcher espousing wisdom and the 'researched' responding. Researchers have to resist the temptation to add their own commentary on the situation they are researching. The conversational style of this interaction facilitates this kind of response. The research methodology, however, is attempting to reflect the participant's experiences and not the interventions of the researcher.

Participatory action research

Participatory action research comes closest to the ideal of praxis: practice and action as research. Participatory action research 'typically involves the use of qualitative interpretative modes of inquiry and data collection by teachers (often with the help of academics) with a view to teachers making judgements about how to improve their own practice ... The emphasis is "practical", that is on the interpretations that teachers and students are making and acting on in the situation' (Kemmis and McTaggart, 2005, p. 561). The focus for participatory action researchers is on improving the situation in which they work, be it a classroom, a hospital or a business. There has been some criticism that this method, founded on the progressivism of the 1970s and 1980s, has fallen short of its ambitious aims of changing the world. In response to this criticism,

Kemmis argues that participatory action researchers 'may not have changed the world but they have changed their worlds' (Kemmis and McTaggart, 2005, p. 600). This research method is suited to film classrooms, as it allows those engaged in film learning to change their worlds in the absence of organised systemic support, and to enrich their own practice by researching it.

In participatory action research, teachers devise a research question that relates directly to their practice, such as 'How can I teach storyboard production to a group of Year 9 students using the principles inherent in productive pedagogies?' The teacher would then (perhaps with the assistance of another researcher) design an intervention (a group of lessons on storyboarding) and then put it into action (teach the lessons). As the lessons take place, data are collected—perhaps through interviews, participant logbooks or observation—to reflect what is going on in the intervention. The concluding reflection provides an in-depth examination of the learning process that may then be linked to advances in theoretical discussions that relate to learning.

Ethical considerations

No discussion of research can or should omit the ethical challenges that face researchers. In education, we are faced with some especially challenging ethical dilemmas, as our research participants are often young children. If we are serious about researching our own classroom practice, we must accept that there are some ethical questions to be reconciled and resolved during research. If you are undertaking research within a school that involves students or teachers, you will need to obtain ethical clearances. This has a twin purpose. It lets your system (university, school, etc.) know what you are doing, and it covers you ethically. While there are whole books devoted to the ethics of research in education, this section deals with those issues that we think are most pertinent to film learning: anonymity and confidentiality, transparency and deception.

Anonymity and confidentiality

Researchers take different views about anonymity in educational research. Punch (1994) argues that 'there is strong feeling among most fieldworkers that settings and respondents should not be identifiable in print and that they should not suffer harm or embarrassment as a consequence of research' (1994, p. 93). Other researchers, such as Shulman (1990, p. 11), take a very different view. They claim that participants' voices should be recognised. However, Shulman also points to the consequences and implications of revealing participant identities that may single them out for ridicule and oppression. Her study into the attitudes of teachers in classrooms left her participants potentially vulnerable, as 'teachers rarely leave the scene [of the research]. They must bear the burden of their written words, for they remain participants long after they complete their roles' (1990, p. 14).

Anonymity often empowers research participants to speak out about their teachers, colleagues or supervisors in ways that would be impossible if they were identified publicly (Shulman, 1990, p. 11). Pseudonyms are useful for the research participants, participants' schools and any other person who could be used to identify the research participants. Broad geographical areas can be used to identify and contextualise the location of the research participants. Our advice is to take the safe course and make your participants anonymous. Your participants may decide that they would like to associate themselves with the research, but that should be left up to them.

Transparency: Informed consent and deception

In research that seeks to include participants as partners in the research, informed consent is crucial. It provides a transparency for the motives of the research that cannot be assured if there is deception in the research process. For instance, if you are exploring whether film learning promotes participation in democratic processes, the following description would appear in your participant information sheet:

> This study will explore whether film learning encourages participation in democratic processes. In this study we will interview you about your participation in politics and your engagement with democratic processes such as voting. At no time during this process will you be asked to reveal your political views.

This clearly, and in plain English, outlines the intent of the study and the expectations of the participants. It also lets the research participants know what they will not be asked to reveal. We cannot think of a reason that participants in film learning research (or any kind of educational research) should be deceived. This approach keeps faith with those with whom we are working and addresses the inherent imbalance between the researcher and the researched. As many of the qualitative approaches we suggest here are not generalisable, we need to search for alternative approaches to validity, reliability and credibility.

Seeking validity and credibility

Validity reflects the extent to which your research is 'sound, cogent, well grounded, justifiable or logically correct' (Schwandt, 2001). If research is credible, it should be trustworthy (Schwandt, 2001) in that it truly reflects the authentic voice of the participants and resonates with others who will be engaged by the research. Many qualitative methodologies seek to remove the traditional researcher and researched status. This partnership can be maintained by ensuring the research participants feel that the research undertaken with them reflects what they feel they wanted to communicate as part of the research. Giving research participants an opportunity to respond to their contribution ensures the reliability and the credibility of the research. Research participants may ask for changes to the research and, even though the researcher may disagree with these sentiments, they have the right to be represented in ways they feel are valid. Naturally this requires negotiation on the part of the researcher and the participants, but the voice and wishes of the participants are central to the validity of the research. The credibility of the research lies in the authenticity and clarity of the research participants' voices and their transferability, creating knowledge that leads to a deeper understanding of the research question. There are some useful measures of credibility here, but in our experience one of the most useful is crystallisation.

Crystallisation

Crystallisation and triangulation, along with the authenticity of the research participants' voice, are important parts of the developing reliability of qualitative research. Triangulation is the use of a variety of data sources in a study (Janesick, 1994, p. 214). It is a useful term, but it does suggest limitations. We prefer the crystallisation method as it has greater scope to validate the data. Laurel Richardson (1994) says the 'central image for "validity" for postmodernist texts is not the triangle—a rigid, fixed, two-dimensional object. Rather, the central image is the crystal, which combines symmetry and substance with an infinite variety of shapes, substances, transmutations, multidimensionalities, and angles of approach. Crystals grow, change, alter but are not amorphous' (1994, p. 522).

Crystallisation seems more able to describe several approaches to validating the research data. The process also reflects the possibility of several reflections from the same source—in other words, several interpretations from the one interview, narrative or case study. The researcher's interpretations may be only one of the many interpretations possible. For instance, if your study examined teachers' experience of the classroom through narratives, you might use several methods of validation for the narratives. First, the teachers in the study could validate the narratives (one facet of the crystal). The teachers might then be asked to read the narratives and respond by indicating whether the narratives reflected their experience. At any point, they could negotiate changes and make additions to the narratives. This validation allows the authentic voices of participants to emerge and ensures the researcher's style or voice does not overwhelm their voices. Another facet of this crystallisation process might be to bring in other researchers to analyse interviews, narratives and case studies, and to suggest other interpretations of the data.

Film learning: Imagining the future

There is an imminent need for those who teach film to justify its place in the crowded curriculum. We know that young people watch and interact with images on the screen more than other activities. We know that there is amazing potential in the intersection of film, education, popular culture and learning. We know that when young people are exposed to the aesthetic principles of making and appreciating film they are engaged and often enthralled by the learning. But there's the rub: it is not enough for 'us' to know, we must develop a strong and sustainable research base from what we know to convince others (policy-makers, school principals, parents and politicians) of the abundant qualities of film learning, not to mention the potential of learning in this area. If we are to make these arguments convincing as film educators and as arts educators, we must build research that speaks of the quantity and quality of our practice. We must use the richness that exists in our classrooms to develop a research base so the potential of the future we imagine may come to fruition for the good of the young people we serve, the community they are now and what they will become.

Appendix: Sample—Scaffolded film learning modules

MODULE 1	FILM LANGUAGE: Form and function, and dramatic action as fundamentals
Learning focus	Students are introduced to the film language of framing, composition and montage, and the fundamental principle that the aesthetic form is related to the function of identification and tension for the viewer. The first module begins with the predominant form of the visual image, and students will attempt to control and create meaning in film only through the visual aesthetic. Dramatic action, intent and belief are introduced as fundamental elements of narrative construction and role.
Making	Students collaborate in small groups of around four members, to create a 30- to 45-second scene without dialogue, sound or music that focuses on and explores how the visual language of framing, composition and montage serves to communicate the purpose of one dramatic action to engage an audience.
Appreciation	Students watch featured extracts from films and will focus on shot choices, composition and conventions. They will also be introduced to fundamental ideas in editing. They will describe the film language used and analyse why it was used and to what effect.

MODULE 2	CHARACTERS IN A LANDSCAPE: Space, cause/effect and dialogue
Prior learning	Students have been introduced to the film language of framing, composition and montage as fundamental principles and have attempted to control and create meaning in film through the visual aesthetic, dramatic intent and belief in role.

Learning focus	A character's action and the landscape or space they inhabit is explored as a means to explore the dramatic purpose and control of the visual aesthetic. Students develop an understanding of how meaning is made from a character's relationship with their surrounding landscape, through the choice of location, the framing and composition of the character in the landscape, the editing of time and space, and the creation of dramatic action and moments for the character. The elements of fabula and syuzhet, cause and effect, tension and expectation are introduced as the principal foundations of narrative construction and the creation of dramatic action and minimal dialogue.
Appreciation	Students will hypothetically problem-solve how a certain character and relationship with the landscape or space can be created through location, shots, composition, time of day, weather, light, dramatic action, editing, sound and music. The hypothetical scenes described are compared with scenes from actual films that capture the same relationship between characters and a landscape or space. Students view a brief film extract that shows a character or characters moving from one landscape to another landscape, and analyse in detail how and why the filmmaker has made certain choices.
Making	Students collaborate in groups to create a 30-second to one-minute scene that focuses on how two characters, a landscape or space, the cause and effect, and heightening of dramatic action come together to create a scene. Music cannot be used, and sound, props and dialogue must be minimal.

MODULE 3	THE ELEMENTS OF *MISE EN SCÈNE*: Focus and tension in the image and the story
Prior learning	Students have been introduced to aspects of *mise en scène* with the film language of framing and composition, and using location, space, time and character placement for dramatic meaning.
Learning focus	The elements of *mise en scène* are introduced: the degree and quality of artifice, framing, the organisation of space in the frame, composition, lighting, character placement and the design of set, location, costume and décor. How these elements control the focus and tension in the image, and contribute to narrative construction, is examined.

Appreciation	Beginning scenes from an eclectic range of films are critically examined to demonstrate specific features in the design of *mise en scène*. Students problem-solve how the elements of *mise en scène* in filmmaking focus dramatic meaning for the audience and contribute to the elements of narrative.
Making	The making task in the next module integrates learning from this module.

MODULE 4	FRAMING the ACTION: The paradigms of a genre, *mise en scène*, montage and music
Prior learning	Students have an understanding of film language and recognise the elements of *mise en scène* and how they contribute to dramatic action and the elements of narrative.
Learning focus	The long take emphasises sustained control of 'composing' or 'staging' dramatic action in the camera frame as an example of manipulating the *mise en scène* without editing. The use of less montage demonstrates how editing can be deemed unnecessary or necessary in contributing to the meaning of the dramatic action. Long takes inform how interest and tension can be sustained and focused through well-staged dramatic action. *Mise en scène* is also related to the concept of genre and recognition through conventions and paradigms or signifiers. The visual and musical signifiers of a scene from a particular genre, such as the high noon shoot-out from a spaghetti Western, are explored.
Appreciation	Students describe what they think are the paradigms of the Western shoot-out. By then viewing small film examples, students examine the similarities and differences that have fulfilled or subverted their expectations. This introduces the ideas of codes, conventions and tropes, and their effect on narrative expectations.
Making	A one-minute shoot-out is filmed as an effectively engaging long take by manipulating the paradigmatic elements and expectations of the Western *mise en scène* and use of music conventions. For example, the Western could be become a football penalty shoot out. The *mise en scène*'s dramatic action and staging, and costumes, must be carefully and artfully controlled. The same scene is filmed again with montage. The differences in rhythm, pace and dramatic focus are examined by comparing the two films of the same scene.

MODULE 5	ACTION, SOUND AND MUSIC: Tension in action and between characters
Prior learning	Students have developed their manipulation of film language and *mise en scène*, without a focus on sound effects.
Learning focus	Sound in film creates sound images that are constructed with the same attention to dramatic intent and detail as visual imagery. Students explore and explain the ways in which sound affects the illusion of a filmic reality, and evokes an atmosphere and effect. The dynamic of cause and effect driving the tension of dramatic and physical action is explored in the choreography of movement in a fight sequence. Music as rhythm is explored to enhance the tension, as well as the relationships between characters in the action scene.
Appreciation	Examples from a range of films will demonstrate the manipulation and intent of sound. Listening to the sound without images requires students to describe the effect of sound images. Viewing the visual images without sound focuses students' awareness on sound's contribution to a filmic reality. Attention is given to how character relationships and tension generated and manipulated in action sequences contribute to narrative.
Making	A one-minute scene without dialogue involving a choreographed fight sequence allows students to create a scene focused on action and reaction (cause and effect) and the building of dramatic dynamics and tension, as well as using post-production sound effects and rhythmic music to heighten the illusion of the fight sequence's physical actions. The relationship between characters has to contribute to the tension of the scene.

MODULE 6	BELIEF IN DRAMATIC ACTION: Acting and writing for film
Prior learning	Students have performed character roles, dramatic action and intent in their filmmaking tasks, but no strong emphasis has been given to acting or writing for film.
Learning focus	Acting for film requires an awareness of and ability to create and communicate complete truth and belief in a situation, and to always play an action that may only be a thought. Acting technique unifies the capability to create the reality of the world of the imagination with the actuality of the filming requirements, such as continuity, timing and positioning.

	Film writing describes the visual and aural information communicated to an audience. It is expressive, clear and precise, and shows rather than tells. Dialogue must drive the dramatic action forward and allow the audience to know what they essentially need to know and be believable as a character's voice.
Making	Students undertake and evaluate belief and the playing of actions through improvisation acting exercises. Some exercises are filmed for class discussion about the acting of internalised truth, conviction and belief on the screen.
	In groups, a short scene of action and minimal dialogue between two characters is created from a brief improvisation exercise. The group transforms the scene into a 30-second to one-minute screenplay that is then filmed by another group of students. The screenplay's intentions and the interpretation of the screenplay are discussed.
Appreciating	Peer and teacher discussion of acting in and writing from the improvisation exercises highlights an appreciation and evaluation of these filmic techniques.

MODULE 7	EXPECTATIONS: Narrative and genre
Prior learning	Students have been introduced to the paradigms and iconography of the Western genre and understand how dramatic action, *mise en scène* and montage can be controlled for meaning.
Learning focus	Genre classification is a way to describe audience expectations and engagement with films. Examples of genres such as the crime thriller, spoof, fantasy, romantic comedy and horror are examined in terms of a film's dramatic intent, subject-matter, style, narrative and structure.
Appreciating	Trailers often use codes and signifiers of genre classification as shorthand to arouse audience interest in and anticipation of a film. Students problem-solve what signifiers in trailers of different film types affect audience expectations.
Making	In groups, students decide on a genre type and create a one-minute trailer or preview to arouse audience expectations through aspects of style, narrative, subject-matter and dramatic purpose through control of the dramatic action, *mise en scène* and montage.

Notes

Chapter 1

1. This is an adapted version of criteria used by the NSW Board of Studies for the Higher School Certificate Drama examination. The original can be found at www.boardofstudies.nsw.edu.au/syllabus_hsc/syllabus2000_listd.html#dance.

Chapter 4

1. Tzvetan Todorov is a structuralist theorist who explains that narrative begins with a state of stable equilibrium that is disrupted by forces of some kind to become disequilibrium. The action of the narrative is to attempt to return to the initial equilibrium.

Chapter 5

1. Simon is a pseudonym, as are all the names of the students mentioned in Chapters 5, 6 and 7. All the quotes relating to the project are taken from a teaching evaluation undertaken as part of the project.

Chapter 6

1. Bertolt Brecht (1898–1956) was a German director and playwright known for his theories in epic theatre, didactic drama and collaborative methods in making theatre.

2. Lars Von Trier and a group of Danish filmmakers committed themselves to the Dogme 95 charter, which is a strict set of rules they chose to apply to their films. These limitations were, for instance, using only a hand-held camera, using nothing artificial in a set, no manipulation of time and place, and using only direct sound.

Chapter 7

1. Brazilian theatre practitioner Augusto Boal used the term 'metaxis' to describe the 'state of belonging completely and simultaneously to two different autonomous worlds' (1995, p. 43).
2. Konstantin Stanislavsky (1863–1938) was a renowned Russian theatre director who developed a systematic approach to actor training. For the actor to be in a 'creative state', he or she focused on the internal and external life of a character, finding specific motivations for every moment and action as a lived truth. The 'magic if' refers to the actor's mental process of being in the 'given circumstances' of the character they are playing.
3. The Russian formalists use 'syuzhet' and 'fabula' to explain narrative construction. The syuzhet is the plot and the events explicitly presented. In a film story, what is presented visually and audibly to an audience is the syuzhet.
4. The fabula is the story of all the events of a narrative that are inferred and explicitly presented.
5. Tzvetan Todorov is a Franco-Bulgarian structuralist who argues that narrative is a transformation through five stages: equilibrium–disequilibrium–recognition–repair–reinstatement of equilibrium.
6. Stanislavsky's approach to acting is essentially based on psychological realism. See note 2 above.

Chapter 8

1. For more information on the work of James Durran at Parkside Community College, please visit www.parksidemedia.net.

Chapter 9

1. In drama education, there are many examples of matriculation examinations that assess students in groups, measuring their individual and group

performance. The New South Wales Higher School Certificate is one such example, and details of this process can be explored in further depth in Anderson (2004).
2. We are referring here to the traditional large-scale pen and paper, often multiple-choice, tests that often control student matriculation. We are not arguing that we should abolish these tests, but rather that they do not always align effectively with learning in arts education.

Chapter 10

1. A cluster analysis is a way of grouping variables that are similar. It allows, for instance, a researcher using a survey to identify unusual relationships between survey items. So in a survey on why film learning is not taking place in certain schools you might be interested in those that have a high interest in film learning on one survey question but reveal in another that they are not teaching the area. When you identify this cluster of schools you can then single them out for further qualitative analysis.

Filmography

A Better Tomorrow (1986)
A Very Long Engagement (2004)
All About My Mother (1999)
Amelie (2001)
American Beauty (1999)
Babel (2006)
Blue Velvet (1986)
Braveheart (1995)
Citizen Kane (1941)
Death's Marathon (1913)
Delicatessen (1991)
Double Indemnity (1944)
Edward Scissorhands (1990)
Eraserhead (1978)
Face/Off (1997)
Fireworks (1997)
400 Blows (1959)
Gladiator (2000)
Gosford Park (2001)
Harry Potter and the Philosopher's Stone (2001)
Hidden (2005)
In the Mood for Love (2000)
Intolerance (1916)
JFK (1991)
Lancelot of the Lake (1974)
Lawrence of Arabia (1962)
Lord of the Rings (2001)
Lord of the Rings trilogy (2001–03)
Lord of the Rings: Return of the King (2003)
Macbeth (1971)
Mad Max (1979)
Memento (2000)
Mission Impossible II (2000)
Moulin Rouge (2001)
Mulholland Drive (2001)
Natural Born Killers (1994)
Ocean's Eleven (2001)
Persona (1966)
Pickpocket (1959)
Platoon (1986)
Pride and Prejudice (1995)
Psycho (1960)
Rabbit-Proof Fence (2002)
Raiders of the Lost Ark (1981)
Rear Window (1954)
Run Lola Run (1998)
Russian Ark (2002)
Sleepy Hollow (1999)

Smiles of a Summer Night (1955)
Star Wars IV: A New Hope (1977)
Strike (1924)
Sunset Boulevard (1950)
Sweeney Todd (2007)
The Battleship Potemkin (1925)
The Blues Brothers (1980)
The Fugitive (1963)
The Godfather (1972)
The Man Escaped (1956)
The Matrix (1999)
The Queen (2006)
The Seven Samurai (1954)
The Seventh Seal (1957)
The Third Man (1949)
The Untouchables (1987)
The Wild Bunch (1969)
Thelma and Louise (1991)
Three Colours Blue (1993)
Time of the Gypsies (1989)
Un Chien Andalou (1929)
Underground (1995)
Volver (2006)
When Father Was Away on Business (1985)
When Harry Met Sally (1989)
Witness (1985)
Women on the Verge of a Nervous Breakdown (1988)
Zatoichi (2003)

Bibliography

Abbs, P. (2003). *Against the Flow: Education, the arts and postmodern culture.* London: Routledge Falmer

Almodovar, P. (2002). 'Dream Weavers'. In L. Tirard (ed.), *Moviemaker's Masterclass: Private lessons from the world's foremost directors.* New York and London: Faber & Faber

Altman, R. (1996). 'Cinema and Genre'. In G. Nowell-Smith (ed.), *The Oxford History of World Cinema.* Oxford: Oxford University Press

Anderson, M. (2002). Journeys in Teacher Professional Development. Unpublished doctoral thesis, University of Sydney

—— (2004). 'Devising Unities: A recent history of drama education in NSW'. In *The State of Our Art: NSW perspectives in drama education.* Sydney: Currency Press

Applebee, A. (1977). 'ERIC/RCS Report: The elements of response to a literary work—what we have learned'. *Research in the Teaching of English,* 11(3), 255–72

Arnold, R. (2005). *Empathic Intelligence: Teaching, learning, relating.* Sydney: UNSW Press

Australia Council for Educational Research (ACER) (2004). *Evaluation of School-based Arts Education Programmes in Australian Schools.* Canberra: ACER

Balázs, B. (1970 [1952]). *Theory of the Film: Character and growth of a new art.* Trans. from the Hungarian by Edith Bone. New York: Dover

Barthes, R. (1977). *Image, Music, Text.* Trans. Stephen Heath. London: Fontana

Benjamin, W. (1935). 'The Work of Art in the Age of Mechanical Reproduction'. In L. Braudy and M. Cohen (eds) (2004), *Film Theory and Criticism,* 6th ed. New York: Oxford University Press

Bennett, A. and Royle, N. (2004). *An Introduction to Literature, Criticism and Theory.* Hallow, UK: Pearson Longman

Bergman, I. (1988). *The Magic Lantern: An autobiography by Ingmar Bergman.* Trans. J. Tate. London: Penguin

Bertolucci, B. (2002). 'Revisionists'. In L. Tirard (ed.), *Moviemaker's Masterclass: Private lessons from the world's foremost directors.* New York: Faber & Faber

BFI Education (2003). *Look Again: A teaching guide to using film and television with three to eleven year olds.* BFI Education. Available online at www.bfi.org.uk/education/resources/teaching/primary/lookagain

Black, P. and William, D. (1998). 'Assessment and Classroom Learning'. *Assessment in Education,* 5(1), 7–74

—— (2004). 'Classroom Assessment is Not (Necessarily) Formative Assessment (and Vice-Versa)'. In M. Wilson (ed.), *Towards Coherence Between Classroom Assessment and Accountability: 103rd Yearbook of the National Society for the Study of Education.* Chicago: University of Chicago Press, 183–8

Board of Studies (NSW) (1998a). *English K–6 Support Document.* Sydney: New South Wales Board of Studies

—— (1998b). *Drama Evaluation Report.* Sydney: New South Wales Board of Studies

—— (1999a). *Stage 6 Drama Syllabus.* Sydney: New South Wales Board of Studies

—— (1999b). *Stage 6 English Syllabus.* Sydney: New South Wales Board of Studies

—— (2000a). *Stage 6 Syllabus.* Retrieved 20 December 2001 from New South Wales Board of Studies website. Available www.boardofstudies.nsw.edu.au/syllabus_hsc/syllabus2000_liste.html

—— (2000b) *Course Statistics.* Retrieved 20 December 2001 from New South Wales Board of Studies website. Available at www.boardofstudies.nsw.edu.au/docs_stats/hsc00_statistics.pdf

Bolton, G. (1984). *Drama as Education: An argument for placing drama at the centre of the curriculum.* Harlow, Essex: Longman

Bordwell, D. (1986). *Narration in the Fiction Film.* London: Routledge

Bordwell, D. and Thompson, K. (2004). *Film Art: An introduction.* Boston: McGraw-Hill

Branigan, E. (1992). *Narrative Comprehension and Film.* London: Routledge

Bresson, R. (1977) *Notes on Cinematography.* Trans. J. Griffin. New York: Urizen

Brindley, S. (2005). 'Are You Sun Literate? Literacy, ICT and education policy in the UK: Literacy—who defines?' In M. Montieth (ed.), *Teaching Secondary School Literacies with ICT.* Maidenhead: Open University Press

Brockett, R.G. and Hiemstra, R. (1991). *Self-Direction in Adult Learning: Perspectives on theory, research and practice.* London: Routledge

Brown, J.S., Collins, A. and Duguid, P. (1989). 'Situated Cognition and the Culture of Learning'. *Educational Researcher*, 18, 32–42

Brownlow, K. (1968). *The Parades Gone By.* Berkeley, CA: University of California Press

Bruner, J (1960). *The Process of Education.* Cambridge, MA: Harvard University Press

—— (1961). 'The Art of Discovery'. *Harvard Educational Review*, 31, 21–32

—— (1977). *The Process of Education.* Cambridge, MA: Harvard University Press

—— (1986). *Actual Minds, Possible Worlds.* Cambridge, MA: Harvard University Press

—— (1987). 'Life as Narrative'. *Social Research*, 54(1), 11–32

—— (1990). *Acts of Meaning.* Cambridge, MA: Harvard University Press

—— (1996). *The Culture of Education.* Cambridge, MA: Harvard University Press

—— (2006) In *Search of Pedagogy. Volume 1: The Selected Works of Jerome S. Bruner.* London: Routledge

Brunner, D. (1994). *Inquiry Reflection: Framing narrative practice in education.* New York: State University of New York Press

Buckingham, D. (2003). *Media Education: Literacy, learning and contemporary culture.* London: Polity Press

Burden, K. and Kuechel, T. (2004). *Evaluation Report of the Teaching and Learning with Digital Video Assets Pilot 2003–2004.* London: Becta

Burton, T. (2002). 'Dream Weavers'. In L. Tirard (ed.), *Moviemaker's Masterclass: Private lessons from the world's foremost directors.* New York: Faber & Faber

Carey, J. (2006). *What Good are the Arts?* New York: Oxford University Press

Carroll, J. (1996). 'Escaping the Abattoir: Critical and transformative research in drama classrooms'. In P. Taylor (ed.), *Researching Drama and Arts Education: Paradigms and possibilities*. London: Falmer Press

—— (2008). 'Mediated Performance: Video production in the English classroom'. In M. Anderson, J. Hughes and J. Manuel (eds), *Drama in the English Classroom*. Melbourne: Oxford University Press

Carroll, J., Anderson, M. and Cameron, D. (2006). *Real Players? Drama, education and technology*. Stoke on Trent: Trentham Books

Carroll, N. (1996). *Theorizing the Moving Image*. New York: Cambridge University Press

Chatman, S. (1990). *Coming to Terms: The rhetoric of narrative in fiction and film*. Ithaca, NY: Cornell University Press

Cherland, M. and Harper, H.J. (2007). *Advocacy Research in Literacy Education: Seeking higher ground*. Mahwah, NJ: Lawrence Erlbaum

Churcher, M. (2003). *Acting for Film: Truth 24 times a second*. London: Virgin Books

Coen, J. and Coen, E. (2002). 'New Blood'. In L. Tirard (ed.), *Moviemaker's Masterclass: Private lessons from the world's foremost directors*. New York: Faber & Faber

Cohen, L. and Manion, L. (2000). *Research Methods in Education*, 4th ed. London: Routledge

Cohen, L. and Manion, L. (2004). *A Guide to Teaching Practice*. 4th ed. London: RoutledgeFalmer

Cope, B. and Kalantzis, M. (eds) (2000). *Multiliteracies: Literacy learning and the design of social futures*. Melbourne: Macmillan

Craft, A. (2002). *Creativity in the Early Years: A lifewide foundation*. London: Continuum

Csikszentmihalyi, M. (1990). *Flow: The psychology of optimal experience*, New York: Harper and Row

Cummings, E.E. (1994). *E.E. Cummings: Complete poems 1904–1962*. New York: Livelight

Daley, E. (2003). 'Expanding the Concept of Literacy'. *Educause Review*, March/April, 33–9

Deasy, R.J. (2002) *Critical Links: Learning in the arts and student academic and social development*. Washington, DC: Arts Education Partnership. Available online at www.aep-arts.org

Deasy, R.J. (2004). *Arts Education Partnership: The arts and education—new opportunities for research*. Retrieved 11 May 2007 from www.gseis.ucla.edu/faculty/files/catterall/catterall.newopportunities

Denzin, N. and Lincoln, Y. (1994). 'Introduction: Entering the field of qualitative research'. In N. Denzin and Y. Lincoln (eds), *Handbook of Qualitative Research*. Thousand Oaks, CA: Sage

—— (eds) (2005). *The Sage Handbook of Qualitative Research*. 3rd ed. Thousand Oaks, CA: Sage

DEST (Department of Education, Science and Training) (2004). *Evaluation of School-based Arts Education Programmes in Australian Schools*. Retrieved 20 October 2007 from www.dest.gov.au/sectors/school_education/publications_resources/other_publications/school_based_arts_education_programmes.htm

Dewey J. (1938). *Experience and Education*. New York: Macmillan

Dewey, J., Ratner, J. and Post, E. (1939). *Intelligence in the Modern World: John Dewey's philosophy*, Published by Modern Library, 1939, original from the University of California, digitised 8 January 2008

Dewey, J. (1954). *Art as Experience*. New York: Capricorn

Disney Institute (2001). *Be Our Guest: Perfecting the art of customer service*, New York: Disney Editions

Donovan, M.S., Bransford, J.D. and Pellegrino, J.W. (eds) (1999). *How People Learn: Bridging research and practice*. Washington, DC: National Academy Press

Early, K. (2006). Video as a Learning Medium. Unpublished Masters of Teaching (Hons) thesis, University of Sydney

Eisenstein, S. (1947). *The Film Sense*. Ed. Jay Leyda. New York: Harcourt, Brace & World
—— (1949). *Film Form: Essays in film theory*. Ed. Jay Leyda. New York: Harcourt, Brace & World
—— (1970). *Film Essays and a Lecture*. Ed. Jay Leyda. New York: Praeger
Eisner, E. (1978). 'Humanistic Trends and the Curriculum Field'. *Journal of Curriculum Studies*, 10(3), 97–204
—— (1993). 'Reshaping Assessment in Education: Some criteria in search of practice'. *Journal of Curriculum Studies*, 25(3), 219–33
—— (2002). *The Arts and the Creation of Mind*. New Haven, CT: Yale University Press
—— (2004). *Artistry in Training: A response to 'The Pedagogy of Making', a cultural comment essay by Elizabeth Coleman*. Retrieved 20 January 2008 from www.culturalcommons.org/eisner.htm
Ely, M. (1991). *Doing Qualitative Research: Circles within circles*. New York: Falmer Press
Erikson, E. (1976). 'Play and Actuality'. In J. Bruner, A. Jolly and K. Sylva (eds), *Play: Its role in development and evolution*. New York: Basic Books
Fabe, M. (2004). *Closely Watched Films: An introduction to the art of narrative film technique*. Berkeley, CA: University of California Press
Film Education Working Group (1999). *Making Movies Matter*. London: British Film Institute
Fischer, G., Giaccardi, E., Eden, H., Sugimoto, M. and Ye, Y. (2005). 'Beyond Binary Choices: Integrating individual and social creativity'. *International Journal of Human–Computer Studies* (IJHCS), Special Issue on Computer Support for Creativity (edited by E.A. Edmonds and L. Candy), 63(4–5), 482–512
Fiske, E. (ed.) (1999). *Champions of Change: The impact of the arts on learning*. Washington, DC: The Arts Education Partnership and The President's Committee on the Arts and the Humanities
Fontana, A. and Frey, J.H. (1994). 'Interviewing: The art of science'. In N. Denzin and Y. Lincoln (eds), *Handbook of Qualitative Research*. Thousand Oaks, CA: Sage
Forster, E.M. (1927). *Aspects of the Novel*. Orlando, FL: Harcourt School.
Freebody, P. (2003). *Qualitative Research in Education: Interaction and practice*. London: Sage
Freire, P. (1972). *The Pedagogy of the Oppressed*. Harmondsworth: Penguin
Garrison, D.R. (1997). 'Self-directed Learning: Toward a comprehensive model'. *Adult Education Quarterly*, 48(1), 18–33
Gee, J. (2005). 'What Would a State of the Art Instructional Video Game Look Like?' *Innovate*, 1(6), para 5
Gillies, R. (2007). *Cooperative Learning: Integrating theory and practice*. London: Sage
Godard, J. (1972). *Godard on Godard*. Ed. and trans. T. Milne. New York: Da Capo
—— (2002). 'In a Class by Himself'. In L. Tirard (ed.), *Moviemaker's Masterclass: Private lessons from the world's foremost directors*. New York: Faber & Faber
Goldfarb, B. (2002). *Visual Pedagogy: Media cultures in and beyond the classroom*. Durham, NC: Duke University Press
Grady, S. (1996). 'Toward the Practice of Theory in Practice'. In P. Taylor (ed.), *Researching Drama and Arts Education: Paradigms and possibilities*. London: Falmer Press
Greene, M. (1995) *Releasing the Imagination: Essays on education, the arts, and social change*. San Francisco: Jossey-Bass
Greenwood, D.J. and Levin, M. (2005) 'Reform of the Social Sciences, and of Universities Through Action Research'. In N. Denzin and Y. Lincoln (eds), *The Sage Handbook of Qualitative Research*. 3rd ed. Thousand Oaks, CA: Sage
Halpin, D., Dickson, M., Power, S., Whitty, G. and Gewirtz, S. (2004). 'Curriculum Innovation

Within an Evaluative State: Issues of risk and regulation'. *Curriculum Journal*, 15(3), 197–206

Hardy, B. (1977). *Narrative as a Primary Act of Mind* in The Cool Web: *The pattern of children's reading*. London: Bodley Head

Hattie, J. (2003). *Teachers Make a Difference: What is the research evidence?* ACER. Retrieved 22 May 2007 from www.acer.edu.au/workshops/documents/Teachers_Make_a_Difference_Hattie

Hayes, D., Mills, M., Christie, P. and Lingard, B. (2006). *Teachers & Schooling: Making a difference—productive pedagogies, assessment and performance*. Sydney: Allen & Unwin

Heathcote, D., Johnson, L. and O'Neill, C. (1984). *Collected Writings on Education and Drama*. London: Hutchinson

hooks, b. (2003). *Teaching Community: A pedagogy of hope*. New York and London: Routledge

Hornbrook, D. (1989). *Education and Dramatic Art*. 2nd ed. London: Routledge.

Jameson, R. (1994). *They Went Thataway: Redefining film genres*. San Francisco: Mercury House

Janesick, V. (1994). 'The Dance of Qualitative Research Design: Metaphor, methodolatry and meaning'. In N. Denzin and Y. Lincoln (eds), *Handbook of Qualitative Research*. Thousand Oaks, CA: Sage

Jefferson, M. (2006). 'Filming *The Boy who Loved Shostakovich*'. *Journal of Education in the Dramatic Arts*, 12(2), 41–6

Jeffrey, B. and Craft, A. (2001). 'The Universalization of Creativity'. In A. Craft, B. Jeffrey and M. Leibling (eds), *Creativity in Education*. London: Continuum

Jeunet, J. (2002). 'Dream Weavers'. In L. Tirard (ed.), *Moviemaker's Masterclass: Private lessons from the world's foremost directors*. New York and London: Faber & Faber

Johnson, R. and Onwuegbuzie, A. (2004). 'Mixed Methods Research: A research paradigm whose time has come'. *Educational Researcher*, 33(7), 14–26

Jones, R. (1941). *The Dramatic Imagination: Reflections and speculations on the art of the theatre*. New York: Duell, Sloan & Pearce

Kaiser Family Foundation (2006). *The Media Family: Electronic media in the lives of infants, toddlers, preschoolers, and their parents*. Menlo Park, CA: Kaiser Family Foundation

Kaufman, J. and Sternberg, R. (eds) (2006). *The International Handbook of Creativity*. Cambridge: Cambridge University Press

Kawin, B. (1992). *How Movies Work*. Berkeley, CA: University of California Press

Kemmis, S. and McTaggart, R. (2005). 'Participatory Action Research'. In N. Denzin and Y. Lincoln (eds), *The Sage Handbook of Qualitative Research*. 3rd ed. Thousand Oaks, CA: Sage

Kidd, J.R. (1973). *How Adults Learn*. Chicago: Association Press

Kitano, T. (2002). 'New Blood'. In L. Tirard (ed.), *Moviemaker's Masterclass: Private lessons from the world's foremost directors*. New York: Faber & Faber

Knowles, M. (1975). *Self-directed Learning*. New York: Association Press

Kolb, D.A. (1984). *Experiential Learning: Experience as the source of learning and development*. Englewood Cliffs, NJ: Prentice-Hall

Kracauer, S. (1973). *Theory of Film: The redemption of physical reality*. London: Oxford University Press

Kress, G. (2003). *Literacy in the New Media Age*. London: Routledge

Kusturica, E. (2002). 'New Blood'. In L. Tirard (ed.), *Moviemaker's Masterclass: Private lessons from the world's foremost directors*. New York: Faber & Faber

Langer, S. (1953). *Feeling and Form*. New York: Scribner's

Lave, J. and Wenger, E. (1991). *Situated Learning: Legitimate peripheral participation*. Cambridge, MA: Cambridge University Press

Leitch, T. (1986). *What Stories Are: Narrative theory and interpretation*. University Park, PA: Pennsylvania State University Press

Lewis, C. (2001). *Literary Practices as Social Acts: Power, status and cultural norms in the classroom*. Mawah, NJ: Lawrence Erlbaum

Lindsay, V. (2006 [1915]). *The Art of the Moving Picture*. Charleston, SC: BiblioBazaar

Luke, A. and Freebody, P. (1997). 'Critical Literacy and the Question of Normativity: An Introduction'. In S. Muspratt, A. Luke and P. Freebody (eds), *Constructing Critical Literacies: Teaching and learning textual practice*. Sydney: Allen & Unwin

Lynch, D. (2002). 'Dream Weavers'. In L. Tirard (ed.), *Moviemaker's Masterclass: Private lessons from the world's foremost directors*. New York: Faber & Faber

Mahn, H and John-Steiner, V. (2002). 'The Gift of Confidence: A Vygotskian view of emotions'. In G. Wells and G. Claxton (eds), *Learning for Life in the 21st Century: Sociocultural perspectives on the future of education*. Cambridge, MA: Blackwell

Manuel, J. (2002). 'Making its Debut: What English teachers think of the new Higher School Certificate English syllabus in NSW'. *English in Australia*, 134, 67–77

Manuel, J. and Brock, P. (2003). 'W(h)ither the Place of Literature? Two key reforms in the senior secondary English curriculum in New South Wales', *English in Australia*, 136, 15–26

Martello, J. (2002). 'Four Literacy Practices Roled into One: Drama and early childhood literacies'. *Melbourne Studies in Education*, 43(2), 53–63

McGaw, B. (1996). *Their Future: Options for reform of the Higher School Certificate*. Sydney: Department of Training and Education Coordination

McQuillan, M. (2000). *The Narrative Reader*. London: Routledge

Metz, C. (1991). *Film Language: A semiotics of the cinema*, trans. Michael Taylor. Chicago: University of Chicago Press

Monaco, J. (2000). *How to Read a Film: The world of movies, media, multimedia—language, history, theory*, 3rd ed. New York: Oxford University Press

Mooney, M. (1989). Drama Education in NSW. Unpublished Master of Arts thesis, Charles Sturt University

—— (2004). 'Morphing into Screen Drama'. In C. Hatton and M. Anderson (eds), *The State of Our Art*. Sydney: EDA of NSW and Currency Press

NACCCE (National Advisory Committee on Creative and Cultural Education) (1999). *All Our Futures: Creativity, culture and education*. NACCCE, Department of Education and Employment. Available online at www.dfee.gov.uk/naccce/index1.htm

Neale, S. (2000). *Genre and Hollywood*. London and New York: Routledge

New London Group (1996). 'A Pedagogy of Multiliteracies: Designing social futures'. *Harvard Educational Review*, 66(1), 60–92

Newman, W.L. (2006). *Social Research Methods: Qualitative and quantitative approaches*, 6th ed. Boston, MA: Pearson Allyn and Bacon

Newmann, F. and Associates (1996). *Authentic achievement: Restructuring schools for intellectual quality*. San Francisco: Jossey-Bass

Nicholson, H. (2002) 'The Politics of Trust: Drama education and the ethic of care'. *Research in Drama Education*, 7(1), 81–91

Nowell-Smith, G. (1972). Cited in P. Wollen, *Signs and Meanings in the Cinema*. London: Secker and Warburg

O'Neill, C. (1995). *Drama Worlds: A framework for process drama*. Portsmouth, NH: Heinemann

O'Toole, J. (1992). *The Process of Drama: Negotiating art and meaning*. London: Routledge

—— (1998). 'Playing on the Beach: Consensus among drama teachers—some patterns in the sand. *NADIE Journal*, 22(2), 5–19

—— (2002). 'Drama: The productive pedagogy'. *Melbourne Studies in Education*, 43(2), 39–52
—— (2004). 'Foreword'. In C. Hatton and M. Anderson (eds), *The State of Our Art: NSW perspectives in educational drama*. Sydney: Currency Press
—— (2006). *Doing Drama Research: Stepping into enquiry in drama, theatre and education*. Brisbane: Drama Australia
Onwuegbuzie A.J. and Leech, N.L. (2005). 'On Becoming a Pragmatic Researcher: The importance of combining quantitative and qualitative research methodologies.' *International Journal of Social Research Methodology* (5), 375–87
Oxford English Dictionary (2006). Creativity, Noun. Oxford English Dictionary Online. Retrieved 28 February 2007 from www.oed.com
Perkins, V. (1972). *Film as Film: Understanding and judging movies*. Harmondsworth: Penguin
Pew Institute (2002). *The Digital Disconnect: The widening gap between internet savvy students and their schools*. Washington, DC: Pew Institute. Retrieved 22 May 2007 from www.pewinternet.org/report_display.asp?r=67
Polkinghorne, D.E. (1988). *Narrative Knowing and the Human Sciences*. New York: State University of New York Press
Pollack, S. (2002). 'Groundbreakers'. In L. Tirard (ed.), *Moviemaker's Masterclass: Private lessons from the world's foremost directors*. New York: Faber & Faber
Posner, D. (2004). 'What's Wrong with Teaching to the Test?' *Phi Delta Kappan*, 85(10), 749–51
Prensky, M. (2001). 'Digital Natives, Digital Immigrants'. *On the Horizon*, 9(5). Retrieved 10 October 2008 from www.marcprensky.com/writing/Prensky%20-%20Digital%20Natives,%20Digital%20Immigrants%20-%20Part1.pdf
—— (2005). 'What Can You Learn From a Cell Phone? Almost anything!' *Innovate*, 1(5). retrieved 26 January 2006 from www.innovateonline.info/index.php?view=article&id=83
Punch, M. (1994). 'Politics and Ethics in Qualitative Research'. In N. Denzin and Y. Lincoln (eds), *Handbook of Qualitative Research*. Thousand Oaks, CA: Sage
Queensland School Restructuring Longitudinal Study (QSRLS) (2001). *School Reform Longitudinal Study: Final Report, Volume 1*. Brisbane: Education Queensland
Ramsden, P. (2003). *Learning to Teach in Higher Education*. London: Routledge.
Read, H. (1932). 'Towards a Film Aesthetic', In R.D. MacCann (ed.), *Film: A montage of theories*. New York: Dutton.
Reid, M., Burn, A. and Parker, D. (2002). *Evaluation Report of the Becta Digital Video Pilot*. October. London: Becta
Richardson, L. (1994). 'Writing: A method of inquiry'. In N. Denzin and Y. Lincoln (eds), *Handbook of Qualitative Research*. Thousand Oaks, CA: Sage
Robinson, K. (1999). *All Our Futures: Creativity, culture and education*. London: Department for Education and Employment
—— (2001). 'Mind the Gap: The creative conundrum'. *Critical Quarterly*, 43(1), 41–5
Rogoff, B. (1994). 'Developing Understanding of the Idea of Communities of Learners'. *Mind, Culture, and Activity*, 1(4), 209–29
Rushkoff, D. (2005). *Get Back in the Box: Innovation from the inside out*. Melbourne: HarperCollins
Safford K. (2005). *Many Routes to Meaning: Children's language and literacy development in creative arts work*. London: CLPE/Creative Partnerships
Schatz, T. (1981). *Hollywood Genres: Formulas, filmmaking, and the studio system*. New York: McGraw-Hill
Schulman, J. (1990). 'Now You See Them, Now You Don't: Anonymity versus visibility in case studies of teachers'. *Educational Researcher*, 19, 11–16

Schwandt, T. (1994). 'Constructivist, Interpretivist Approaches to Human Inquiry'. In N. Denzin and Y. Lincoln (eds), *Handbook of Qualitative Research*. Thousand Oaks, CA: Sage
—— (2001). *Dictionary of Qualitative Inquiry*. Thousand Oaks, CA: Sage
Scorsese, M. (1995). *A Personal Journey with Martin Scorsese Through American Movies*. DVD. A BFI TV production for Channel 4 in association with Miramax films.
—— (2002). 'Revisionists.' In L. Tirard (ed.), *Moviemaker's Masterclass: Private lessons from the world's foremost directors*. New York: Faber & Faber
Scorsese, M. and Wilson, M.H. (1997). *A Personal Journey with Martin Scorsese Through American Movies*. London: Faber & Faber
Sheingold, K. (1991). 'Restructuring for Learning with Technology: The potential for synergy'. *Phi Delta Kappan*, 73, 17–27
Shernoff, D.J., Csikszentmihalyi, M., Schneider, B. and Steele, E. (2003). 'Student Engagement in High School Classrooms from the Perspective of Flow Theory'. *School Psychology Quarterly*, 18, 158–76
Slade, P. (1954). *Child Drama*. University of London Press: London
Sobchack, V. (2000). 'The Scene of the Screen: Envisioning cinematic and electronic presence'. In R. Stam and T. Miller (eds), *Film and Theory: An anthology*. Nantucket, MA: Blackwell
Stafford, K. and Barrs, M. (2005). *Creativity and Literacy: Many routes to meaning—children's language and literacy learning in creative arts projects*. London, CLPE. Available at www.clpe.co.uk.
Stake, R. (1994). 'Case Studies.' In N. Denzin and Y. Lincoln (eds), *Handbook of Qualitative Research*. Thousand Oaks, CA: Sage
—— (1995). *The Art of Case Study Research*. Thousand Oaks, CA: Sage
—— (2005). 'Qualitative Case Studies'. In N. Denzin and Y. Lincoln (eds), *The Sage Handbook of Qualitative Research*. 3rd ed. Thousand Oaks, CA: Sage
Sternberg, M. (1978). *Expositional Modes and Temporal Ordering in Fiction*. Baltimore, MD: Johns Hopkins University Press
Stone, O. (2002). 'Big Guns'. In L. Tirard (ed.), *Moviemaker's Masterclass: Private lessons from the world's foremost directors*. New York: Faber & Faber
Thompson, J. (1991). 'Assessing Drama: Allowing for meaningful interpretation'. In J. Hughes (ed.), *Drama in Education: The state of the art*. Sydney: Educational Drama Association
Todorov, T. (1981). *Introduction to Poetics*. Trans. Howard. Minneapolis: University of Minnesota Press
UNESCO (2003). Website: http://portal.unesco.org/culture/es/ev.php-URL_ID=29870&URL_DO=DO_PRINTPAGE&URL_SECTION=-465.html
UNESCO (2006). *Road Map for Arts Education*. Retrieved 2 January 2008 from http://portal.unesco.org/culture/en/ev.php-URL_ID=30335&URL_DO=DO_TOPIC&URL_SECTION=201.html
Von Trier, L. (2002). 'New Blood'. In L. Tirard (ed.), *Moviemaker's Masterclass: Private lessons from the world's foremost directors*. New York: Faber & Faber
Vygotsky, L. (1976). 'Play and its Role in the Mental Development of the Child'. In J. Bruner, A. Jolly and K. Sylva (eds), *Play: Its role in development and evolution*. New York: Basic Books
—— (1978). *Mind in Society: The development of higher psychological processes*. Cambridge, MA: Harvard University Press
Watson, P. (2003). 'Authorship, Genre and Stars in Hollywood'. In J. Nelmes (ed.), *An Introduction to Film Studies*. London: Routledge
Way, B. (1967). *Development Through Drama*. London: Longman

Wenders, W. (1988). 'Why Do We Make Films?' in *The Logic of Images*, New York: Faber & Faber
—— (1991). *The Logic of Images: Essays and conversations*. Trans. M. Hofmann. New York: Faber & Faber
—— (2002). 'Revisionists'. In L. Tirard (ed.), *Moviemaker's Masterclass: Private lessons from the world's foremost directors*. New York: Faber & Faber
Wenger, E. (1997). *Communities of Practice: Learning, meaning and identity*. Cambridge: Cambridge University Press
Wiggins, G.P. (1993). *Assessing Student Performance*. San Francisco: Jossey-Bass
Wiltshire, K. (2006). 'In Defense of the True Values of Learning.' *The Australian*, 23 September
Wollen, P. (1972). *Signs and Meaning in the Cinema*. London: Secker and Warburg
Woo, J. (2002). 'Big Guns'. In L. Tirard (ed.), *Moviemaker's Masterclass: Private lessons from the world's foremost directors*. New York: Faber & Faber

Index

400 Blows 44–5, 129, 130

A Close-Up View (Eisenstein) 49
A Personal Journey with Martin Scorsese 38, 90
A Voyage to the Moon 37–8
abstract films 61, 62
acting 81, 95, 116, 121, 130–3, 146
    learning from 133–5
    and the 'magic if' 121–2
    shaped by camera 131–2
    'technical actors' 122–3, 130
active learning 28
aesthetic control 16–17, 24, 26, 84–5
aesthetic understanding 18, 19, 24, 26
All Our Futures 27
Almodovar, Pedro 46, 75, 112
Altman, Robert 127
American Arts Education Partnership 170–1
American Beauty 4, 43
appreciation, of film 17–18, 34, 82, 149
    critical 18–19, 144
Arnold, Roslyn 4
art films 148
arts 1–2, 23
    assessing 154
    central role in schooling 34
    experiencing 78
    good teaching of 128
    like play 121
    role 23, 133
Arts Education Partnership 169
arts education research *see* research
arts learning 82
assessment 152–4, 166
    in the arts 154
    authentic and relevant 155–6
    avoiding dichotomies 160–1
    of collaborative learning 158–60
    examples 162–6
    five principles 154, 161–2
    interaction between making and appreciation 157–8
    for learning 156–7
    process/product 161, 166
    'trained subjectivity' 154
associational films 61, 62
audience 121, 126–7, 133, 140, 148
    role of 114
auteur theory 74–5, 98, 99
authentic learning 103–4

Babel 4, 5, 65, 67, 70, 129, 130
Balázs, Béla 38, 57
Bambi Meets Godzilla 61
Barthes, Roland 42, 119
Battleship Potemkin 51
    Odessa Steps massacre 52–3, 65, 92–3, 94, 148–9
Benjamin, Walter 57

Index   207

Bennett, A.   119
Bergman, Ingmar   74, 77, 78, 79
Bertolucci, Bernardo   99, 115, 122
blockbusters   72
Boal, Augusto   193n
Bolton, Gavin   118, 121
Bordwell, D.   62, 67, 92, 126, 127
Branigan, Edward   63, 66–7
Brecht, Bertolt   192n
Bresson, Robert   108
Brindley, Sue   33
British Film Institute   138
Bruner, Jerome   7, 83, 84, 119–20, 179
Buckingham, David   14, 15, 18
    on creativity   24
    on media literacy   29
'Buffalo Bill's'   21
Burton, Tim   112

camera
    captures 'moments'   133
    invisible character   122, 123, 132
    manipulates perspective   38, 51
    proximity of   89
    psychic strength of lens   38
camera shots   81, 83, 84–5
    dramatic purpose   89–90
    types   90
Carroll, J.   155
Carroll, Noel   47–8
case studies   142–3, 150–1
    Newtown High School of the Performing Arts   147–50
    Parkside Community College   143–7
categorical films   61, 62
cause and effect   63, 68, 70, 125–6, 127
Chapman, Seymour   69
characters
    desires   70
    dramatic intent   132
    identifying with   89–90
    motivations   69, 70, 132
chase scenes   158
Child Drama   19
children
    media exposure   31–2
    screen literacy   31
Churcher, M.   131, 133

cineliteracies, defined   28
cinema   57, 69
Citizen Kane   43–4, 55–6, 150
close-up semiotic theory   49–50, 55, 56, 58
close-up shots   89–90
cluster analysis   194n
codes   53–4, 58
    as conventions   54–5
    as innovations   55–6
    and learning   56
Coen, Joel and Ethan   114
collaborative film project, assessing   164–6
collaborative learning   98–9, 101–3
    and filmmaking   103–4
    self-directed   105–7
    teacher's role   101
    Vygotsky's ideas   98, 99–100
comedy films   72
Coming to Terms   69
communication, in film   47
community of practice   172
composition   91–2, 96, 125, 149
conflict   68–9, 70
continuity   133, 145, 146
control *see* aesthetic control
creative thinking, in institutions   23
creatives   24
creativity   22–3
    collaborative process   25–6
    defined   23
    in film learning   27, 128
    and literacy   21–2, 34–5
    open to all   24–5
    and schooling   23–4
    teaching   26–7
critical literacy   28–9
cross-cutting   40, 41, 52
crystallisation   185–6
Csikszentmihalyi, Mihaly   11, 12
Cummings, E.E.   21, 22
curriculum, film in   3, 19–20, 136–7, 147, 148, 151

Daley, Elizabeth   30
Death's Marathon   40, 41, 52
deep focus   55–6
deep knowledge   39
Denzin, N.   179, 180

detective films   127
Dewey, John   8, 83
dialogue   45, 47
disaster movies   72
discovery learning   84, 103
Disney, Walt   167–8
Doing Drama Research (O'Toole)   169
drama   9, 23
drama education   14, 19, 102, 103, 107–8, 118, 160
dramatic action   124, 127, 131
    exercise   96–7
Durran, James   143, 150

early film   37, 38, 40, 45, 90–1
Early, Kate   172
eclecticism   72
editing   17, 81, 113–14, 123–4, 146, 153
Eisenstein, Sergei   49, 51, 52–3, 54, 55, 57, 93, 118
Eisner, Elliot   1–2, 34, 78, 82, 102, 120–1, 128, 134, 177, 179
empathy   4
ensemble theatre   107, 108
equilibrium, of the situation   68, 126, 192n
Erikson, Erik   120
expectation, in audience   66–9, 127
experiential learning   8
exposition   69–71

fabula   63–6, 68, 123, 127, 193n
Fassbinder, Rainer Werner   74
Fellini, Federico   74
fight sequences   149
film
    beginnings/middles/ends   69–71, 126
    capacity to influence   57, 58
    Carroll's five necessary conditions   47–8, 58
    collaborative art form   74
    components   45–6, 49, 87
    in the curriculum   3, 19–20, 136–7, 147, 148, 151
    elements of   39
    forms of   62
    pervasiveness   19, 148
    Read's definition   41
    self-exploration   116
    social role   23, 57
    students' familiarity with   6
    understanding   36, 84–5
film aesthetics   40–1, 54, 87
film analysis, Eisenstein's viewpoints   49, 50, 55, 57
Film Education Working Group   33–4
    Cineliteracies for Stage 5   33–4
film language   40–1, 54, 61, 148
    defined   87
film appreciation   92–3
    first module   87–9, 90, 97
film learning   2, 134, 151
    with 3–5 year olds   138–9
    collaborative process   31, 160
    creative process   25
    developing a continuum   137–8
    experiential   7–8
    as flow experience   11–13
    in junior secondary school   140–1
    place in curriculum   3
    in primary school   139–40, 144
    productive pedagogy   8–11
    scaffolded modules   187–91
    in senior secondary school   141–2
    social nature of   30–1
    as sociocultural approach   7
film literacy   32–4
film noir   54, 72
film stills, theatrical   37
film stories   116
    and audience   126–7
    defined   130–1
    self-understandings   118
film teaching   1–2, 6
film teaching framework   13–14
    appreciating   17–19
    critical engagement   19
    making   15–17
film trailer production   146–7
filmic codes *see* codes
filmmaking   8, 39
    aesthetic experience   82
    authentic learning   103–4
    collaboration   80–1, 102, 118, 166
    first attempts   15
    professional   15, 155
    self-expression   114

stages of 108–9
as storytelling 127
flow theory 11, 13
concentration 11
enjoyment 12
interest 11–12
Fontana, A. 182
Ford, John 74
formative assessment 158, 160, 161, 166
Forster, E.M. 70
framing 50–2, 88–9, 91–2, 132
Freire, Paulo 28, 167
French New Wave 74, 98
Frey, J.H. 182
frozen frame 44

genre 71–2
analysis 73–4
defining 72–3
hybridity 72
referencing 72
genre-based trailer, assessing 162–3
George, Ula 147
gesture 54
Gladiator 43
Godard, Jean-Luc 53, 61, 74, 98, 99
Gosford Park 127, 130
Grady, S 179
graphics 46, 47
Greene, Maxine 129, 133
Griffith, D.W. 40, 41, 91
group work 100, 101, 118
shared roles 107–8
Guide to Teaching Practice (Cohen & Manion) 3

Halpin, D. 136–7
Hardy, Barbara 134
Harry Potter and the Philosopher's Stone 46
Hawks, Howard 74
Heathcote, Dorothy 15, 107
Hidden 67
Hirsch, E.D. 73
Hitchcock, Alfred 52, 55, 66, 74, 98
Hollywood films 54–5, 71
hooks, bell 28
Hornbrook, David 19

horror films 72, 146
hospital dramas 145–6

identification, of viewer with film 38, 58, 67, 70, 89–90
images *see* visual imagery
imagination 128–9, 139
unlocking 129–30, 131
In the Mood for Love 67
intertextuality 72
Intolerance 91

Jackson, Peter 67
Jeunet, Jean-Pierre 112
John-Steiner, Vera 26

Kaiser Family Foundation 138
Kawin, Bruce 74
Kim, Isabelle 180
kinaesthetic storyboarding 110–11, 130, 131
Kitano, Takeshi 117, 120
Kolb, D.A. 8
Kracauer, Siegfried 57–8
Kusturica, Emir 122

Langer, Susanne 80
language, of film *see* film language
Lawrence of Arabia 43
Leitch, Thomas 61, 70
Lévi-Strauss, Claude 72
lighting 122
limericks 64, 68, 130
Lincoln, Y. 179, 180
Lindsay, Vachel 40
literacy 28–30, 32–3
and creativity 21–2, 34–5
defined 27
as social practice 30–1
literacy pedagogy 29–30
literature review 174
identifying relevant material 175–6
literature search 174–5
word budget 174
long-shot analysis 49, 55, 90
and social context 57–8
longitudinal studies 176–7
Lord of the Rings 67, 68, 70
Return of the King 70

Luhrmann, Baz   72, 145
Lynch, David   74, 133–4

machinima   22
Mahn, Holbrook   26
Malle, Louis   98
meaning   49, 58, 70–1, 145
   by association   52
   and *mise en scène*   50–2
   and montage   52–3
   and stories   60, 62
measurement   35
media   137, 138
   children's exposure to   31–2
media arts colleges   143
media literacy   29, 143
Méliès, George   37–8
melodrama   46
Memento   65
metonymy   52
Metz, Christian   36, 41, 42
mid-shot view of narrative   57, 58, 90
Minority Report   147
mise en scène   43, 44, 53, 56, 58, 65
   making meaning   50–2
   techniques   53–4
mobile phones   2
Monaco, James   36, 49, 55, 58
montage   44–5, 53, 56, 58, 65
   learning   93–5, 96
   making meaning   52–3
   techniques   53–4
Moulin Rouge   72
movement, in visual imagery   41–5, 58
moving pictures   40–1, 42
multiliteracy   22, 32
   beyond the written word   30
   and children   31–2
   defined   27–8
   as social practice   30–1
music   46, 47
Muybridge, Eadweard   42

Narrative Comprehension and Film
   (Branigan)   63
narrative construction   124–5
   and the audience   126–7
   cause and effect   125–6

narrative films   61, 62–3, 148
   schema to construct   66–7
   'through line'   70
narratives   3–5, 21–2
   causality   63
   constructing reality   119–20
   creating   22
   space and time   65
   see also film stories
Nash, Ogden   64, 68
Neale, Steve   72, 73–4
New London Group   22, 29–30, 31
New South Wales Higher School
   Certificate   159
New Wave   74, 98
Newland, Marv   61
Newtown High School of the Performing
   Arts   147–51
Nicholson, Helen   102, 103
non-creatives   24

Ocean's Eleven   127
originality   25
O'Toole, John   9, 107, 169
over-testing   161

panning shots   90
Parkside Community College, Cambridge
   143–7, 150, 151
participatory action research   182–3
pedagogy   40, 47, 58, 130, 151
performance   123, 140
perspective   37–8, 54
play   9, 120–1, 139
plot   64, 123, 127, 130
Pollack, Sydney   132
portfolios   158
Posner, D.   152
post-production   108, 113–14
postmodernism   18, 150
praxis   167, 177
pre-production process   108, 109–11
Prensky, Marc   2
print material   32
production process   108, 112–13
productive pedagogies   8–11, 39
proxemics   54, 89
proximity, in *mise en scène*   54

Psycho 55, 146
public expression 118–19
Punch, M. 183

qualitative research 176, 177, 179, 185
quantitative research 176, 177–8
Queensland School Reform Longitudinal Survey 8–11

Rabbit-Proof Fence 4, 5
Read, Herbert 41, 45
Rear Window 43, 52, 65, 66
    opening sequence 69–70, 94
Renoir, Jean 74
research 167–8, 186
    anonymity/confidentiality 183–4
    case studies 181
    creating a *bricolage* 180–1
    credibility 185
    crystallisation 185–6
    ethical issues 183
    finding a research question 171–2
    informed consent 184
    interviews 181–2
    longitudinal studies 176–7
    methodology 176–7
    mixed-method approaches 178
    motives for 169
    need for 170–1
    participatory action research 182–3
    qualitative 176, 177, 179, 185
    quantitative 176, 177–8
    refining the research question 172–4
    transparency 184
    validity 185
    see also literature review
resource management 104–5
responsibility 104–6
rhetorical films 61, 62
Richardson, Laurel 185
Rivette, Jacques 98
road movies 72
Robinson, Ken 23, 32
Rohmer, Eric 98
role-playing 131
Romeo and Juliet 145
Royle, N. 119

Rushkoff, Douglas 12
Russian Ark 65

scaffolding 82–4, 85–7, 95, 97, 100, 101
Schatz, Thomas 72, 73
schooling
    and lived experience 137
    outmoded 32, 34
science fiction 72
Scorsese, Martin 38, 74, 112, 117
screen learning 39–40, 156
    overlooked in school 32
    see also film learning
screen literacy 22, 32, 138–9
    defined 28, 30
screen practice 58–9
screen theory 58–9
screening 114–15, 118–19
search engines 174
self-expression 118–19
semiotics 49–50, 94, 109, 113
Seven Samurai 129, 130
shooting 81, 83, 84–5, 112–13, 122–3, 125, 149
    see also camera shots
Shostakovich Film Project 77–82, 83, 99, 101–3, 106, 110, 117–18, 122–3, 135
Shrek 146
Shulman, J. 183–4
silent films 46
Slade, Peter 19
Soderbergh, Steven 127
sound 45, 47, 129–30
speech 45, 47
Spiderman 147
Stake, R. 181
Stanislavsky, Konstantin 121, 193n
    acting questions 132
Star Wars 64
Stone, Oliver 107
stories 124–5
    learning from 133–5
    need to tell 119–20
    playing 120–1
    source of 128–9
story construction 126–8
storyboarding 31, 110–11, 112, 144
    kinaesthetic 110–11, 130, 131

storytelling   60–1, 62, 63
   in film   117–18, 149
Strike   54
summative assessment   161
Sunset Boulevard   130
surrealism   71, 149
suspense   68
synecdoche   52
syuzhet   63–6, 68, 123, 127, 193n

talkies   45
teacher effectiveness   6
Teachers and Schooling Making a Difference (Hayes et al.)   39
teaching   100
   aim   6
   effective   26–7
technical actors   122–3, 130
technicians   24
technology, and making film   2, 18
tension   66–9, 89–90, 124, 125, 127
The Art of the Moving Picture (Lindsay)   40
The Blues Brothers   158
The Boy Who Loved Shostakovich   77–8, 81, 113, 117
The Fugitive   158
The Matrix   71
The Queen   4
The Untouchables   18
Thelma and Louise   71
Theory of Film (Kracauer)   57–8
Thompson, K.   62, 67, 92, 126, 127
thrillers   72
Todorov, Tzvetan   68, 126, 192n, 193n

Toland, Gregg   55–6
Towards a Film Aesthetic (Read)   41
triangulation   185
tropes   55, 56
Truffaut, François   44–5, 98
trust   102–3

Un Chien Andalou   71
UNESCO, future of arts education   169–70

visual imagery   47, 87
   framing   50–2, 88–9, 91–2
   learning to appreciate   92–3, 96–7
   reading   36
Volver   46
von Trier, Lars   114, 193n
Vygotsky, Lev   7, 83, 98, 99–100, 120

Watson, P.   72, 73, 75
Welles, Orson   43, 55–6, 74
Wenders, Wim   60–1, 74, 117, 118
What Stories Are (Leitch)   61
Wiggins, G.P.   155
Williams, John   46
Wiltshire, Kenneth   28–9
Witness   43
Woo, John   116, 117
workshopping   131

youth videomaking projects   180

zoetropes   42
zone of proximal development   100, 101, 103

For Product Safety Concerns and Information please contact our EU representative GPSR@taylorandfrancis.com
Taylor & Francis Verlag GmbH, Kaufingerstraße 24, 80331 München, Germany

www.ingramcontent.com/pod-product-compliance
Lightning Source LLC
Chambersburg PA
CBHW051522230426
43668CB00012B/1702